THE SPANISH-AMERICAN FRONTIER
1783–1795

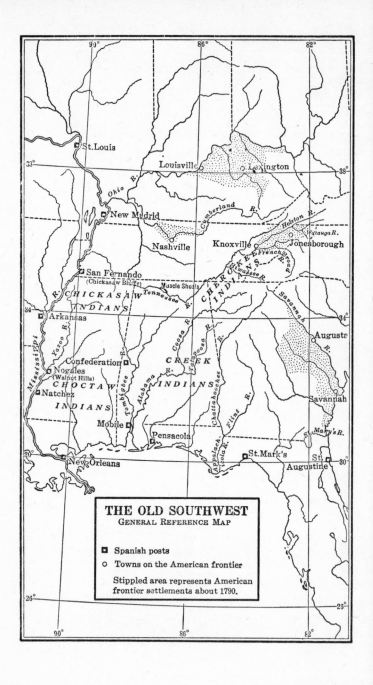

THE OLD SOUTHWEST
GENERAL REFERENCE MAP

◼ Spanish posts
○ Towns on the American frontier

Stippled area represents American
frontier settlements about 1790.

THE SPANISH-AMERICAN FRONTIER : 1783-1795

The Westward Movement and the Spanish Retreat in the Mississippi Valley

BY

ARTHUR PRESTON WHITAKER

Sometime Amherst Memorial Fellow

WITH AN INTRODUCTION BY

SAMUEL ELIOT MORISON

Professor of History at Harvard University

AND WITH MAPS

GLOUCESTER, MASS.

PETER SMITH

1962

TO
FREDERICK JACKSON TURNER
HISTORIAN OF THE AMERICAN FRONTIER

ACKNOWLEDGMENT

THE writing of history is no longer an individual achievement, if indeed it ever was. It is the work of many hands, some living and some dead. Archivists, collectors, benefactors, other historians, and the persons whose correspondence chance and foresight have preserved, all play their part in determining what monuments of the past the writer shall see and how he shall regard them.

My own debit column is a long one. The present work could not have been written at all but for the indefatigable labors of Lyman C. Draper, the establishment of the Archive of the Indies by Charles III, the publication of its voluminous records by the state of North Carolina. The writings of earlier historians, such as Theodore Roosevelt, Justin Winsor and Archibald Henderson have been of invaluable assistance. One of the most noteworthy of recent contributions in this field is *Pinckney's Treaty*, by Professor Samuel Flagg Bemis, a book which it was my privilege to read in manuscript (not in its final form) towards the end of my fifteen months' residence in Spain. Important additions to the bibliographical resources of Spanish history have been made within the last few years by B. Sánchez Alonso (*Fuentes de la historia española*), and R. Ballester y Castell (*Bibliografía de la historia de España*). The bibliographical aids on the American side are so familiar that it does not seem necessary to name them here.

It was under an appointment as Amherst Memorial Fellow (Amherst College) that I spent two years in France, Spain, England and the United States in the preparation of this book, the plan of which was conceived in 1922. It was also the generosity of the Amherst Memorial Fellowship Committee that enabled me to make the present arrangement for publication. My first studies in the history of the Old Southwest were carried on under the guidance of Frederick Jackson Turner, to whom this book is dedicated as a mark of esteem for a great historian and of gratitude to an unfailing friend.

For reading and criticising my manuscript, I am indebted to Dr. James A. Robertson, editor of the Hispanic American Historical Review; Professor Samuel Eliot Morison of Harvard University; Professor Laurence B. Packard, on behalf of the Amherst Memorial Fellowship Committee; and Professors Isaac J. Cox and J. A. James of Northwestern University.

I may add that I am planning a companion volume to the present one, carrying through to its conclusion the story of the Spanish retreat from Louisiana and the Floridas in the face of the advancing American frontier. The present work, while complete in itself, needs the sequel.

A. P. W.

June 20, 1927

CONTENTS

MAPS

INTRODUCTION

THROUGH an amazing web of intrigue and diplomacy the irrepressible frontiersmen of the old South-West burst their way to the Mississippi. When Roosevelt wrote his *Winning of the West*, little that was certain could be told of this story. Dr. Whitaker has pursued every clue to the Spanish archives, where the servants of a declining empire carefully recorded every letter and interview and bargain concluded in their colonies on the Gulf of Mexico and the Mississippi. From the material so gathered, he has reconstructed a fascinating story of relations between rough-necked backwoodsmen of the Daniel Boone breed and courtly representatives of the King of Spain; Scots fur-traders and the half-breed chiefs of the Creek and Cherokee; picturesque rascals like O'Fallon and Tom Washington, and venal legislatures. The influence of this frontier underworld on the formal diplomacy between Spain and the United States has been clearly brought out; and the significance of it, as a conflict between two different civilizations, adequately appreciated. Twelve eventful years of this conflict are concluded by the Madrid negotiations of 1795 between Thomas Pinckney and Manuel de Godoy, and the treaty of San Lorenzo, which cleared Spanish obstructions from our westward advance.

S. E. MORISON

THE SPANISH–AMERICAN FRONTIER

1783–1795

∴

CHAPTER I

RIVAL EMPIRES

IF ever a peace failed to pacify, it was the peace of 1783. The international settlement at the close of the American Revolution was incomplete, for no treaty defined the relations or restrained the rivalry of the oldest and newest empires in America, Spain and the United States. The treaties that did form a part of that settlement were mutually conflicting or silent on matters of vital import to these two powers. And yet the most comprehensive and definite treaties could have done nothing more than postpone the ineluctable conflict between the old order and the new. This conflict, indeed, had been in progress for generations before the Revolution. It merely entered upon a new phase when the thirteen colonies of British North America won their independence.

THE EIGHTEENTH-CENTURY RENAISSANCE
OF SPAIN

Since the day when the destruction of the Armada baffled Spain's attempt to protect its American empire against English invasion by invading England, Spain had been compelled to surrender first at one point and

1

then at another her arrogant claim to universal empire in the New World. Virginia, Jamaica, Georgia, Campeche, the Floridas, had one by one fallen into English hands.[1] By 1775 England had built up the most numerous, the richest and most powerful colonies in America. Through economic penetration, whether contraband trade or legitimate commerce under the treaty of Utrecht, she was threatening Spain's hold on her remaining dominions on the Mississippi and the Gulf of Mexico.

At the same time, Spain seemed to be emerging from her age-long lethargy. Throughout the eighteenth century the Bourbons had striven to revive the energies of the nation. By the third quarter of the century their efforts seemed to be producing results of permanent value. The reign of the austere Charles III (1759–88) is the one which in all the history of Spain since the sixteenth century is least wounding to national pride. Government finances were reduced to order and commerce and industry encouraged by tariffs, the building of roads, and the founding of such corporations as the Philippine Company and a national bank. Splendid individual achievements illuminate these years: the statesmanship of Floridablanca, Goya's brush, the economic writings and reforms of Campomanés and Jovellanos.[2] In the colonial field, in which our immediate interest lies, talent and energy abounded. Even England's colonial service could boast no abler men than Charles III's colonial secretary, José de Gálvez, or José's nephew, Bernardo de Gálvez, conqueror of British West Florida, or the viceroy of New Spain, the Marqués de Revillagigedo.[3] As for Spain's colonial policy, the commercial regulations of 1778 liberalized the old monopolistic system in some important respects, and seemed to promise an era of progressive reform.

This national revival was accompanied by a resumption of the territorial advance of Spain in North America. Northwestward the Spanish flag was carried into Upper California; northeastward, into the Floridas and up both banks of the Mississippi. The acquisition of Louisiana (1762), the conquest of West Florida (1779–81), the recovery of East Florida (1783), the establishment of forts San Marcos, New Madrid, Nogales, Confederation and San Fernando de las Barrancas in the Mississippi Valley region (1787–95), were paralleled by the founding of San Diego, Los Angeles, Santa Bárbara and San Fernando Rey de España on the Pacific coast (1760–97).[4]

Spain's recovery, coinciding with the territorial and commercial expansion of England, led to numerous wars and incessant contention between the two powers throughout the eighteenth century. In the first six decades of the century the Spanish Bourbons had met with one reverse after another, although supported by their royal cousins of France. They were driven from Guale to the northward of St. Augustine, from St. Augustine itself and from Pensacola, and by the close of the Seven Years' War (1763) the Spanish frontier in North America had been forced back from the Savannah River to the Mississippi.

The American Revolution seemed to offer the Bourbon monarchies of France and Spain a providential opportunity to shatter England's power, and in 1783 a superficial observer might have thought that Spain had taken full advantage of the opportunity and had won a substantial reward. East and West Florida were in her possession, giving her control of the Bahama Channel and the Mississippi River and making the Gulf of Mexico a Spanish lake. In reality, Spain found herself in a more dangerous situation than ever, for she was left face to face with the first independent power of the New World, a power possessing a numerous and energetic population animated by the British urge to expansion and liberated from that intimate participation in the European state system which had so often checked England's spoliation of Spain. Had the sole object of the English government been, as many Spaniards thought it was, to destroy the Spanish empire at all costs, and had it possessed the Machiavellian cleverness attributed to it, England would have granted without delay the American demand for independence.

THE REVOLUTION AND THE AMERICAN FRONTIER]

The economic system and social ideals that had carried the English colonists from the Atlantic coast across the mountains into the Mississippi Valley emerged with undiminished vigor from the Revolution. More than this, the eight years' war gave a fresh impulse to the expansionist movement in the Old Southwest, a name we use to designate the region south of the Ohio, east of the Mississippi and west of the Appalachian ranges. In the first place, the restraining hand of imperial control was removed. Indian relations, frontier advance, land grants, had all been in the hands of a British superintendent of Indian affairs or of colonial governors responsible to the crown. The control of these matters now devolved upon the state governments, except in so far as the feeble Congress of the Confederation could extend its vague grant of power in Indian relations. The result was favorable to the advance of the frontier, for the chain of restraint was no stronger than its weakest link, and the state governments were less able to resist land speculators or to

intimidate recalcitrant frontiersmen than the British
government had been before the Revolution. This
very weakness of the federal government was, as we
shall see, an advantage to the republic in its conflict
with Spain.

In the second place, the area of settlement was
extended during the Revolution, whether by the establishment of new communities (*e.g.*, those on the Cumberland River), or by the legalization and growth of
settlements already made in defiance of law at the
outbreak of the Revolution (*e.g.*, Kentucky and
Watauga).[5] This revolutionary advance was made in
such a way that, as a glance at the map will show,
further extension was required by the communication
and transportation necessities of these settlements.
Any further extension must be made at the expense of
the Indians, as was always the case, and the Revolution
left a heritage of real and fancied grievances against the
savages that facilitated their dispossession.

In the third place, the states found that the easiest
way to pay their war debts was to release the frontier.
Money was scarce and land plentiful. During the Revolution land bounties were given to encourage enlistment,
and after the Revolution the paper currency was extin-
guished by conversion into Western lands. Some of
these grants were located in regions already open to
settlement, some of them within the Indian hunting
grounds. The economic readjustment during and after
the Revolution sent merchants as well as farmers westward.[6] The result was an increase in the population
of the frontier settlements and in popular pressure on
the state governments to extinguish Indian rights and
make Indian hunting grounds available for white colonization. Other forces that sent men westward were

the heavier taxation consequent upon the war, and the natural and acquired taste for combat.

The result was that the land passed with amazing rapidity from public into private possession. In the decade following the close of the Revolution, more land was entered in the land office of North Carolina than in the previous hundred years of its existence as a colony.[7] The process was by no means unconscious. A frontiersmen's interpretation of the Revolution as a release of expansive energy is found in a letter written by a Holston settler in 1785. Recording the defeat of the Cherokee Indians and the rapid extension of settlement down the Holston, he concluded: "Such are the fruits, such the foretastes of the glorious American Revolution."[8] Human material for frontier extension abounded, and such observers as William Grayson of Virginia and Hugh Williamson of North Carolina were struck by the "immense spirit of emigration" to the West, and by its concomitant, the "epidemic" fever of making new states.[9] The political designs of the Southerners, many of whom planned an early extension of their system to the Mississippi, were indicated during the progress of the Revolution by Virginia's erection of Kentucky into a district and by a provision in the North Carolina constitution of 1776 authorizing the legislature to permit the organization of a separate state in its western territory. The spirit of westward-straining Georgia found expression in 1785 in the charge of Judge Walton to the grand jury of Wilkes county: ". . . I look forward to a time, not very far distant, when . . . the whole [of Georgia] will be settled and connected . . . from the shores of the Atlantic to the banks of the Mississippi." What would become of the Indians and Spaniards actually occupying the territory in question, Judge Walton did not vouchsafe to say.[10]

At the close of the Revolution, the American settlements in the Mississippi Valley were firmly established, rapid growth seemed assured and statehood was promised. Continued extension was ingrained in the nature of the Anglo-American frontier, and the finger of destiny seemed to point down the Mississippi Valley. Even before further territorial extension was possible, the use of the river was essential to the prosperity of the existing settlements. Hardly had the Revolution begun when Patrick Henry, governor of Virginia and speculator in Western lands, opened a correspondence with governor Gálvez of Louisiana in the interests of American commerce on the Mississippi.[11]

The policy of the Spanish government was directly opposed to the ambitions of the Americans. Its objects in entering the war against England in 1779 were, in Europe, to reconquer Gibraltar and Minorca, and, in America, to recover Florida and "to expel from the Gulf of Mexico some neighbors who are causing us infinite vexation";[12] in other words, to put an end to English contraband in the Gulf, contraband that was made possible by the English settlements in Honduras and Campeche, at Pensacola and on the Mississippi, and by the right, secured to England in 1763, to the free navigation of that river throughout its course. To wipe out illicit trade by closing the river to all but Spanish shipping was one of Spain's principal war aims. It was not a purpose that Spain would lightly surrender, for it grew out of the long, determined fight that the crown had for decades been waging against contraband in Spain itself as well as in America. The prevalence of illicit trade throughout the empire was galling to Spanish pride, injurious to Spanish business and a most striking proof of Spain's maladjustment to eighteenth-century conditions of life. Its monopolistic system was opposed in principle to commerce between its colonies and foreign nations, and there were few exceptions to the principle; and yet Spanish shippers, merchants and manufacturers were utterly unable to satisfy the needs of the Spanish colonists. The attempt to enforce an unnatural monopoly led to the corruption of government officials and the disaffection of colonists, and involved Spain in endless controversy with other nations. And yet the ancient system could not be abandoned, for it was believed that it was essential to the maintenance of a favorable balance of trade, and it was hallowed by immemorial custom.

With the United States a peculiarly acrimonious controversy arose out of this question at the end of the Revolution. In three years of fighting, Spanish arms under the leadership of Bernardo de Gálvez had conquered all of British West Florida, Fort Bute and Natchez on the Mississippi as well as Mobile and Pensacola on the Gulf. Both banks of the Mississippi in its lower course, and consequently the navigation of the river, were now in the hands of Spain. Gálvez's conquest made possible, and the possibility made certain, the closing of the Mississippi to all but Spanish shipping. This measure could not fail to precipitate a conflict with the United States. Not only did the Americans consider the free navigation of the river essential to the prosperity of their Western settlements: through long use they had come to regard it as an inalienable right. From 1763 to 1779 the river was open to them as British subjects. From 1779 to the end of the war Spain continued, as a war measure, to permit the rebellious colonists to use it. It was in this period of free navigation that the settlements of the Old Southwest — Kentucky, Holston and Cumberland — were established. Custom had by 1783 become inalienable right, and this conviction was reinforced by the application of a principle of private law to an international problem. It was argued that the Americans had as much right to the continued use of the Mississippi as a proprietor to the thoroughfare on which he has built his house.

THE DIPLOMATIC SETTLEMENT, 1783

Spanish ministers sensed the danger of the situation and shaped their policy accordingly. Count Aranda, the Spanish ambassador in Paris, and Martin Navarro, the intendant of Louisiana, warned their government to be on its guard against the turbulent, ambitious Americans, and Navarro further pointed out that the free navigation of the Mississippi would foster the growth of the American West.[13] Floridablanca, Charles III's secretary of state, turned a deaf ear to Vergennes's assurances that the bucolic Americans would never be dangerous neighbors, and used all his diplomatic resources to close the Mississippi to them and to keep their settlements as far as possible from its banks. Hence Jay's negotiations with Floridablanca were sterile, for his famous offer on behalf of the United States to submit to the closing of the Mississippi was hedged about with conditions altogether inacceptable to Spain.[14]

When Jay's abrupt departure from Madrid in May, 1782, broke off this negotiation, Aranda was instructed to renew it in Paris. Floridablanca directed him to establish Spain's exclusive right to the navigation of the Mississippi, to fix the western boundary of the

United States as far to the eastward of the Mississippi as possible, and to leave England in possession of a part of East Florida — that is, the east coast from Cape Cañaveral to Georgia — as a buffer between Spain's colonies and the restless Americans. On Rayneval's advice Aranda tried to create another buffer by neutralizing the Indian country south of the Ohio River. Supported by Vergennes he was making things very uncomfortable for Jay and his colleagues when England's clever stroke of diplomacy detached the United States from France and forced the conclusion of a general peace on terms most unwelcome to Spain.[15]

It was the treaties negotiated by England and the consequent policy of Spain that brought on an immediate controversy between the latter power and the United States. England's treaty with the United States granted the Americans the free navigation of the Mississippi throughout its course, reserved the same right for British subjects, and fixed the southern boundary of the republic at the thirty-first parallel.[16] In England's treaty with Spain, no mention was made of the navigation of the Mississippi. East Florida was ceded to Spain, which, it was provided, should "retain" West Florida. The treaty made no stipulation with regard to the boundaries of these provinces, but one thing was certain: Spain had failed to interpose either of the buffers and was left face to face with the United States.

There was an obvious conflict between the provisions of these treaties. By using the word "retain" in the Spanish treaty, England apparently recognized Spain's right to West Florida as a conquered province. Now West Florida was conquered in its whole extent by Spain, and its extent, as fixed by a British order in

council of 1764, included Natchez and all the territory as
far north as the parallel passing through the junction
of the Yazoo and Mississippi Rivers, that is, about 32°
26'.[17] Thus both Spain and the United States could
claim under treaties with England signed on the same
day (September 3, 1783) a broad band of territory
extending, between the parallels 31° and 32° 26', from
the Mississippi to the Chattahoochee and embracing the
important post of Natchez and the heart of the Southern
Indian country. Both in this case and in that of the Mississippi, Spain asserted that the English cessions to the
United States were void since England ceded what was
not hers to give.

No conclusive evidence has yet been produced to
prove that the object of English diplomacy at this point
was to embroil Spain and the United States, but circumstances certainly indicate that it was. Such was
the conclusion drawn by the Americans when their
preliminary treaty with England was first published in
Philadelphia,[18] and such was the common assumption
by Americans in later years.

Spain fell readily into the trap, if trap it was. Indeed,
it is not easy to conceive of anything more maladroit
than Floridablanca's policy towards the United States
at this juncture as well as throughout the next three
years. It is true that his foreign envoys did not serve
him well, for, contrary to the common assumption of
American historians, he never knew of the secret clause
in the preliminary treaty between England and the
United States (1782) fixing the boundary of the United
States at the mouth of the Yazoo River in case British
arms should recover West Florida before the final
treaty;[19] nor was he informed of the British order of
1764 moving the northern boundary of West Florida

up to the mouth of the Yazoo River. The lack of this important information weakened Spain's case and may be pleaded in extenuation of Floridablanca's excessive caution and subtlety. Even in larger matters of policy, however, where no lack of accurate information or sound advice can be urged, he adopted what seems to have been almost the worst possible course. Disregarding the repeated and urgent advice of Aranda and of France in the years 1777 and 1778 that he sell Spain's aid to the United States in return for an advantageous treaty with the republic, he let slip the unique opportunity and followed a course that alienated the United States, led to war with England and gave great offence to Spain's one ally, France.[20] A similar ineptness marks the Spanish diplomacy during the negotiations of 1782 and 1783. At no time did the government make a formal protest against England's concessions to the United States, nor was any attempt made to insert in the treaty with England a definition of the boundaries of West Florida or any clause relating to the navigation of the Mississippi.

Floridablanca's policy in this crisis is easy to state: it was one of studied silence; but it is difficult to understand. He explained it by saying that England was pretending to do something which in its nature could not be done, granting territory and a right that had already been lost by the Spanish conquest of West Florida, and that consequently no action on his part was necessary to protect the rights of Spain. Furthermore, he said, the points in question concerned Spain and the United States alone, and should be settled, not at the general peace conference at Paris, but in a subsequent treaty negotiated either in the United States or at Madrid.[21] Even if we admit Floridablanca's assumption of the utter incompetence of England to make the grants in question, we still wonder why he did not take exception formally and publicly to the Anglo-American treaty. His omission to do so enabled the Americans to argue that Spain had given the consent of silence to their treaty with England. As time went on, this not altogether convincing argument gathered strength and was finally one of the chief considerations advanced by Godoy in 1795 to justify his surrender of the disputed points.[22]

STAKES OF THE CONFLICT

The foregoing survey has shown that the Spanish-American conflict was a direct result of the Revolutionary War. That war gave birth to an energetic republic in North America, and flung the unfortunate Spain across the path of its progress. The stage was set for the renewal of the struggle between the English and Spanish systems. A conflict was certain to come sooner or later, and it came immediately because the diplomatic settlement at the end of the war gave a semblance of legal validity to important and irreconcilable claims of the two nations. Which of the two should control land grants at Natchez, trade and treaties with the Southern Indians, shipments of tobacco down the Mississippi? Behind these immediate issues was a larger stake, the destiny of the Mississippi Valley.

In the conflict for this stake was tested each of the rival empires' power of incorporation, its power to produce a living social synthesis out of bewildering diversity. The conflict was waged in both Europe and America, by the two powers' diplomats and their frontiersmen, who sometimes worked in harmony with each other and sometimes at cross-purposes. The most striking contrasts are presented by the personages who move across the stage in this drama. A hard-headed Philadelphia republican is torn from his romance with a French duchess to follow the dusty peregrinations of the Spanish court in pursuit of a will-o'-the-wisp treaty about the Mississippi Valley. A suave Spaniard is sent from his master's embassy at Lisbon to keep open house for backwoods emigrants at Natchez, and to smoke the peace pipe with Choctaw headmen and warriors. A British fur trader is one of the chief bulwarks of Spanish power against the Anglo-Saxon tide sweeping down the Ohio and the Tennessee; and one of the pilots of these simple Anglo-Saxon frontiersmen comes of a French family, plays cards, attends balls, and calls his wife his "lady" and his backwoods clearing a "plantation." And yet despite this confusion of races and nationalities, despite the surface aimlessness, despite the venality or shortsightedness of many a Spaniard and many an American, there were both Americans and Spaniards who knew that out of this welter there would emerge the destiny of one of the world's richest valleys, and more than that, the destiny of a continent.

Though all the world knows that in this conflict Spain had at last to yield, the conflict is not for that reason devoid of interest. All the world knows of Œdipus' tragic end, and yet there are many who will read and read again his tortured story. Spain's defeat has in it something of the quality of a Greek tragedy, for a relentless hand seemed to drive the monarchy on to work its own destruction. Energy and intelligence were of no avail. Turn and twist as it might, there was no escape, and its very virtues contributed to its undoing.

CHAPTER II

PROTAGONISTS AND FIELD OF ACTION
WHALE OR SHARK?

HENRY ADAMS's Gothic trope in which he likens the Spanish empire at the end of the eighteenth century to a whale, huge, helpless, and charming to its captors,[1] was never struck off as an image of the Spain of our period. The figure is misleading if we apply it — as Adams never intended it to be applied — to the Spain of 1785 or 1790 as seen through Yankee eyes. To the United States Spain may have taken on the aspect of that charming monster as the century drew towards its close, but before the wars of the French Revolution helpless whale it never was. Down to the battle of Trafalgar (1805) Spain was one of the chief maritime powers of Europe, while the United States, though it possessed a magnificent merchant marine, had no navy at all until the very end of the century. Americans were painfully conscious of this fact, for Spain's sea power would render futile the conquest of New Orleans by land forces descending the Mississippi, and would in case of a rupture wipe out the growing trade of the United States in the Mediterranean. Nothing but the neutralization of Spain's sea power could give the United States the upper hand. Consequently the chief anxiety of Spanish ministers in our period was lest the United States should secure England's alliance and England's navy, and the hope of the Americans lay in the expectation of a European crisis that would array England, or perhaps France, against Spain. The situation was complicated by France's alliance with both Spain and the United States. In 1783 the realization of either the Americans' hope or the Spaniards' fear seemed remote, and to American eyes the Spanish whale looked very like a shark.[2]

A less invidious and perhaps more faithful figure would be the description of Spain as the sick man of America, a patient whose condition permitted one to hope for the worst and yet gave discouragingly persistent indications of recovery. Austrian jealousy of Russian designs on Turkish Constantinople and the Straits is matched by the agitation of Washington's government whenever it was rumored that England or France might acquire New Orleans. In its dealings with Spain throughout these dozen years the United States observed a perfect bedside manner. Its attitude was one of watchful waiting. So much is said of the dilatory Spaniard that one is inclined to think that the fault is Spain's if delay occurs in a negotiation in which Spain is concerned. Those who read the following pages will see that the long delay in the settlement of the controversy was caused by the United States even more than by Spain. Delay was the essence of the American policy in this dispute. Afraid to risk an open break, Jefferson, Jay and Washington believed that time would give the United States an overwhelming superiority in numbers in the Mississippi Valley, and that time would also bring a European diplomatic crisis favorable to their designs.[3] Far from seeking, they avoided a settlement of the controversy, hoping that changed circumstances would force Spain to make a complete surrender.

This time factor was one of the most important of the conditions of the conflict. A kind of organic law seemed to decree the continued growth of the United States and the continued decline of Spain. Spanish ministers as well as those of the United States were aware of the former tendency and made a valiant effort to turn it to their own advantage. They accepted, after a brief resistance, the inevitable development of the next natural field of American expansion, the Mississippi Valley, entering into competition with the United States for colonists and opening a political intrigue with the Western Americans. The success of either of these two measures would have neutralized or reversed the operation of the time factor so far as the frontier phase of the struggle was concerned.

FORMS OF GOVERNMENT

In regard to political organization, neither country had an appreciable advantage over the other, for it happened that each government was adapted to the execution of its designs. The Spanish government regarded Louisiana and the Floridas as a barrier for the protection of its other possessions in America. To render them responsive to imperial needs, their control must be highly centralized. This requirement was met by the existing Spanish system. Every village and town in Louisiana and West Florida was under the command of an army officer responsible to the governor of Louisiana, who was fortified with the double authority of the civil and military command of the provinces. He in turn was responsible to the governor of Havana, who was captain-general of Louisiana and the Floridas and directly under the control of the king's ministers.[4]

The administration of colonial affairs in Spain was twice altered during the period under consideration. At the outset, there was a colonial secretary, José de Gálvez, ennobled as the Marqués de Sonora, who had general control of all colonial affairs. On his death in

1787 the business of the colonial office was divided between two ministers.[5] In 1790, the colonial office was
suppressed and colonial affairs were distributed among
the appropriate ministries.[6] Another important change
was effected by an order which directed that the governors of Louisiana and West Florida and of East Florida,
who were required in general to communicate with
the court through the captain-general at Havana, should
correspond directly with the secretary of state about
all matters relating to Indian affairs and the American
frontier.[7] In our period this was as far as the court
would go towards increasing the powers of its frontier
governors, though in August, 1795, the king authorized the secretary of state to erect Louisiana into a
captaincy-general in order to facilitate resistance to the
sinister designs of the United States.[8] Even the limited
concession of direct correspondence produced important results, for it gave unity and coherence to Spain's
policy towards the United States. It was Floridablanca
who guided Gardoqui's negotiation in New York with
Jay, and it was also Floridablanca who shaped Spain's
immigration policy in Louisiana and the Floridas and
who directed the intrigue with the frontier Americans.
Godoy, Floridablanca's successor after Aranda's brief
ministry, continued to coördinate Spain's frontier and
diplomatic policies.

Moreover, under this system the affairs of Louisiana
and the Floridas received a more expeditious handling
than is generally supposed. Even Spanish historians
have exaggerated the dilatoriness of their government
in the eighteenth century. On the whole, the Spanish
governmental system worked with as much despatch
as could be expected in an age when transportation
facilities and business methods were in such a rudi-

mentary stage of development. It was well adapted
to the requirements of the situation in so far as co-
ordination and action on a large scale could be effective. In the suppression of disorder, in the management
of the Indian trade, in intrigue, in the extension of the
military frontier, Spain excelled. The very virtues of
her militaristic system, however, became vices in the
competition for colonists. The legendary despotism
of Spain was reproduced in the petty tyranny of its
post commanders, a tyranny brought out in striking
relief by the proximity of the turbulently free American
settlements. If we add the restrictions placed on land
grants and on the commerce of the Floridas and Louisiana, which will be discussed in their place, we can
begin to understand the utter failure of the Spanish
immigration policy. This failure was fatal to the
Spanish cause.

The government of the United States was well
adapted to its needs in the conflict with Spain. Its
very weakness was a source of strength.[9] In the first
place, it was the turbulence, the lawlessness, the violence
of the American frontiersmen and land speculators,
and not the feeble threats of the federal government,
that alarmed Spain. Had the dominant majority in
the United States government had its way, there would
have been no demonstrations of frontier turbulence,
no Yazoo companies, no French legion on the Ohio.
In the second place, the majority in Congress would
probably have submitted to the closing of the Mississippi but for the fear that such action would bring about
the secession of the West. In other words, the contest
with Spain would have been ended by surrender in 1786
but for the realization of the majority that the United
States government could not enforce its will upon the

Mississippi Valley settlements.[10] The United States escaped a premature surrender and gained an ultimate victory in this conflict because the people were stronger than their government.

The relative efficiency of the Spanish and American systems of colonial government can be determined only by observing them in operation. We may anticipate in order to call attention to the interesting contrast between the simultaneous administrations of Carondelet in Louisiana (1792–97) and William Blount in the Southwest Territory (1790–96). Without the slightest knowledge of conditions in the province, Carondelet was sent to Louisiana apparently because of his influential connections and because his rank and services entitled him to promotion at the time when the governorship of Louisiana fell vacant. Appointed for five years, his further promotion depended partly upon his rendering some signal service to the crown, and one gets the impression from his whole administration that the interests of the colony were sacrificed, unconsciously perhaps, to his desire to distinguish himself. Neither king nor colony was well served by such a system, although, as we have seen, it possessed many excellent qualities. Blount, on the other hand, was no doubt chosen by Washington because of his long intimacy with the people and the affairs of the Southwest Territory. Without hope of promotion in the service of the federal government, but bound to it by his oath of office and his salary, he saw the situation in the Southwest from both the national and local points of view, rendered an important service by interpreting each to the other, and was a tower of federal strength on the Spanish frontier.

In point of population as well as of sea power Spain

had an advantage over the United States, for the king-
dom alone, without including its dependencies, had
about ten million inhabitants in 1790 as against some
three millions in the United States. This advantage,
however, was offset by the diffusion of Spain's energy
throughout the four quarters of the globe, in Europe,
Africa, North and South America and the Philippines,
and by its remoteness from the scene of conflict.

THE SPANISH FRONTIER

Of the two competing frontiers, the American was
far stronger than the Spanish. Spain's border settlements extended in a thin, L-shaped line about the
southern and western extremities of the United States.
St. Augustine, Pensacola, Mobile and New Orleans
carried the line westward from the Atlantic to the
Mississippi. North of New Orleans the only Spanish
posts of any consideration in 1783 were Natchez, Arkansas and St. Louis, and Natchez was in the territory
claimed by the United States. Altogether a dozen
ruinous forts and palisaded blockhouses, garrisoned by
an incomplete and ill-equipped regiment of the worst
troops in the Spanish army, were the sole support of
Spanish authority in all Louisiana and West Florida.
In East Florida the only post of any consequence was
the capital itself, St. Augustine.

There was little to be expected from the support of
the handful of colonists in this vast territory. In 1786
the total population of East Florida was less than 1500.
Some of these were negro slaves, and most of the rest
were British, Greek and Maiorcan.[11] West Florida's
population was probably somewhat larger. In Louisiana
there were some 20,000 inhabitants, nearly half of whom
were slaves.[12] Of the white inhabitants of these two

provinces the majority were French, although, after the conquest of West Florida, there were several hundred Anglo-American Protestants permitted to remain on sufferance. Besides the colonial officials and the army, there was hardly a Spaniard to be found in the whole length and breadth of Louisiana and the Floridas. If Spain might perhaps count on the French colonists to defend New Orleans against an attack by the United States, as they had aided in the conquest of British West Florida, there was no certainty as to the course the Anglo-Americans at Natchez might follow in such an event. On the other hand, when the French Revolution arrayed Spain against France in 1793 and the Natchez planters were ready to support the colonial government against the Jacobins, the French of lower Louisiana threatened rebellion and became a serious liability.

Economically and financially these provinces were unprofitable to Spain. Their principal products were furs and hides, indigo, rice, lumber and tobacco. None of these commodities had a market in Spain, except for a time tobacco, nor could Spanish merchants supply the wants of the colonists with Spanish goods. The wines of Bordeaux, the guns of St. Etienne, the silks of Lyon for the masters, British linseys and osnaburgs for the slaves: such were the goods required by the colonial market, in which, moreover, American flour undersold flour from Spanish sources whenever a pretext could be found for its importation. From Spain hardly anything was taken but inconsiderable quantities of olive oil and sausage. The one Spanish merchant who invaded the field with a full stock lost heavily and never repeated the venture.[13]

The expenditures of the Spanish government in Louisiana exceeded its revenues there. About $500,000 was sent to New Orleans in 1785 for the support of the colonial government, civil and military, and the amount had to be increased each succeeding year. Most of this represented a dead loss to the government, for the revenue from customs duties, the principal source of income, amounted to about $50,000 a year. In other words, Louisiana represented a net loss of about half a million dollars every year to the home government. This amount passed into circulation in the colony, some of it into the hands of merchants who, violating the law against the exportation of specie, used it to settle the unfavorable balance of their legitimate trade with France and of their illicit trade with England and the United States. And so in effect the Spanish government found itself paying for the maintenance of law and order in a colony disaffected and economically unprofitable to the Spanish nation. The continuance of such a state of affairs was intolerable to Spanish pride and irreconcilable with its interests, and yet to cut off foreign commerce entirely would put an end to the prosperity of the colony and might well cause a revolution, besides offending France.[14]

We shall see how in the regulation of commerce, as well as in local government, the Indian trade, and even religion, the Spanish government made a valiant effort to adapt its colonial system to the needs of alien colonies and the frontier conflict with the United States, but was fettered by tradition and prejudice. The consequent half-measures and inconsistency tantalized the colonists and, together with persistent rumors of the cession of the Floridas to England and Louisiana to France, created a feeling of uncertainty, of insecurity, that discouraged the immigration of capital and labor into these provinces.

HEADMEN AND WARRIORS

Between the thin line of Spanish posts and the clusters of American frontier settlements lay four formidable Indian tribes far more numerous than the Spanish colonists and almost equal in numbers to the American frontiersmen. In the Creek towns were some 6000 warriors; in the Cherokee, 2000; in the Chickasaw, 500; in the Choctaw, 5000. In all, their braves numbered about 13,500, and their total population was about 45,000.[15] More numerous than Cornwallis's army at Yorktown and hardened by a life of incessant warfare, what part would these tribesmen play in the Spanish-American conflict? The Creek and Cherokee could hardly be otherwise than hostile to the Americans, for the occupation of the Southern piedmont and the beginning of the trans-Appalachian movement had for a full generation before the Revolution kept up constant strife between them and the "Virginians," as they called all their backwoods neighbors indiscriminately. Neither French nor British nor Spanish instigation was necesssary, in all the years from 1740 to the end of the century, to set these Indians against the "Virginians." The disappearance of game, which in reality was largely due to the demands of the fur traders upon the short-sighted and compliant Indians, was attributed by the latter to the advance of the American settlements. In the face of the flight of this means of livelihood, the Indians had recourse to three remedies: They might take to farming, or they might permit the white men to pauperize them, or they might move westward across the Mississippi. All three of these things they had already begun in some measure to do, the last least of all. By the beginning of our period, they had all passed out of the nomadic stage. Their corn-fields were extensive, stock-raising was not uncommon, their villages were seldom moved except in response to external pressure, and they bitterly resented the expropriation of their lands, vaguely though their several territorial claims were defined.

The fur trade was still an important factor in the control of these Indians, although fifteen years had passed since the British superintendent of Indian affairs, John Stuart, had declared it incapable of further extension.[16] About 1785 it still required $80,000 worth of goods a year to supply the Indians whose trade was carried on through Mobile and Pensacola, and $20,000 worth for the trade of St. Augustine,[17] not to mention that which was in the hands of Americans in Georgia and on the Holston and Cumberland Rivers, and of interlopers on the Yazoo and Tennessee Rivers, whose value it is difficult to estimate. The situation in 1783 was favorable to Spain's supremacy in this commerce, for the Creek and Cherokee had been involved in the recent war against the United States, the Choctaw were too remote to be brought easily under American influence, and the Chickasaw tribe, though friendly to the United States, was so small that its trade was of no great value. Moreover, it was already clear before the Revolution that the control of the fur trade was shifting from Georgia to Mobile and Pensacola. This tendency was strengthened by the fact that most of the British Indian agents and traders were loyalists during the Revolution and that many of them took refuge in East and West Florida.[18] American traders from Georgia, the Holston and Cumberland were active among the Creek, Cherokee and Chickasaw respectively, but throughout our period Spanish control was substantially maintained by trading houses at St. Augustine, St. Mark's, Pensacola, Mobile, and San Fernando (Chickasaw Bluffs).

Economically the Southern fur trade was of doubtful value, for it was highly speculative, and while the profits were often large the risk was always great. Politically their trade was of dubious utility, contrary to the common assumption of their white neighbors, for the Indians could not be thrown into the fray and withdrawn at the convenience of their white instigators. A present was easily forgotten by them, but not the shedding of blood. In fact, neither the Americans nor the Spaniards knew enough of their customs or mental processes to understand them. The Americans solved the problem by declaring flatly that the Indians were not human beings, and by acting accordingly. The misunderstanding was mutual, for the Indians comprehended little or nothing of treaties, kings or private property in land.

THE AMERICAN FRONTIER

The frontier communities of the United States present a very different picture from the one that we have sketched of the Floridas and Louisiana. These communities were four in number: Georgia, Holston, Cumberland and Kentucky. Their population in 1785 may be estimated at not more than 75,000, or about three times that of the neighboring Spanish provinces. Of these 75,000 frontiersmen, somewhat less than 30,000 were in Kentucky, somewhat more than that number in Georgia, about 10,000 on the Holston and its tributaries, and about 4000 in Cumberland.[19] For military purposes, however, this advantage must be considerably discounted. The points of strategic importance in the Spanish colonies were Natchez and New Orleans, and the Georgians were too remote to be very dangerous, even had the Southern tribes not intervened. The remaining 45,000 frontiersmen living on the waters of the Mississippi had almost as formidable obstacles to overcome before they could hope to conquer lower Louisiana. The Mississippi afforded them at once a highway and the motive power to traverse it, and, up to the beginning of the Wilkinson intrigue with Spain (1787), their preparations could be completed without the knowledge of the Spanish government, whose first information service in Kentucky was established in the person of Wilkinson himself. Here the advantages of the frontiersmen ended. Louisville and Nashville, the logical points of concentration for expeditions against Louisiana, were a thousand miles distant from New Orleans. The maintenance of a service of supply would be extremely difficult. There were no settlements of any consequence on the Mississippi except those of Spanish subjects, and even these were few above the fortified post of Natchez. To support a large body of troops by hunting was out of the question. Only an immediate and overwhelming victory would solve the problem of supply, and such a victory was extremely doubtful. There was little or no artillery in the American settlements with which to silence the numerous six and twelve pound guns at Natchez and New Orleans. Behind these garrisons were Cuba and Mexico, from which Spain would certainly send reinforcements. The frontiersmen, on the other hand, could expect nothing but opposition from their own unwarlike government. The uncertainty as to the attitude of the neighboring Indians made the outcome of an invasion still more dubious; and there was always in the background the inescapable fact, which we have already noted, that Spain's navy, the third largest in Europe, would still control the Gulf and render useless the conquest of the Mississippi.

These were the most formidable of the many obstacles to an invasion of Louisiana. It is only by keeping them in mind that we can understand why the frontiersmen never carried out their windy threats against that province, although they boasted that success was certain, although they were in need of the free navigation of the Mississippi and although they boiled with indignation at its closure by Spain. As the most discerning Spaniards saw, the only immediate danger to Louisiana lay in the greed of freebooters who would be content with plunder and had no larger end in view.[20] Without the support of Congress the frontiersmen had little power to inflict a real injury upon Spain, and Congress without a navy was hardly more dangerous. The real danger to Spain lay in an alliance between the United States and England, or simply between the American frontiersmen and England.

The economic situation of the backwoodsmen furnished an added reason for the cultivation of friendly relations with Spain. As settlement progressed and the fur trade declined, their exports became bulkier and their imports more numerous and expensive. Cheap transportation became a matter of increasing importance to them, and the Mississippi seemed to offer the only cheap means of transportation. Since the merchants of Philadelphia could undersell those of New Orleans in Kentucky, and since the bulky exports of Kentucky could not be returned with profit over the mountains to Philadelphia, the frontiersmen's chief hope of prosperity lay in the development of a triangular trade, his imports coming from the Atlantic states and his returns being made by way of New Orleans and the French West Indies to Philadelphia or Baltimore.

There was another possibility. Even in the Atlantic States gold and silver coin were scarce. Spanish milled dollars were highly prized, and the merchants, Robert Morris among them, were eager to cultivate trade with Spain as a means of increasing the gold and silver supply of the United States. In the West, where the scarcity of gold and silver coin was much greater than on the Atlantic coast, the desire for Spanish gold was even keener. The navigation of the Mississippi only so far south. as Natchez or New Orleans would be of great value to the Kentuckians, despite the danger of the return trip up the Mississippi, if only they could exchange their flour, salt pork and tobacco for pesos. Such commercial ambitions were capitalized by James Wilkinson and formed the substantial basis of the Spanish intrigue.

Georgia stood somewhat apart from the rest of these frontier communities. Since all its inhabitants lived on the Savannah and Ogeechee Rivers, it was merely an extension of the contiguous South Carolina settlements, and as much an Atlantic state as New York or Massachusetts; and since it already possessed statehood it lacked one of the chief grievances of the other frontier communities of that day. As an expanding society, however, it was keenly interested in the chief concerns of the American Southwest. Its advancing frontier brought it into conflict with the Creek Indians, and its territorial claims, extending westward to the Mississippi and embracing most of the other tribes of Southern Indians, made it a paradise of land speculators, a claimant to the Natchez district and the navigation.

of the Mississippi River, and a determined foe of Spain, which added fuel to the flames by harboring fugitive slaves in the Floridas. Finally, while tobacco planters were beginning to settle in large numbers in upper Georgia, Augusta still hoped at the close of the Revolution to regain its former preëminence in the Southern fur trade.

Kentucky, Cumberland and Holston were purely frontier communities, and were more completely isolated than any founded since the settlement of Jamestown. Indian relations, land speculation and the navigation of the Mississippi and Mobile Rivers were matters of common interest among them, and all three aspired to political autonomy. Established without the aid or in spite of the opposition of the colonial and state governments, and separated from the Atlantic States by the Appalachian ranges, they seemed to many observers destined by nature to secession from the United States and to union with Spain. This belief was based on current conceptions regarding natural frontiers and geographical influence on political institutions, and on an economic interpretation of politics. Men of sound judgment in the East, such as George Washington and Rufus King,[21] expressed the fear that the opening of the Mississippi to the United States would create an economic bond between its Western inhabitants and Spain that would in the end disrupt the Union. A better knowledge of Louisiana would have shown how little ground there was for this fear, for, as we have seen, the trade of New Orleans was in the hands not of Spaniards but of Frenchmen, and was in constant conflict with Spanish interests and Spanish law. Furthermore, even if Spanish officials could fit the American frontier settlements into Spain's colonial system or its system of alliances, the frontiersmen were by no means certain to be docile subjects or tractable allies. Most of them were Protestants, if they professed any religion at all. Few if any of them spoke Spanish. Even James Wilkinson, with all his long and intimate intercourse with Spanish officials, seems never to have learned the language. There was no spiritual affinity between the American frontiersman and the Spaniard. Still, while the incorporation of these communities into the Spanish empire might be extremely difficult, it was not at all impossible that Spanish intrigue might secure their erection into an independent power which could be played off against the republic on the Atlantic coast.

In reality the American frontier was more securely bound to the United States than were Louisiana and Florida to Spain. At first glance this does not seem to be the case, for, while every village in the Spanish colonies had its Spanish garrison and its Spanish flag, there was nowhere in Kentucky, Holston or Cumberland in 1784 any material evidence of the authority of the United States government. Yet, while evidences of royal authority in its frontier provinces were abundant, Spain's grip on them was not strong, since it depended upon inadequate military force in the midst of an alien population. In the American frontier settlements the population was certainly heterogeneous enough, but it was drawn largely from the Southern and Middle States, and the overwhelming majority spoke the same language, which was the language of their government.

The Spanish colonial system was cast in an imperial mould, and, despite the efforts of the ministry, could not be adapted to the requirements of these provinces on the Gulf and the Mississippi. The American system of local government, of land-ownership, of commerce had been evolved from an English basis by the older colonies when they were frontier communities, and was admirably adapted to the needs of the new frontier communities across the mountains. It is remarkable how little the law and constitutions of Kentucky and Tennessee differ from those of Virginia and North Carolina, how few changes the frontiersmen had to make. It is still more remarkable how little they desired to change. The explanation is no doubt that they were not given to speculation, that they came westward not because of discontent with the older societies but because of discontent with their own place therein. Their purpose was not creative but reproductive. They were indeed state-builders, but they found their plans and specifications ready made.

The most lasting impression that one gets from contemplating their words and deeds is that of an intense materialism shot through with mystic exaltation. Grimly they drove the Indians out before them, and exploited natural resources, slaves and public office, trampling down with pitiless determination every obstacle to prosperity. In these same men we perceive an equally intense devotion to the republican faith, a mystic sense of union with the deity of republicanism, and a conviction that their god would let none but the faithful prosper. They had their rainbow, and at its end was a pot of gold. This strange dual ideal, communicated by a common language and strengthened by common institutions, maintained the unity of the new republic despite all the dissolvent forces of the times, and gave the United States what Spain lacked, a living idea.

CHAPTER III

THE SPANISH BARRIER

BUFFERS AND BULWARKS

THE war of the American Revolution was hardly ended when the Spanish government began to execute a series of measures which would have proved to demonstration, had there ever been any doubt on the point, that sympathy for the American republic had had nothing whatever to do with Spain's entering the war against England. For all its lack of sympathy, however, Spain's intervention had contributed in a modest way to establish the independence of the rebellious colonists of England, to create a Frankenstein against which Spain must now defend herself. Spain's participation in the war had not affected the general military decision, but it had led England to grant the United States the boundary and navigation right now in dispute between His Catholic Majesty and the republic. Spain's own actions, therefore, had brought the Americans knocking at the back door of her empire.

That the thirteen jarring states, debt-ridden and exhausted by the war, should have been a source of uneasiness to the Spanish government may seem to indicate an extreme degree of timorousness on the part of the latter. We must remember, however, that the Spaniards of that day hardly distinguished between the English and the Americans, calling the latter Anglo-Americans, and that two centuries of bitter experience had convinced the Spanish government of the Briton's restless ambition. Floridablanca had two good reasons for believing that a mere change of government had not diminished the ambition of the

Anglo-Americans: first, the terms of the treaty between the United States and England; and second,
the rapid advance of the "Anglo-American" frontier
during the Revolution. The boundaries claimed by
the new republic seemed paradoxically to the Spaniards
a proof of its limitless ambition. That this ambition
was in train of execution seemed patent to any Spaniard
who so much as glanced at the new settlements of
Kentucky, Cumberland, the Holston and Georgia.
Alexander McGillivray found in the American advance
at the Indians' expense a powerful means of frightening
the Spanish government for his own purposes.[1] His
dire forebodings had been anticipated by Spanish
officials in America, for Martin Navarro, the intendant of Louisiana, and Francisco Rendón, Spanish
agent in Philadelphia, had warned the ministry repeatedly from 1780 to 1783 that the rapid growth of
the American frontier settlements was a menace to
Spain's empire in North America, and their warnings
had received the personal attention of the King's
chief minister, Count Floridablanca.[2]

After the peace of 1783, that minister took up again
the task of circumscribing his ambitious and turbulent
neighbors. He adopted five measures in order to secure
his purpose. With the first of these, his attempt to sell
St. Augustine back to the British in return for Gibraltar
or some other concession, we are not concerned, as it
belongs to the diplomatic story. We merely record
the fact. Two of his measures will be discussed in connection with Gardoqui's mission to the United States,
namely, the closing of the Mississippi to the commerce of the United States, and the assertion of a claim
to the east bank of the Mississippi as far to the eastward and northward as the Flint, Hiwassee and

Tennessee Rivers. His fourth and fifth measures require our attention at this point. One was the encouragement of commerce and immigration in Louisiana and West Florida; the other, the conclusion of treaties of alliance with the Southern Indians. The reader will observe that he resumed his effort of 1782 to insert an insulation of alien territory between Spain's possessions and those of the United States. This insulation, as he planned it, would run in an unbroken line northwestwardly from the Atlantic to the Mississippi, and would consist of upper East Florida in British possession, and of the contiguous territory of the Creek, Choctaw and Chickasaw Indians. Up to 1792, the Spanish government made no effort to include the fourth Southern tribe, the Cherokee, within its political system. Furthermore, Floridablanca's policy was designed to weaken the American West and strengthen Louisiana and West Florida, thus fortifying Spain's hold on the Mississippi Valley and erecting a bulwark for the protection of Mexico.

THE CÉDULA OF 1782

Spanish merchants and manufacturers were, as we have already seen, unable to supply the colonies with the commodities that they required, and Spain was unable to consume their products. Since most of the people of Louisiana were French and since the Bourbon king of Spain was bound by intimate ties to his royal cousin of France, it was provided in 1768 and again, on more liberal terms, in 1778 that under certain conditions trade might be carried on between Louisiana and France.[3] Since experience soon proved these concessions inadequate, and since the colonial minister, José de Gálvez, was a particularly warm partisan of

France, a *cédula*, or order in council, was issued in 1782 amplifying the privileges of trade with France and permitting trade between New Orleans and Pensacola and the French West Indies in urgent cases.[4] The *cédula* was to remain in effect for ten years. It was felt that if Louisiana was to be a dependable barrier against the United States, its population must be increased, for its vast extent made its defence by Spanish troops almost impossible. Besides these commercial concessions, direct encouragement was given to Catholic immigrants to settle in Louisiana and West Florida, the slave trade was legalized, and the government even permitted the British Protestants of West Florida to remain there as Spanish subjects.[5]

BRITISH LOYALISTS AND THE INDIAN TRADE

The 45,000 Indians on the frontier of the Floridas and the still more numerous American backwoodsmen beyond them to the north and east constituted both the problem and the opportunity of Spain. Upon her relations with these two groups depended in a large measure the success of her diplomacy, of her effort to keep the United States at a safe distance from the Mississippi, the Gulf of Mexico and Mexico itself. Indian relations and the frontier intrigue, and commerce, which was inseparably linked with them, therefore play a leading part in the history of Louisiana and the Floridas in the period from 1783 to 1795.

The Indians were nearer neighbors than the American frontiersmen, and so they required Spain's first attention in order to forestall the United States. The government adopted provisionally a method of securing European goods for the Indians which was in accordance with its general commercial policy in these border provinces, but even more liberal, for the goods were secured not from Spain's ally, France, as the Gálvez family and their Creole connections, the Maxents, wished, but from England. The system of managing Indian affairs that the government adopted was based partly on its own experience in Louisiana and partly on the British system as it already existed in the Floridas.[6]

During the Revolution, Indian supplies by way of Charleston and Savannah had been cut off and the trade thrown into the hands of loyal Britons in St. Augustine, Mobile and Pensacola.[7] At the end of the war it was a question which of their former enemies, Spain or the United States, the British leaders of the Indians would favor with their trade. Their decision was in accordance with the tendency, which we have already noted, for the trade to move southwestward from Augusta to Pensacola. Most of the traders and agents among the Southern Indians had remained loyal to the British government during the Revolution and had seen their property confiscated and their lives threatened by the Americans. The war with Spain, on the other hand, had been their government's rather than their own, and had left no such bitter feuds behind it as the barbarous fighting on the frontier of the United States.

That Spain succeeded in getting control of the Southern Indian trade was largely due to the activities of two of these Loyalists. The first was Alexander McGillivray, a quadroon Creek, the son of the powerful Georgia trader and politician, Lachlan McGillivray, and a half-breed Indian woman. The elder McGillivray's name headed the list of Loyalists who were exiled and whose property was confiscated by the state of Georgia.[8] Alexander, who had been employed as a British Indian agent, apparently fell heir to this claim on his father's retirement to Scotland, and freely admitted to the Spaniards that the loss of this property, valued at more than £25,000, was one of the principal reasons for his hostility to the Georgians.[9]

The younger McGillivray's life was as varied and his character as many-sided as his Scottish-Creek-French ancestry was heterogeneous. Far better educated than such American frontiersmen as John Sevier and James Robertson, he lived not the life of an Indian chief or even a white trader, but that of a prosperous Southern planter, with numerous slaves, horses and cattle, and broad acres of farm land on the Coosa River, near the present Montgomery, Alabama. He seldom if ever took part in the fighting that he instigated. He was a Mason, his garb was a white man's and his abode a house, and he possessed and used a well-stocked sideboard and spread a lavish table. But the lady who presided at his table was an Indian squaw, and there were other squaws. He was a heavy drinker — a fault common among eighteenth-century gentlemen — was subject to fearful, blinding headaches, and was sometimes seized by gusts of primitive passion, as on one occasion when he could scarcely restrain himself from scalping the backwoodsmen of Georgia in order to avenge a slighting remark made by an Indian commissioner from Connecticut. His hold over the Indians gave him great weight in Spanish counsels and enabled him to render Panton invaluable service in securing concessions from Spain; yet he seems to have been in a kind of tutelage to Panton and at his death was heavily in debt to the Scotchman.[10]

The other Loyalist was this William Panton, whose

name as well as that of the elder McGillivray was
on the list of confiscation and banishment of the
state of Georgia. Going to St. Augustine just after the
outbreak of the Revolution, Panton and his fellow-
countryman Robert Leslie formed a trading company.
They prospered, and by the end of the Revolution
Panton, Leslie and Company was the largest mercantile house in East Florida. At the beginning of 1783 the
first step in the firm's great expansion was taken when
Charles McLatchy, one of the partners, established
a store at St. Mark's, then still within the province of
British East Florida.[11]

The firm's first success in securing a privileged
position under the Spanish government was won at
St. Augustine. When the Spaniards took possession
of the province in 1784, the new governor, Zéspedes,
found himself with a paucity of funds and a super-
abundance of Indian beggars on hand. Accustomed
by British liberality to expect a present whenever they
visited the governor, these Indians would have returned home with bitter hearts had Zéspedes sent them
away empty-handed, and the consequences to Spain
might have been serious. With no alternative, the
governor sought the aid of Panton, Leslie and Company, got a large supply of goods from them on credit,
and was forever after their close friend and ardent
advocate. It was he who forwarded their first memorial
with vigorous support to the Spanish government.
Deploring the necessity of permitting English traders
and English goods to dominate Spain's trade with the
Indians, Zéspedes assured the court that the services
of Panton's company were indispensable in order to
hold the Indian trade against competition from the
United States until Spanish merchants and traders

were able to take it over. He supported in detail the
various requests made in the memorial. The most
important of these were that the company be permitted
to remain in East Florida on taking an oath of obedience, not of allegiance, that it be permitted to import
a certain amount of Indian goods directly from England to East Florida each year, and that it be permitted
to export directly to England the commodities taken
in payment from the Indians, chiefly furs, paying a six
per cent duty on imports and on exports.[12]

The court returned a favorable reply. By a royal
order dated May 8, 1786, the requests contained in the
memorial were granted provisionally, but without the
specification of a time limit.[13] Thus the British firm
began its career as an instrument of the Spanish
government to combat the influence of the United
States among the Southern Indians.

In East Florida, the company's success in securing
the government's support was due to its own resources, its control of the machinery of Indian trade,
and its conquest of Governor Zéspedes' good will. In
West Florida, the situation was quite different. Panton, Leslie and Company were newcomers in this
province, where Gálvez and Miró, the permanent
governor and *ad interim* governor respectively, had
protégés of their own for whom they wished to secure
the plum of Indian trade. The concession was much
more valuable here than in East Florida, for Mobile
and Pensacola were trade centers for most of the Creek
as well as the Chickasaw and Choctaw towns, and it
became still more desirable when in 1784 St. Mark's
was separated from East and added to West Florida.

Bernardo de Gálvez, captain-general of Louisiana
and West Florida, had spent seven troubled years in

his two provinces, and was convinced of the importance to Spain of maintaining friendly relations with the neighboring Indians and of controlling their supply of blankets, munitions and mirrors. Bernardo was also aware of his family obligations. In 1781 his father-in-law, Gilberto Antonio de Maxent, was sent to Spain, where, through the influence of José de Gálvez, he concluded a contract with the king for supplying the Indians of West Florida with French goods. Disaster soon overtook him. On his return to America he was captured by the British and lost a shipload of his goods; and hardly had the British released him when Spanish officials brought against him a charge of smuggling, in which Francisco de Miranda, later the revolutionizer of Venezuela, was also implicated. Other provision must be made for supplying the Indian trade of West Florida.[14]

PROTECTORATES AND SPHERES OF INFLUENCE

Already before Maxent's failure the Creek, Choctaw and Chickasaw Indians had been summoned to congresses with representatives of the king of Spain for the purpose of establishing peace and friendship, of regulating trade and fixing prices, and of excluding American traders from the Indian country. The first of the two congresses [15] was held with the Creek at Pensacola (May 31–June 1, 1784). Governors Miró and O'Neill, the latter in command at Pensacola, and Intendant Navarro urged McGillivray to agree that the New Orleans firm of Mather and Strother should supply all the Indians of West Florida. Though the half-breed held out resolutely for his partner, Panton could secure nothing more than the bare permission to remain at St. Mark's, Mather and Strother being commissioned

to supply Mobile and Pensacola with a shipload of
goods each for the next year's trade. It soon proved,
however, that the New Orleans firm's credit was un-
equal to the strain, and in 1785 Panton took over the
trade at Pensacola.[16] The permission was for one year
only, but it was renewed again and again for many
years, and the firm remained at Pensacola, with an
occasional change of name, until the Florida purchase
in 1819. Its conquest of the Southern fur trade after
1785 was rapid. In 1788, Mather and Strother gave up
their concession at Mobile, and again Panton, Leslie
and Company succeeded them, thus securing the bulk
of the Choctaw and a part of the Chickasaw trade.[17]

After the Creek Congress of 1784, Miró and Navarro
went to Mobile, where in July they concluded treaties
with the Chickasaw and Choctaw. We need not linger
over the terms of these various treaties, by which
Spain brought all the Southern Indians except the
Cherokee under her protection. It is enough to note
that the Choctaw, Chickasaw and Creek all agreed to
acknowledge the protectorate of Spain, and to exclude
all traders who could not show a Spanish license. This
is the only clause in either of the two treaties at which
the United States could justly take offence, for most
of their towns lay within the territory in dispute between the two powers. This latter fact, indeed, was
one of the chief reasons why Spain cultivated their
friendship.

The striking thing about these congresses is their
defensive, pacific character; a thing that is particularly
striking in comparison with the mad policy of aggression adopted a few years later by Miró's successor
in Louisiana. Far from encouraging Indian hostility
towards the United States, Miró even refused McGil-

livray's request at Pensacola for arms with which to resist American encroachments, and would do no more than forward McGillivray's request to the court.[18] Not military but economic aggression was the keynote of the policy of Miró and Navarro, and their course met with the court's approval. While the ministry, with every appearance of sincerity, instructed the governors of these border provinces to restrain the Indians from attacking the American frontier, it made every effort to monopolize the trade of the Southern Indians. One of its principal objects was to destroy the influence of the United States with these tribes lest the Americans incite them to harass the Spanish settlements or persuade them in any way to coöperate in the conquest of Louisiana and the Floridas; [19] in other words, Spain's purpose was to accomplish through trade what her diplomacy had failed to do: to erect the Southern Indian tribes into a barrier between the United States and the Spanish empire in North America.

By the conclusion of these arrangements for supplying, regulating and monopolizing the Indian trade, the Spanish government succeeded in its purpose of anticipating the Americans; but the means that it had to employ in order to insure success revealed an organic weakness in the Spanish empire, a weakness of which we have already had occasion to speak. Spain was unable to carry on the commerce of her own colonies. In order to prevent Americans from trading with her Indian neighbors, she had to permit Englishmen to trade with them through her own ports. There was hardly a Spaniard to be found who had any acquaintance with the country or the language of the Indians. There was nowhere to be found a Spanish

merchant who knew what goods the Indians required
and how to get them. The Indians had long been
accustomed to British goods, and it was out of the
question to try to satisfy them with Spanish or even
French goods. Hence if a Spanish merchant would
trade with these Indians, he must send to England for
his wares, bring them to Spain and reship them to
Pensacola. Without the necessary knowledge as to the
choice of a cargo, the Spanish merchant labored under
the additional disadvantage of having to pay higher
freight rates, port charges and duties. He must then
have reliable traders and a large capital, for a year's
credit must be extended to the traders. The latter were
accustomed to get their goods on credit and to pay for
them at the end of the next hunting season.[20]

If we suppose the hunting season over and the
Spanish merchant's debts happily collected in the
shape of the skins of deer, bear and beaver, he must
turn these into cash and buy a new supply of goods for
the fall hunting season. Here a new problem con-
fronted him. He had no market for his skins in Spain.
He might ship them to France, or, provided his ship
flew the British flag, to London. Since he would find
a better market and his next season's goods there, England would no doubt be his choice. Here arose his next
difficulty. If the Spanish colonial laws were enforced
and he had to call at a Spanish port on his way to
England, he would probably lose his cargo of skins
through warm weather and worms. If an exception
were made and his call at a Spanish port dispensed with,
the colonial system would be in so far suspended.
British goods would supply the Indians, Indian furs
would go in payment to England and would be carried
in British ships. A Spanish merchant conducting such

a trade would be Spanish in name only. The commerce itself would be British.

Several courses were open to the Spanish government. It might drive British trade out by simply expelling the English merchants and prohibiting further imports. The Indians would then go unsupplied, or would pay a higher price for inferior Spanish goods. Such a course, however, would throw the whole Indian trade into the hands of the Americans, the very calamity that the Spanish government was striving to avert. Again, the government might resort to subventions, but such a policy would be very expensive. Another alternative was to leave the trade in the hands of the English for the time being, with careful governmental supervision, and to prepare a gradual substitution of Spanish merchants, traders and goods for those of England. This was the course that the government adopted. It did so reluctantly, and only after its attempt through the agency of Maxent to supply these Indians with goods from France, its ally, had ended in dismal failure. Even then, the court stipulated at first that Panton, Leslie and Company should use none but French or Spanish goods in their trade with the Indians.[21] Finally in 1786 it yielded to the repeated assurances of Miró and Zéspedes, reinforced by those of the converted Bernardo de Gálvez, that for the present at any rate none but British goods and British traders could prevent the Americans from gaining control of the Indian tribes lying on the border between Spain and the United States.

An organic weakness thus left the Spanish government no alternative but to turn over to two English firms the whole of the Indian trade of the two Floridas. The vital significance of this fact cannot be understood unless we remember that during the whole of the period with which we are dealing the Southern Indian tribes were relied on by Spain as one of her chief defenses against the aggression of the United States and that the conduct of these Indians exercised a powerful influence in determining the attitude of the American frontiersmen towards Spain. That Spain would be badly served by her British protégés was foreseen by more than one intelligent observer. That she was badly served will appear in the following chapters.

CHAPTER IV
THE WESTWARD COURSE
CAPITALISM ON THE FRONTIER

THE conflict between Spain and the United States in its frontier phase seemed at times to reduce itself to a conflict between fur trader and land speculator. The fur trader of the Floridas was no quicker to prepare for the coming struggle than the land jobber of the young republic was to precipitate it. It is not to be understood that in this struggle the government of the United States identified itself with the one or that of Spain with the other. On the contrary, both governments strove to maintain their independence of action, and even on occasion opposed their self-appointed agents; but the latter represented the stage of economic development reached by their respective communities, and their services were indispensable. The governors of Louisiana might write eloquently to their home government about the danger of permitting Englishmen to supply the Indians, and yet in a crisis they always protested that for a few years at any rate nothing must be done to offend Panton. Again, President Washington might hurl his proclamations against speculator O'Fallon and his Yazoo associates, but at the very same time he was appointing speculator Blount governor of the Southwest Territory.

The importance of the land speculator in the history of westward extension in the United States, and specifically in the conflict with which we are now concerned, can hardly be exaggerated.[1] That he created the westward movement no one would pretend, nor does the recognition of his importance involve depreciation of the hunter, trader and Indian fighter. They are both manifestations of the same vital principle of national growth, useless each without the other. There was ample room for both Henderson and Boone, for both Blount and Robertson, in the Mississippi Valley, and neither can be understood without the other. Indeed the folly of opposing the complementary types becomes apparent at once when we observe — as we might expect in a region where specialization existed in only a rudimentary form — that the two types are fused in a single person, as in the case of John Sevier. "Nolachucky Jack" was both a constant harrier of the Indians and an inveterate speculator in frontier lands.

The hunter and fighter, the pioneer of white civilization, was by very definition a transient. He must either march on in pursuit of retreating game, whether it were four-footed or two-footed, or he must change his whole scheme of life and cease to be a pioneer. That the speculator appeared early on the scene is not to be wondered at. A capitalistic society was occupying new lands, and the land speculator merely applied to westward extension the methods of capitalistic organization. The purchase of presents for the Indians, of tools, arms and flatboats for the settlers, the payment of surveyors, the securing of grants from state legislatures — such essential steps in the establishment of a new colony required concerted action and extensive financial resources, and were therefore beyond the power of any individual frontiersman, no matter how brave in conflict or cunning in woodlore he might be. The land speculators, who possessed these resources, were something more than mere real estate agents; or at any rate they were real estate agents cast in a heroic mould. Now they intoxicated a whole Indian tribe, now corrupted a state legislature, now erected a new state when they found none ready to serve their purpose. Although not one of their major projects was successful in the period under consideration, these speculators played a most important part in it, and did something that was much more important than the mere establishment of another colony or two in the already populous Mississippi Valley. They advertised the West and pointed the way not only for later American settlement, but also for the immediate establishment of posts by the jealous Spaniard. They stirred up Western indignation against Spain and Western discontent with the Union, and one of their number, Patrick Henry, very nearly prevented the adoption of the present federal constitution because of his dissatisfaction with the Northern States' attitude towards the development of the Southwest. Finally, it was these speculators who forced the issue of the controversy between their government and Spain, for the success of their speculative schemes depended upon the free use of the Mississippi.

It has already been observed how the American Revolution not only freed the expansive forces in the South from imperial restraint, but also gave the frontier a further impulse towards the Mississippi. This was due in part to the political decentralization which accompanied the Revolution, facilitated the operations of land speculators, and was in turn strengthened by the tendencies of land speculation; but at the same time that the Revolution destroyed imperial restraint, it raised up a new obstacle to expansion in the Old Southwest. Spain's recovery of British West Florida created a competing frontier on the east bank of the Mississippi in the very region most coveted by land speculators of that day. Actually in possession of

Natchez, Spain extended her claim northward to the
Tennessee River [2] so that it embraced not only most of
the Southern Indian villages, but also every one of the
sites most desired by speculators of the United States.
These were Muscle Shoals on the Tennessee, and Chickasaw Bluffs and Walnut Hills on the Mississippi. Although the extent of the Spanish claim as formulated
by Floridablanca was known only in confidential
Spanish circles, the land speculators of the Southern
States fell to work in 1784 as if they had divined it and
were determined to teach the crown of Spain a thing
or two in the fixing of boundaries. There is, indeed,
reason to believe that the legislature of Georgia sanctioned one of these enterprises, the Muscle Shoals
project (1784), because of a report that the Spaniards
were occupying that region.[3]

FRONTIER EXTENSION AND STATE-MAKING

The expansive energy of the Southwestern frontier
expressed itself in two forms at the close of the Revolution : first, in the extension of existing settlements;
second, in the projection of new colonies across the
wilderness. The area of continuous settlement was
extended further into the Creek country by the Georgians through "treaties" (1783, 1785 and 1786) with
a handful of those Indians, and into the Cherokee country by similar cessions of land further down the Holston
extorted by the new state of Franklin from its helpless
neighbors.[4] In the interval between the collapse of
British power in West Florida and the arrival of the
first large supply of Spanish munitions in 1785, these
two tribes could offer little resistance to the land-hungry
frontiersmen. The Georgia frontier was pushed forward to the Oconee, and the Holston settlements soon

advanced down the river of that name to the site of the present Knoxville. Several new "stations" were established on Cumberland River in the first two years of peace; and it was reported by Campo, the Spanish chargé in London, that 8000 immigrants settled in Kentucky alone in 1783.[5] The state governments encouraged these new settlements by the creation of counties and the erection of county governments, the incorpoation of towns, the appointment of militia officers, and the extension of the state judicial system. In one case, that of North Carolina, the state actually raised a standing "army" of one hundred and fifty men to protect the frontiersmen against the Indians.

Even these concessions, however, failed to satisfy the frontiersmen's ambitions. Already the creation of new states in the Southwest was under discussion. A separatist movement had been on foot in Kentucky since 1782, if not earlier, and it met with some encouragement in Virginia. In 1784 there was a movement in Southwestern Virginia to form that valley into a separate state.[6] In December of the same year the state of Franklin [7] was erected by the Holston settlers in the region ceded by North Carolina to Congress in June, although the cession act was repealed by the state legislature in November. Particularism and expansionism, religiosity and hatred of the Indians, imitativeness and individualism, all played their part in the complex movement that produced this frontier state; but the dominant interest was in land. A cession of lands south of the French Broad was extorted from the Cherokee by the Franklinites, who also expected to dispose of the vacant lands ceded by North Carolina to Congress and planned to establish a greater state of Franklin by occupying the Muscle Shoals region.

The first and only governor of Franklin, John Sevier, was one of the most interesting men in the Southwest of his day, for he possessed in a high degree the qualities that distinguish the American frontiersman. If we are to trust his diary and the other extant records concerning him, his life was almost completely external and objective.[8] Of introspection, emotional self-consciousness, intellectual inquiry there is hardly a trace. A monument erected to him in Knoxville, Tennessee, bears the significant inscription : "Thirty-five battles, thirty-five victories," which, though not altogether accurate, expresses adequately the lifelong Indian fighter, the soldier who recorded in his diary a conversation with Napoleon on a high mountain overlooking the kingdoms of this earth. To complete the picture, however, the inscription should add : "He was an inveterate land speculator, despite many failures." His hold over his fellow-frontiersmen was due in part to their belief that he could lead them triumphantly against the Indians and into the Promised Land, but it was due also to the charm of his free, generous nature, to his overflow of abundant vitality. He had little in common with the negative, repressive, sectarianism that later dominated his community. His feet frequently trod those twin roads to hell, card-playing and dancing. It is recorded that on one occasion he was arrested for drunkenness and disorderly conduct,[9] and there are rumors of other irregularities in his private life. He bought, sold and used slaves without compunction, winked at if he did not openly permit the cold-blooded murder of unoffending Indians, intrigued with Spain, and while governor of Tennessee (1796) openly condoned the violation of a federal proclamation. And yet he was an industrious farmer and storekeeper, a churchgoer, careful to provide for the education of his children, foremost in Indian warfare when the settlements were threatened, and always ready to lend a helping hand to his poorer neighbors. His were the virtues of a frontier community.

None of these Western communities realized its dream of statehood at this time. The North Atlantic States were loath to increase the political power of the South and West. North Carolina opposed the Franklinites, and Virginia, while more compliant in the case of the Kentuckians, moved slowly. Circumstances soon arose that gave a new direction to Western particularism, but in order to understand those circumstances we must first give our attention to the schemes of land speculators in the Southwest in the years 1784 and 1785.

PROJECTED COLONIES : CHICKASAW BLUFFS, MUSCLE SHOALS, BOURBON COUNTY

The second manifestation of expansive energy in the Southwest was the projection of new colonies. In these enterprises the land speculators played a prominent part, for Muscle Shoals, Chickasaw Bluffs, Walnut Hills and Natchez offered a tempting field for speculative endeavor. Immigration into the Mississippi Valley was assuming such proportions that property-owners in the Atlantic States were alarmed, those in the Western settlements elated, Spanish statesmen disturbed and neutral observers dumbfounded. Peace seemed assured by the crushing defeat inflicted on the hostile Indians in the Revolutionary War, prosperity by the free navigation of the Mississippi, permitted to the Americans by Spain during the war, granted by England in the treaty of peace, and still undisturbed at the beginning of 1784. Above all, no Spanish counterclaim to the territory in question had ever been publicly asserted. Spain had made no protest against the treaty with England which fixed the southern boundary of the United States at the thirty-first parallel. It is not surprising that under these circumstances many new colonies were projected, or that when at length Spain closed the Mississippi and challenged the boundary claim of the United States the projectors of these colonies refused to relinquish tamely their dreams of profit and empire.

One of the first and most persistently prosecuted of these plans, and one of the last to be realized, was that of James Robertson and other North Carolinians to establish a settlement at Chickasaw Bluffs.[10] Since this site lay within the hunting grounds of the Chickasaw Indians, with whom Robertson and the other Cumberland settlers were on excellent terms, success seemed more than likely; but the Spanish treaty with the Chickasaw at Mobile in June, 1784, the menace of war and the remoteness of Chickasaw Bluffs prevented the plan from being carried into effect. The chief importance of the project is that its discovery called the attention of the Spanish government to this spot, increased its alarm at the territorial ambitions of the frontiersmen, and finally in 1795 led the governor of Louisiana to establish a fort there.

Another of the colonies projected during this period was one at Muscle Shoals.[11] Both because of the number of prominent persons in the South engaged in the enterprise and because of the events connected with the long and persistent attempt to establish the colony, the Muscle Shoals venture is one of singular importance in the history of the Old Southwest. Three future governors were members of the original company:

Richard Caswell of North Carolina, William Blount of the Southwest Territory, and John Sevier of Franklin and Tennessee. Others engaged were Joseph Martin, agent of Patrick Henry and of the state of Virginia, General Griffith Rutherford, and Wade Hampton of South Carolina. In the first phase, William Blount was the head of the company, corresponding with his frontier associates, who secured the Cherokee title to the site of the proposed colony, and visiting Georgia, where he persuaded the legislature to provide (February, 1784) for the settlement of the Shoals district and the organization of a county government there. The "District of Tenasee," as it was called, including all the land lying between the Tennessee River and the southern boundary of the present state of Tennessee, was erected into a county called Houston, and all the offices were filled with members of the company and their relatives.

Everything was apparently ready for an exodus from the older Holston settlements to Muscle Shoals when in August, 1784, the progress of the enterprise was halted by the separatist movement which resulted in the establishment of the state of Franklin. This movement was at first opposed by Sevier, for it diverted attention from the speculative project; but, finding the separatist tendency too powerful to resist, he put himself at its head and was elected governor of the infant state. Once in the saddle, he returned to his favorite scheme with the force of the new government behind him. This later phase of the project will be discussed in another place.

The third of the projected colonies lay on the Mississippi. This was Bourbon County, erected by the state of Georgia in 1785, and including, besides Natchez itself, which was at the time garrisoned by Spanish troops, all the territory on the Mississippi between the thirty-first parallel and the mouth of the Yazoo River.[12] This curious episode is typical of the situation in the whole Southwest at that time, and reveals some of its complexities. There were three claimants to the territory in which Bourbon County was erected: Georgia, Spain and the United States. Though actually in possession of the district, which Bernardo de Gálvez had conquered during the Revolution, Spain had made no protest against its cession by England to the United States in 1783. Gardoqui, however, was on his way from Spain to New York to take up the matter with Congress. His coming had been long expected, his object was easy to guess, and it was precisely while he was in Havana (February, 1785), waiting for a ship to take him to New York, that the Georgia legislature granted the request of persons from Natchez and erected that district into a county of the state of Georgia under the name of Bourbon.[13]

Four commissioners were appointed to proceed to Natchez and organize the county government. Two of them made their way down the Ohio and Mississippi rivers, and the other two traveled overland through the Indian country, where they tried to reëstablish the former commerce between Augusta and the towns of the Chickasaw and Choctaw. Although the Georgia legislature had strictly ordered the commissioners not to commit any act of hostility against Spain, it was persistently rumored that they were planning the use of force, and that George Rogers Clark was to lead an army of 2500 Kentuckians to rout the Spaniards out of Natchez.

The enterprise was an utter failure. The first of the commissioners to arrive in Natchez exceeded his powers, violated the pacific instructions given him by the Georgia legislature, abruptly demanded the surrender of the district by the Spanish commander, and threatened violence when he was refused. The people of the district, many of whom were British Loyalists, showed no enthusiasm for the rule of revolutionary Georgia. This was especially true of the wealthier planters. When Governor Miró was first informed of the commissioners' arrival in Natchez, he played for time, afraid to deal with them as summarily as he wished; but later, on the receipt of orders from his energetic chief, Captain-General Gálvez, now Viceroy of New Spain, and of assurances that the people of Natchez would not aid the Georgians, he expelled the commissioners from the district. In the meantime Gardoqui had arrived in New York, and had protested to Congress against the proceedings of the commissioners. Congress, itself a claimant to the district, was not disposed to prejudice the negotiation with Gardoqui for the benefit of its rival, the state of Georgia. Since not even Georgia's delegates in Congress could deny that the Bourbon County commissioners had violated their instructions, the affair·ended to the entire satisfaction of Gardoqui and the complete discomfiture of the Georgians.[14]

Yet the affair was ominous for Spain. The union of land speculators and fur traders of Georgia and the Carolinas with the frontiersmen of Kentucky and North Carolina was a formidable one, and there was nothing to prevent its being formed again on more definite and more aggressive terms and with a better chance of success. Such a menace Spain might of course resist by strengthening her military defences, as Miró did on this occasion, but such measures were very costly. The extraordinary expenses occasioned by the Bourbon

County episode were about $50,000,[15] which was not a small sum for a province already burdensome to a none too prosperous government. As the frontier conflict became more acute, the expense of bolstering up the military defences of Louisiana became greater and greater, until finally, at a critical period in Spain's international relations and in her finances, the burden became intolerable.

"INCROCHEN TYRENTS"

Although not one of these projected colonies was established at any time in our period, and although on the contrary Spain anticipated the speculators and their frontier agents by establishing forts first in the Yazoo district (1791) and then at Chickasaw Bluffs (1795), the projects produced results of the very first importance in the history of the Spanish-American conflict. That the enterprises were not mere paper prospectuses was shown by the fact that agents were actually on the site of the intended settlements in 1784–85, making surveys, marking trees, and preparing for colonization, and that the commissioners of Bourbon County presented themselves in Natchez with the evident — though unaccountable — expectation of taking over the government from the Spanish commandant. The resolute opposition of Spain to these designs, the expulsion of the Georgia commissioners from Natchez, the Indian attacks on the speculators at Chickasaw Bluffs and Muscle Shoals, enraged the frontiersmen and led Thomas Green, one of the Bourbon County commissioners, to warn his fellow-countrymen that if they did not look about them a few "incrochen tyrents," namely the Spaniards, would soon be in possession of all the choicest places in the New World.[16]

In the face of the unexpected obstacle of determined and effective Spanish resistance, the frontiersmen and speculators changed their tactics and began to take Spain into account. Some of them intrigued with Spain, some against Spain, and some, such as John Sevier and George Rogers Clark, did both. It was the intrigue against Spain, the planning of a devastating invasion of Louisiana and the Floridas, that appealed most powerfully to the imagination of the frontiersmen. Sevier, Clark, Green, Sullivan, O'Fallon — these and many other names are associated with designs of expelling the "haughty and indolent Spaniard" from the mouth of the Mississippi and establishing in his place the beneficent rule of the long-haired frontiersman. Reports of these hostile designs soon reached the Spanish court, and, as we shall see, were influential in determining Floridablanca to adopt as a defensive measure against frontier hostility an intrigue with the frontiersmen themselves.

A FUR TRADERS' WAR

A more immediate result of the frontier advance and the speculative enterprises of 1784–85 was the outbreak of war between the Georgians and the Creek Indians. This was primarily a fur traders' war. In every one of the schemes that we have discussed the speculators seem to have been almost as much interested in fur trading as in colonization. The Georgia commissioners, both on their way to Natchez and after their expulsion from it, made strenuous efforts to reconquer for Georgia the trade of the Choctaw and Chickasaw. Sevier's letters to the Chickasaw are full of allusions to the trade that would be provided them by the projected colony at Muscle Shoals. The Cumberland settlers were trying to divert the Southern fur trade from Mobile and Pensacola to Nashville, and their projected post at Chickasaw Bluffs was probably a part of their plan.[17]

As one might expect, the half-breed chief Alexander McGillivray and his partner William Panton lost no time in launching a counter-offensive against their rebel cousins in Georgia and the Carolinas. McGillivray had made the American frontier menace the text of a letter to Miró in 1784. In 1785 he was one of the first to warn the governor of the Bourbon County project. In July of the same year he protested to the Spanish government, in the name of the Creek, Choctaw and Chickasaw nations, against the encroachments of the Americans, specifying the recent creation of counties within the Indian's hunting grounds and demanding the restoration of the boundaries of 1772 — that is, the evacuation of a large part of Georgia, of most of the Holston settlements, of all those on the Cumberland River, and of half of Kentucky.[18]

In July, 1785, Congress appointed commissioners to negotiate treaties of friendship, commerce and limits with the Southern tribes.[19] In November the commissioners arrived in Georgia, where they attempted to treat with the Creek Indians, but were baulked by the opposition of the state of Georgia and McGillivray. Both of the latter apparently preferred to fight it out. More successful elsewhere, the commissioners negotiated treaties with the Cherokee, Chickasaw and Choctaw in the winter of 1785–86. The significance of the most important of these treaties, the one with the Cherokee, will be discussed in another place.

The unwillingness of the Creek to compromise their dispute with Georgia was no doubt increased by the fact that through William Panton's concession from the Spanish government they had received in the summer of 1785 their first large supply of munitions since the outbreak of the war between Spain and England. In April of the following year, without awaiting the court's reply to his protest against American encroachments, McGillivray let loose his warriors upon the Georgia frontier and upon Cumberland.[20] It was only after the decision had been made and the warriors had set out on the war-path that he informed Miró of the accomplished fact, styled the war a defensive one on the part of the Indians and demanded Spain's aid. It is significant that the war began with the murder and expulsion of Georgia traders among the Creek; and if any doubt remained that this was a fur traders' war, it would be set at rest by a letter written by William Panton two years later in which he said: ". . . Our house expended by the struggle we had with the Georgia merchants in the years 1784, 1785 and the beginning of 1786 before we obtained their expulsion from the Indian nation, no less a sum than thirty thousand dollars. . . ." [21]

Contrary to the general impression, this war was not willed or ordered by the Spanish government or any of its officials. On the contrary, it came as a shock even to Miró and placed him in a most embarrassing position, for he suspected that not all the fault was on the side of the Georgians. Though he granted McGillivray's request for munitions, he directed that they be delivered with the utmost secrecy and on the understanding that they were to be used for defensive purposes only.[22] He further urged McGillivray to make peace with the Americans as soon as possible. His action was ulti- mately approved by the court, which, with every appearance of sincerity, enjoined upon Miró and all the frontier officials a pacific policy.[23] The Spanish government never, either at this time or at any other, authorized the Indians to begin hostilities against the Americans, and while Miró remained in Louisiana he complied faithfully with the orders of his government, even to the detriment of Spain's interests among the Indians.[24]

Thus the activity of American speculators and frontiersmen forced the first public indication of Spain's territorial claims east of the Mississippi, precipitated an Indian war, compelled the definition of Spain's Indian policy, and prepared the way for frontier intrigues both with and against Spain. By bringing out in high relief the conflict of interest between Spaniard and American and by sharpening their mutual antagonism, this activity showed that the interests of peace required an early adjustment by treaty of the points at issue between the two countries.

CHAPTER V

GARDOQUI'S MISSION

THE FRONTIER ORIGIN OF GARDOQUI'S MISSION

THE Spanish government's uneasiness at the growth of the American West was a constant factor in its diplomacy from the beginning of the Revolution throughout the period with which we are concerned. It will be seen again and again in the following pages how this uneasiness, justified and increased by the reports of its agents in North America, shaped the course of Spain's policy with regard to the United States and its Western settlements. To begin with, it was one of the chief reasons for Gardoqui's mission to the United States.

We have already seen how Floridablanca deliberately postponed an adjustment with the United States until after the peace settlement of 1783. In the negotiations of 1782–83 he had failed first in his attempt, with French assistance, to have the western boundary of the United States fixed well to the eastward of the Mississippi, and then in his effort to beguile England into playing the buffer between the Spanish dominions and the United States. After this double failure he had no recourse but to settle the points at issue with the United States by a separate treaty. This he postponed until after the general peace settlement of September, 1783, in order, no doubt, to avoid as far as possible the danger of coöperation between the United States and England. Thus a Spanish-American treaty was conspicuous by its absence from the general settlement, and Floridablanca seemed in no hurry to supply the deficiency.

Less than ten months later — that is, before the end of July, 1784 — he had decided to take the initiative in resuming the negotiation with the United States, and had drawn up the instructions for that purpose. Within another three months he had chosen Gardoqui to represent Spain in the negotiation and had ordered him to the United States to open it. This sudden zeal for an accommodation is explained by the pressure of Spanish officials in North America, and their insistence in turn is explained by their uneasiness at the activity of their republican neighbors in the Mississippi Valley.

One of the first officials to warn Floridablanca was Bernardo del Campo, then chargé d'affaires and later ambassador in London, who, under Floridablanca's direction and with the assistance of Gardoqui, had conducted the fruitless negotiation with Jay in Spain (1780–82). Writing from London in November, 1783, he reported that swarms of discontented Americans were crossing the mountains into the Mississippi Valley, where they might soon become a serious menace to Spain's neighboring possessions. Floridablanca was sufficiently interested by this information to refer it to José de Gálvez, the colonial secretary,[1] but did nothing further in the matter until he was prodded into action by similar warnings from many other sources.

On March 2, 1784, Bernardo de Gálvez, then in Madrid, wrote his uncle, the colonial secretary, requesting in his capacity as governor of Louisiana and the Floridas instructions as to the boundaries of West Florida.[2] Such instructions were necessary, he pointed out, in view of the conflicting provisions of England's treaties with Spain and the United States on that subject. He warned the colonial secretary that the line claimed by the United States would give them Natchez "which I had the honor to place under the obedience of my sovereign in the late war," most of the Southern Indian tribes and their fur trade, and access to Mobile Bay, leaving Spain with nothing but a thin strip of territory along the Gulf coast. Such a situation, together with the free navigation of the Mississippi River, which the United States claimed as a right, would be a perpetual source of discord between the two powers.

The navigation of the Mississippi, mentioned in passing by Count Gálvez, was the principal theme of letters to José de Gálvez from the acting governor of Louisiana, Estevan Miró, and the intendant, Martin Navarro.[3] Writing from New Orleans in March, 1784, they reported the recent arrival at that city of the *America*, Captain Christopher Whipple, from Providence, Rhode Island, with a Rhode Island passport. Undert Article 8 of the treaty of 1783 between England and the United States, Whipple claimed the right to pass freely up the Mississippi to the possessions of the United States, which, he declared, extended as far south as the thirty-first parallel. Miró and Navarro had no instructions that would cover such a case. Their latest order from the court relating to the Mississippi was dated October 29, 1781, and opened its navigation to the Americans for the duration of the war. Now that the war was over, the governor and intendant were in doubt as to the course that they should follow. Suspicious of Whipple, who had his cabin fitted up as a shop with shelves and weights, they put a detachment of soldiers on board his ship in order to prevent illicit trade with the plantations in Spanish territory along the Mississippi; but, since they had no orders to the contrary, they gave Whipple permission — with their tongues in their cheeks, no doubt — to sail up the Mississippi, turbulent with the spring floods, to the American settlements at the Illinois. Navarro advised strongly against opening the river to the commerce of the United States, for, said he, the *cédula* of 1782 permitting trade between Louisiana and France made adequate provision for the needs of the province, and the admission of any other nation would facilitate contraband and injure the merchants of Louisiana.

As the Mississippi problem was presented to Floridablanca for decision in the summer of 1784, it presented two aspects, one familiar and vexatious, the other new and alarming. In the first place, Navarro's letter of which we have just spoken made it clear that if Spain admitted the validity of Article 8 of the Anglo-American treaty of 1783, an immediate consequence would be the revival of that contraband trade whose eradication had been one of Spain's principal war aims, and that now two nations instead of one would "cause her infinite vexation" on the lower Mississippi and in the Gulf, as Floridablanca had complained of England in 1778.

In the second place, the case of the *America* called attention to a new aspect — new since 1775 — of the Mississippi problem : its relation to the rapidly growing American settlements in the Ohio Valley. While the Revolution was still in progress, Navarro had written José de Gálvez on this subject, and Gálvez had, by order of the king, transmitted his letters to Floridablanca. If the Spanish government followed Navarro's advice, it would close the Mississippi River to American commerce in order to stifle the Western settlements. In this letter and another of the same year (1781),[4] Navarro reported the rapid growth of Kentucky and of the American settlements at the Illinois, and shipments of American corn down the Mississippi. The Americans were an active, enterprising people, he said, citing by way of illustration the case of a former South Carolinian, Gaillard, who had emigrated from that state to Natchez by way of Pittsburg with his family and slaves, stopping in Kentucky long enough to make a crop for their support. Such energy and resourcefulness, said Navarro, combined with the greedy ambition of the Americans, made them a menace to Mexico. Spain had a remedy, however, for it could strangle the American West by closing its only commercial outlet, the Mississippi.[5]

Further evidence of the alarmingly rapid development of the American West was contained in a letter from Francisco Rendón, the agent of Spain in Philadelphia. Writing in December, 1783, he reported that Kentucky had applied to Virginia for permission to form a separate state in conformity with the general principles of the Confederation, and that Connecticut was preparing to make use of the territory claimed by it in the Ohio Valley. These indications of the rapid extension of the American system across the mountains, confirming earlier reports, disturbed the colonial secretary, who submitted Rendón's letter to his nephew, Bernardo, for his opinion. The latter replied briefly that if the territory between the Mississippi and the Appalachians belonged to Spain, the Americans should by no means be permitted to settle in it; but that if it belonged to the United States, Spain could not prevent their occupation of it. Clearly a definition of Spain's territorial claim and of Spanish policy was necessary, and José de Gálvez, forwarding Rendón's letter and the Count's report thereon, reminded Floridablanca of the urgency of the matter.[6]

STRANGLING THE AMERICAN WEST

To meet this situation, Floridablanca adopted three measures. A royal order was issued closing the Mississippi River to all but Spanish ships; a formal statement was drawn up setting forth Spain's position in regard to the navigation of the Mississippi and the boundary of its possessions on the east bank of that river; and Gardoqui was sent to negotiate a treaty with the United States.

The order closing the Mississippi was, at Floridablanca's suggestion, drawn up by the colonial secretary without waiting for the completion of the formal statement of Spanish claims then in preparation. On June 26, 1784, Gálvez wrote the governor and the intendant of Louisiana and Spain's agent in Philadelphia, Rendón, directing them respectively to announce in the colonies and to inform Congress of Spain's exclusive right to the navigation of the Mississippi and to warn the Americans not to expose themselves and their property to arrest and confiscation pending the settlement of the questions at issue between Spain and the United States. A proclamation to this effect was published in Louisiana, and Rendón communicated the substance of the order to Congress through the agency of the French chargé, Marbois.[7]

Not only was this the first, but it was also by all odds the most important, of Floridablanca's three measures, and the other two were subsidiary to it. In drawing the boundary line, the object was to give Spain possession of both banks of the river as far north as possible; and the chief purpose of Gardoqui's mission was to secure the acquiescence of the United States in the closing of the Mississippi. By this means he expected,

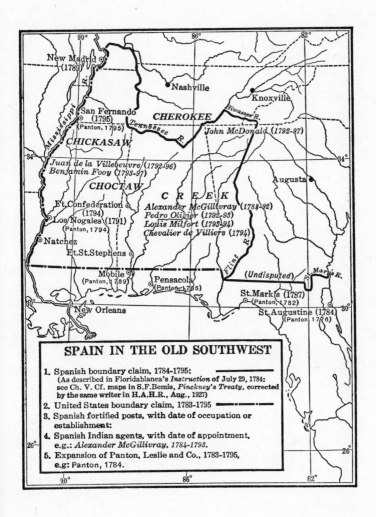

New Madrid
(1789)

Nashville

Knoxville

San Fernando
(1795)
(Panton, 1795)

CHEROKEE

Hiwassee R.

Tennessee R.

John McDonald (1792-97)

CHICKASAW

Augusta

Juan de la Villebeuvre (1792-96)
Benjamin Fooy (1793-97)

CHOCTAW

C R E E K

Ft.Confederation
(1794)
Los Nogales (1791)
(Panton, 1794)

Alexander McGillivray (1784-92)
Pedro Olivier (1792-93)
Louis Milfort (1793-94)
Chevalier de Villiers (1794)

Natchez

Ft.St.Stephens

Flint R.

St. Marys R.

Mobile
(Panton, 1789)

Pensacola
(Panton, 1785)

(Undisputed)

New Orleans

St.Marks (1787)
(Panton, 1782)

St.Augustine (1784)
(Panton, 1786)

SPAIN IN THE OLD SOUTHWEST

1. Spanish boundary claim, 1784-1795: ▬▬▬▬
   (As described in Floridablanca's *Instruction* of July 29, 1784:
   see Ch. V. Cf. maps in S.F.Bemis, *Pinckney's Treaty*, corrected
   by the same writer in H.A.H.R., Aug., 1927)
2. United States boundary claim, 1783-1795 ▬ ▬ ▬
3. Spanish fortified posts, with date of occupation or
   establishment:
4. Spanish Indian agents, with date of appointment,
   e.g.: *Alexander McGillivray, 1784-1793.*
5. Expansion of Panton, Leslie and Co., 1783-1795,
   e.g: Panton, 1784.

on Navarro's assurance, to strangle the American settlements in the Mississippi Valley.

The comprehensive statement of Spain's position on the boundary and navigation questions was issued by Floridablanca on July 29, 1784.[8] It took the form of an "Instruction" to the captain-general, Gálvez, and was intended to govern both the colonial officials of the Floridas and Louisiana and the plenipotentiary to be sent to the United States. Stating that the time had now come to settle these two questions, the Instruction announced that His Majesty accepted the the boundary of East Florida as claimed by the United States, but that from its western extremity the Spanish boundary followed the Flint River up to its source, thence in a straight line to the Euphassee (Hiwassee), thence down the Euphassee, Tennessee and Ohio Rivers to the Mississippi, and thence to its source. This claim was based on the conquest of West Florida by Gálvez during the Revolution, the Spanish treaty with England of 1783, the subrogation by Spain of France's rights as ceded to England in 1763, the dependence of the Chickasaw on Pensacola, and the fact that the Spanish commandant of Arkansas had on November 22, 1780, taken formal possession of the east bank of the Mississippi in the name of the king of Spain. It is curious to note that, so far as this Instruction and all other available evidence show, the Spanish government was still not aware of the secret article in the preliminary treaty between the United States and England (1782),[9] or of the proclamation of 1764 moving the northern boundary of West Florida up to the mouth of the Yazoo River.

As for the navigation of the Mississippi, the Instruction declared Spain's exclusive right to it so far as she owned both banks of the Mississippi. England's right to the navigation of the Mississippi, it was said, depended on the possession of the eastern bank; and since Spain had conquered this bank during the war, England's pretended cession of the free navigation to the United States was an attempt to cede something that England did not possess. Not even in order to reach their possessions on the Upper Mississippi were the Americans to be permitted to navigate its lower waters.[10] In view of Spain's boundary claim, this was equivalent to the assertion that the United States had no right to navigate the Mississippi below its junction with the Ohio.

His Majesty's intention of sending a plenipotentiary to treat with the United States was referred to in the foregoing Instruction. After it was drawn up, and apparently before the final orders to Gardoqui were issued, another letter from Rendón, with still more alarming reports about the American West, was received by José de Gálvez and transmitted by him to Floridablanca. In this letter Rendón reported that Americans were said to be going from Kentucky down the Ohio River and up the Red River to carry on contraband trade with Mexico. Proceeding from this point of departure to observations of greater importance, Rendón gave warning that the Americans would not respect any treaty unless they were granted "a free mutual commerce," that they regarded the free use of the Mississippi as essential to the prosperity of the West, and that their resentment at Spain's conduct during the Revolution made precautionary measures indispensable if serious disturbances were to be avoided.[11]

By October 2, 1784, Gardoqui's instructions had been drawn up.[12] He was given for his guidance a copy of the Instruction of July 29, and was directed to correspond with Count Gálvez, with whose consent he might make some concession to the United States with regard to the boundary, provided that the settlements of Louisiana and West Florida were protected as far as the Bahama Channel. In other words, his instructions indicated that the king would assent to the cession of St. Augustine to the United States and to some modification of the boundary in the Mississippi Valley as set forth in the Instruction of July 29. Gardoqui was further directed to insist on the exclusive navigation of the Mississippi so far as Spain held both banks, and to inform the United States that it was useless for them to request admission to the commerce of the Spanish colonies, since that was prohibited by treaties from Utrecht (1713) down to 1783. They might, however, be offered most favored nation treatment in Spain itself and the Canaries. In order to facilitate the negotiations, Gardoqui might agree to a defensive alliance and a mutual territorial guarantee. These terms, said Floridablanca, should prove satisfactory to the United States, since they were practically the same as those proposed by Jay in 1781, with the territorial guarantee and the commercial concessions the equivalent of Jay's demand for immediate recognition of the independence of the United States and aid in the war against England. Gardoqui was given the rank of *encargado de negocios* (chargé d'affaires), and was empowered to negotiate a treaty in accordance with the foregoing instructions. He was to correspond with Floridablanca by the roundabout way of Havana, which was connected with the court by a monthly mail service, but might send his despatches by commercial vessels going direct to Spain, in case he were satisfied that they were reliable. Rendón was to be his secretary, and two lads, Jáudenes and Viar, were sent with him to assist in the work of the legation. His salary was fixed at $12,000, and he was allowed a secret service fund. His credentials were drawn up in the same style as those of the Spanish ministers to Holland, and in presenting them he was to follow the same ceremonial as the French minister to the United States.

Gardoqui's mission and the resumption of the negotiation were clearly due to the initiative not of the United States but of Spain,[13] and the Spanish government was actuated partly by a desire to prevent the recrudescence of contraband trade on the Mississippi, but above all by its uneasiness at the rapid growth of the American West. The policy that it adopted at this time in the face of the American menace remained, despite occasional reluctant deviations, substantially the same throughout our period: namely, to secure the acquiescence of the United States in a system that would protect Spain against the American frontier. The terms His Catholic Majesty was willing to offer changed with changing circumstances, but Spain usually relied for success upon an appeal to the provincial interests of the Atlantic States, a course suggested as early as 1778 by the first Spanish agent in the United States, Juan de Miralles.[14]

The instructions given to Gardoqui and the correspondence relating to his mission show that the possibility of a converse policy, an appeal to Western sectionalism, played no part in Floridablanca's calculations at this stage of the game. Although the possibility of a British intrigue with those people was mentioned by Miralles, no Spanish official proposed before 1786, so far as the records show, that Spain undertake such a measure. Intrigue was indeed a hazardous alternative to negotiation, and it is not surprising that it was not considered while there seemed to be any hope of concluding a satisfactory treaty with Congress.

Don Diego de Gardoqui found his way into diplomacy through the tradesman's entrance. The Bilbao firm of which he was a member had traded with the United States, then colonies, for a full generation before the Revolution,[15] and was the screen behind which the Spanish government furnished arms and clothing to the rebellious colonies of England when Spain was still ostensibly a neutral power. Don Diego was the company's representative in arranging these matters with the Spanish government. His knowledge of English made the transition to diplomacy easy. He was Grimaldi's interpreter at the time of Arthur Lee's unwelcome visit to Spain (1777), and in 1780 he formally entered the government service. When John Jay and his secretary, William Carmichael, arrived in Spain. Gardoqui not only had charge of financial arrangements with them, but also discussed purely diplomatic questions. As early as 1780 the Spanish government planned to send him to the United States, and in 1782 John Jay wrote that Congress had long been expecting his arrival in the capacity of minister plenipotentiary to the United States.[16] For various reasons the mission was postponed. In 1784 developed the disquieting situation described above, and Gardoqui was finally despatched. For a detailed account of his negotiation with John Jay, Congress's secretary for foreign affairs, the reader is referred to a formal diplomatic history of the period. It is enough for our purpose to sketch the situation in the barest outline and to note the results of the tedious negotiation, which lasted from 1785 to 1788.

THE CONFLICT OF SECTIONAL INTERESTS

Despite the indignation aroused in the West and on the Atlantic coast by Spain's announcement of the closing of the Mississippi, and despite Gardoqui's isolation — his only regular channel of correspondence with Spain was by way of Havana, and his sources of information in the United States were scanty and unreliable —[17] he found conditions favorable in several respects to the success of his mission. In the first place, the usual post-war economic depression was settling down upon the United States.[18] American shipping and exports, with former markets in the British empire wholly or partially lost, were seeking compensation elsewhere. Commercial concessions for the United States in Spain and its colonies, vainly sought by Jay during his Spanish mission (1780–82), were more important to the country than ever now that the Revolution was over. Rendón had transmitted to his government a plan outlined by Robert Morris for the development of trade between the two countries, and Gardoqui wrote home that nothing could give the Americans more pleasure than a trade that would bring Spanish gold and silver into their ports.[19] Moreover, the whole of the United States' growing Mediterranean trade would be benefited by the interposition of Spain's good offices with the vexatious Barbary States.

In the second place, there were many influential people in the United States who were opposed to the rapid development of the American West. Contempt for the lazy, shiftless backwoodsman; sympathy for

the dispossessed Indian tribes; the self-interest of
landlord and employer; Northern jealousy of the agri-
cultural South and West; the conviction that the
ultimate secession of the Mississippi Valley settlements
was a certainty — one or more of these considerations
disposed such representatives of the commercial states
as Rufus King, Timothy Pickering and Gouverneur
Morris in favor of any measure that would check the
alarming exodus of population from the Atlantic coast
and the equally alarming spread of settlement in the
West.[20] In the period 1786–88 the Mississippi question was the subject of even bitterer controversy within
the United States than between the United States and
Spain, and the controversy assumed a dangerously
sectional character. William Grayson, speaking in the
Virginia ratifying convention of 1788, voiced the sentiments of many in the South and West when he said:
"I look upon this as a contest for empire. Our country
[Virginia] is equally affected with Kentucky. The
Southern States are deeply interested in this subject.
If the Mississippi be shut up, emigrations will be
stopped entirely. There will be no new states formed
on the western waters. . . . This contest of the Mississippi involves this great national contest; that is,
whether one part of the continent shall govern the
other. The Northern States have the majority, and
will endeavor to retain it."[21] So long as this "national
contest" remained unsettled and the Americans were
unable to decide whether or not they wanted the free
navigation of the Mississippi, there was little likelihood
that Spain would concede it.

In the third place, Gardoqui's offer of a territorial
guarantee was equivalent to an offer that, if the United
States would yield to Spain a part of its claims in the

Southwest, Spain would join the United States in forcing England to evacuate the posts that it still occupied in the Northwest. Since the Northwest had been ceded by the claimant states to Congress, and since the Southwest had not, the majority in Congress was inclined to give more weight to the interests of the former than of the latter.

Well might Jay declare, as he did in a notable address to Congress in August, 1786, that the treaty with Spain was the most important treaty the United States could negotiate with any power.[22] With this preface, he proceeded to describe the hopeless state of his negotiation with Gardoqui, for both the plenipotentiaries were bound by instructions that left them little discretion and made agreement impossible. Diplomacy had failed to move Spain, and the United States was in no position to go to war. It was impossible, said Jay, to secure both the navigation of the Mississippi and the thirty-first parallel; but, by yielding the former for a term of years, the United States might secure the latter, as well as valuable commercial concessions in the ports of Spain. At the end of the period of suspension the United States could renew the assertion of its claim to the navigation of the Mississippi with even better reason than at present. After a long and bitter debate on this proposal, in which the opposition was led by the Virginia delegation, Congress empowered Jay to negotiate such a treaty, leaving undetermined in its instructions the number of years for which the navigation of the Mississippi might be closed to the United States.[23]

No treaty was ever negotiated under this revised instruction. According to Gardoqui, who was himself not overbold, Jay was intimidated by the widespread denunciation of Congress' decision, which, though taken in secret session, soon became public property. Now and then the two plenipotentiaries conferred, but without result. Jay held that such a thorny question should be reserved for the new federal government then forming, and such was the decision of Congress in 1788 upon the ratification of the federal constitution by nine states.[24]

The result of this new turn of affairs was twofold. The decision of Congress to surrender for twenty or thirty years the navigation of the Mississippi precipitated a secessionist movement in the West. On the other hand, Gardoqui warned Floridablanca from the moment Congress adopted this resolution that it was a moral certainty such a treaty would never be negotiated, so great was the popular clamor against it.[25] Out of this situation, as we shall see, grew the intrigue between the American frontiersmen and Spain, but not before Floridablanca had made one more attempt to secure a treaty with the United States government.

CHAPTER VI

THE CHEVALIER OF THE ORDER OF ST. LOUIS

FLORIDABLANCA's last effort to secure a treaty with the Congress of the Confederation was made in 1787 and was intimately connected with certain proposals that he had recently received in regard to the American frontier. The first of these plans in order of importance came from a Frenchman by the name of Pierre Wouves d'Argès; the other, which was hardly more than a suggestion, was offered by James White, a delegate of North Carolina in Congress. By a judicious combination of their proposals with diplomatic pressure, Floridablanca hoped to find a way out of the *impasse* of the American negotiation and to strengthen Spain's position in the Mississippi Valley.

FROM KENTUCKY TO SAN ILDEFONSO

In the spring of 1787 this d'Argès, a middle-aged French gentleman of misfortune and a chevalier of the Order of St. Louis, emerged from a three years' residence in the backwoods of Kentucky and presented himself to the Spanish ambassador in Paris, Count Aranda.[1] Explaining how ill health and ambition had led him in 1783 to wander so far from the accustomed haunts of chevaliers as to settle in Kentucky, he warned Aranda that the weakness of Louisiana and the rapid increase of the American West in population and in hostility to Spain made it imperatively necessary for the Spanish government to adopt a new defensive system in the Mississippi Valley if it did not wish to lose its North American dominions. He proposed a twofold remedy: Spain should strengthen Louisiana and weaken the American West by attracting to its own territory as many of the American frontiersmen as possible; and the frontiersmen who resisted this seduction and remained in the American settlements should be mollified by a partial opening of the Mississippi, whose closure was their chief grievance against Spain. Both these results could be accomplished, he said, by manipulating commercial regulations on the Mississippi and by liberal land grants. The river should be opened to the frontiersmen's commerce subject to a twenty-five per cent duty, for such a duty would be low enough to placate them and yet so high that they would find it more advantageous to emigrate to Spanish territory, where, d'Argès proposed, they should be admitted as Spanish subjects and enjoy the use of the river without the payment of any duty whatsoever. The American immigrants should be concentrated in Natchez, which was the cynosure of American eyes and an important strategic point. D'Argès, who according to Aranda spoke excellent English, requested that he be sent back to the United States as the agent of Spain in this affair. He mentioned as one of his chief qualifications the fact that he was already the agent of some five thousand Kentucky families who wished to emigrate to Spanish territory.

Aranda, who had from the beginning of the American Revolution warned his government in season and out of season against the restless ambition of the Americans, gave this project vigorous support. He emphasized the value of Natchez as a bulwark against the rising republican tide and suggested that Floridablanca summon d'Argès to Spain and hear him in person. After consulting José de Gálvez, who now bore the title of

Marqués de Sonora, reminiscent of his distinguished services in Mexico, Floridablanca agreed to hear the Chevalier, but urged that the affair be kept a profound secret, especially from the Americans.

The secretary of state's interest in these propositions was not due solely to the advocacy of the powerful Aranda. In the first place, war with England was threatening.[2] In the second place, two despatches from Gardoqui had already prepared him for some such measure as that proposed by the Frenchman. In August, 1786, Gardoqui had a conversation with James White, delegate of North Carolina in Congress.[3] After remarking on White's education, judgment and influence and his connections among the American frontiersmen on the Cumberland, Gardoqui related how in this conservation White assured him of the Western frontiersmen's intense interest in the navigation of the Mississippi, of their surprise and resentment at Congress's approval of Jay's proposals relative to its suspension, and of the probability that the Western settlements would secede from the Union and put themselves under Spanish protection in return for its free use. At the same time Gardoqui informed Floridablanca that it was impossible to secure a treaty on the terms hitherto demanded by Spain and that Jay would never dare to make use of the power granted him by Congress to surrender the navigation of the Mississippi for a term of years.

A NEW DEVICE

Faced by a deadlock in the negotiation with Congress and by a backwoods menace that, together with an English war-scare, made every day's delay dangerous, Floridablanca welcomed d'Argès's project as a possible

solution of both the diplomatic and the frontier problem. Conversing with d'Argès while with the court at
San Ildefonso, he was reminded by the Frenchman of
the significance of George Rogers Clark's recent
spoliation of Spanish merchants at Vincennes. Such
measures, said d'Argès, were avowedly adopted by the
frontiersmen by way of reprisal for the closing of the
Mississippi. With the Bourbon County episode a
recent memory, Floridablanca lost no time in consulting the other members of the cabinet, notably Valdés,
who on the recent death of José de Gálvez had taken
over the colonial office, and in drawing up the necessary
orders and instructions.[4] Under the date of August 23,
1787, a royal order relating to d'Argès's commission
was transmitted to the governor of Louisiana, and on
September 5 another to the same effect was sent
Gardoqui.

According to d'Argès's instructions, he was to go by
way of New York to Kentucky, under the title of His
Majesty's commissioner for adjusting the boundary.
While there he was to listen to the complaints of the
people against Spain and encourage them to expect the
opening of the Mississippi as far as New Orleans,
subject to a twenty-five per cent duty. He was also
instructed to consult and be guided by Gardoqui at
New York and by Miró at New Orleans. Although he
was being sent to Kentucky as an immigration agent
to secure settlers for Louisiana, his instructions made
no mention of that fact. This omission, it was explained
to d'Argès, was made so that they might give no
ground for an official protest by the United States in
case they should fall into unfriendly hands. In reality,
Floridablanca did not have perfect confidence in either
the discretion or the fidelity of his French agent.

One of the most notable by-products of d'Argès's project was that the post of Natchez was converted into a government, and that the post of governor was filled, after several months' delay, by the appointment of Manuel Gayoso de Lemos, later governor of Louisiana and probably the ablest of all the Spanish officials who served their king in the conflict with the United States. Even Gardoqui lacked Gayoso's versatility and his penetrating insight into the American character. His winning manner and thorough knowledge of English fitted him for the command of a district that the Spanish government expected to fill with thousands of emigrants from the American frontier.[6]

The order informing Gardoqui of d'Argès's appointment and its objects reveals the intimate connection between Spain's Mississippi Valley policy and its negotiation with the United States.[7] In a letter to Valdés, Floridablanca had declared that d'Argès's commission should facilitate Gardoqui's negotiation with Congress. Just before his departure that gentleman let it be seen that he regarded the opening of the Mississippi as a *fait accompli* to be announced by himself in the United States. In order to set him right and to prevent any further misunderstanding in the matter Floridablanca wrote him that he was to adhere literally to his instructions and that Gardoqui was to determine when effect should be given the order opening the river. At the same time, the secretary of state wrote Gardoqui warning him of d'Argès's impetuosity, and directing the chargé categorically to make use of the concession with regard to the Mississippi in order to facilitate his negotiation with Congress, or, if that were impossible, to get some advantage for Spain from the Western Americans.[8]

There can be no doubt that Floridablanca's principal object was still to conclude a treaty with Congress. While the possibility of bringing about Western secession by manipulating Spain's control of the Mississippi had been suggested to him by James White's conversation of August, 1786, with Gardoqui, there is no indication in any of the papers of Floridablanca's office that he had the slightest intention of opening an intrigue with the Western Americans at this time. We certainly stand here on the threshold of the "Spanish intrigue," but we have not yet crossed it. Of the three objects of d'Argès's mission — to assist Gardoqui's negotiation, to attract immigrants to Louisiana and West Florida from Kentucky, and to encourage the secession of the American West — the first was undoubtedly foremost in Floridablanca's calculations. The immigration policy was left incomplete: The conditions to be offered the immigrants were not specified, Gayoso did not sail for America until the following year, and d'Argès was sent not directly to Kentucky, but to New York, where Gardoqui was engaged in his negotiation with Jay. The bid for Western secession was to be made not by means of intrigue and conspiracy, but by a change in Spanish commercial regulations on the Mississippi. James White's name does not occur anywhere in the orders relating to d'Argès nor did Spain make any move at this time to accept the obvious invitation to intrigue contained in his conversation with Gardoqui. Further proof of the true object of Spanish policy at this time is contained in Floridablanca's statement in a letter written to Gardoqui that His Majesty hoped for the adoption of the new federal constitution in the United States and the erection of a stronger central government with which he might negotiate a lasting treaty.[9] The d'Argès project carried with it a threat of intrigue with the West, and it was this threat, as well as the actual concessions on the Mississippi, that Floridablanca expected to give it force with Congress. He merely threatened the intrigue in order to obtain the treaty.

It was in accordance with this design that Florida-blanca drew up a new plan for a treaty with the United States.[10] The date of the letter transmitting this plan, when compared with that of the order relating to d'Argès's commission, indicates the intimate connection between the two. Both documents were dated September 5, 1787. The proposed treaty was to be of indefinite duration, though at the end of ten years it might be denounced by either power. It contained important concessions to the Americans. The southern boundary of the United States was fixed at the thirty-first parallel, except for the district of Natchez, which was to remain in Spain's possession. Floridablanca's previous insistence on Spain's exclusive control of the Southern Indian tribes was abandoned. Even in regard to the navigation of the Mississippi some concession was made, for it was stipulated that a joint commission be appointed to inquire into the validity of the American claims. While this concession would have brought no immediate relief to American commerce on the Mississippi, it nevertheless involved an important surrender of principle by the Spanish government, for hitherto it had refused even to discuss the claim of the United States. This retreat was an evidence of the terms Floridablanca was prepared to agree to in the face of simultaneous threats from England and the American frontiersmen. With the united force of the d'Argès project and the new treaty plan, of intimidation and conciliation, he hoped to enlist the Atlantic States in the defense of the Spanish empire against its two most dreaded enemies, England and the American frontiersmen.

ANOTHER FAILURE

The story of d'Argès's mission is soon told. Cultivated by the Spanish ambassador in Paris, treated with consideration by the secretary of state in San Ildefonso, enabled by the royal bounty to replenish his meagre wardrobe and to secure a servant and three horses, and given his passage on the royal packet from Coruña to New York, the poor man began to encounter from the day of his arrival in America a systematic frustration of his and the ministry's plans that embittered his life for the next year and ended only with his return in disgust to Paris in 1789. He was to find how obedient servants of the king could prevent the execution of His Catholic Majesty's express orders.

The ship that brought d'Argès to New York brought Gardoqui a double mortification. The new treaty plan caused him by its very reasonableness the exquisite anguish that comes from thinking of achievements that might have been. For more than two years he had labored vainly to win the distinction of success in this his maiden effort in diplomacy, but the inflexibility of his government's demands had prevented agreement at the favorable moment when economic depression and political chaos inclined the United States to conciliation. Now that his government had at last moderated its demands there was no longer an American government with which Gardoqui could negotiate. With a world of feeling latent in his discreet reticence, he assured his chief that had the terms contained in this new plan been offered in the beginning he could have concluded the treaty without difficulty and to the court's complete satisfaction.[11] In the spring of 1788, however, the old government of the United States would not act pending the establishment of the new, and yet the establishment of the new was still problematical. In the field of diplomacy nothing could be done to restrain the American frontier. Floridablanca's new plan fell on stony ground. The only hope left Gardoqui was that he might convince his chief that he was not to blame for the fruitlessness of his long negotiation.

Not only was Gardoqui's past embittered by a vain regret. His future as well was clouded by the ministry's well-meant effort to assist him in his task. The d'Argès project, which came too late to forward his negotiation, threatened to strike from his hand the new instrument with which he hoped to serve his king and secure his own advancement in the royal service. Ever since his confidential interview with James White in 1786, Gardoqui had continued to take a lively interest in the affairs of the American frontier, but pending Floridablanca's reply to the report of that conversation he could take no further step in the matter. By the late fall of 1787 Gardoqui had heard through Governor O'Neill of Pensacola of James Wilkinson's favorable reception at New Orleans. Renewing his leisurely conferences with White, he was brought up with a turn by d'Argès's arrival with a commission to visit the Western settlements of the United States. For all the chargé knew, d'Argès might gather into his hands the threads of the Western intrigue. In order to understand Gardoqui's relentless animosity to the Frenchman, one must remember that he had nothing whatever to do with calling d'Argès to the attention of the Spanish court, and consequently could claim none of the credit for any benefit that Spain might derive from the mission. The chargé had not taken any part in initiating the project, nor could he insinuate himself into it. D'Argès's orders stated that Gardoqui might give him a companion for the Western journey, but they also stated expressly that d'Argès might precede his companion to Kentucky and summon him when it seemed expedient to him.

Gardoqui's treatment of the court's agent was annihilating. He first insisted that d'Argès take as his companion one of the officials of the legation, Jáudenes and Viar, and when the Chevalier objected that the secretaries knew very little English and nothing about Kentucky, Gardoqui darkly hinted to Floridablanca that his reluctance indicated a guilty conscience and treacherous designs. He then forced the Frenchman to give up the itinerary approved by the court, and, instead of going by way of Fort Pitt and the Ohio directly to Kentucky, to take the absurdly long détour by way of Havana and New Orleans. Instead of a few weeks, many months would elapse before d'Argès's arrival in Kentucky, if indeed he did not lose his scalp on the dangerous path from Natchez through the Indian country and Cumberland to Lexington. Gardoqui wrote Floridablanca letters bristling with charges and innuendoes against him, suggesting, among other things, that he probably had been and might still be in the pay of France.[12] The chargé then wrote Miró a letter designed still further to delay d'Argès on his arrival in New Orleans.[13] Then having by these measures kept the field clear — or so he thought — for his own agent, he hastened to despatch that agent, James White, to the Western settlements. How White fared we shall see in another place.

THE SHADOW OF JAMES WILKINSON

Resentful, but obedient since Gardoqui held the purse-strings, d'Argès left by sea to encounter fresh disappointments in New Orleans. Miró also had his project of intrigue from which he hoped to win promotion and perhaps undying fame, and needed no instigation from Gardoqui to induce him to interpose further delays in the Chevalier's slow progress to the American frontier. His pretext for delaying d'Argès's progress was much better than Gardoqui's, for his conspiracy with James Wilkinson, to which we shall return presently, was further advanced than the chargé's with White, and he was really justified in expecting an answer from the court at almost any time, and therefore in detaining the Chevalier until the answer arrived.[14]

Through no fault of Miró's, since the court's decision on Wilkinson's memorial was long delayed, d'Argès was kept waiting for almost a full year after his arrival at New Orleans in May, 1788. In the interval he lost patience and received permission to go to French Santo Domingo on business pending further instructions. When the order finally arrived from Spain, it showed that d'Argès had been replaced by Wilkinson as Spain's agent in Kentucky. At the same time, the order expressed His Majesty's sense of obligation to the Chevalier and directed Miró to employ him as a captain of militia at some frontier post in Louisiana. Miró accordingly offered him the command of the post just established at New Madrid in the proposed colony of George Morgan. Spurning this offer, d'Argès retired to Paris, and we hear no more of him in the history of the Mississippi Valley.[15]

Gardoqui's despatches made it clear that d'Argès's mission had no chance of success in its principal object, for Congress was too weak even to be frightened. The negotiation could not be renewed until the new government was established, and no one could say how long that might be. In the interim Spain could not afford to remain inactive, for the American West was in a turmoil of excitement, full of resentment against both its own government and Spain. A storm was brewing on the Ohio, and it was Floridablanca's duty to see that it did not break over the Spanish empire.

CHAPTER VII

INTRIGUE AND IMMIGRATION

THE intrigue between the American frontiersmen and the Spanish government has usually been regarded as something essentially Spanish. Its very name, "The Spanish Intrigue," indicates the interpretation put upon it by American writers.[1] This may be due to the conviction that intrigue is something essentially un-American; that the countrymen of the Borgias could reach a given objective only by a détour, while the American frontiersman always moved, as did the bullet from his trusty rifle, straight to the target. Whatever the reason for its currency, the phrase is rather misleading, for it gives the impression that the intrigue was primarily the work of Spain. As a matter of fact, the frontiersmen made the first overtures, deceived the Spanish government as well as their own, and were the sole gainers by the intrigue. A much more appropriate designation would be "the frontier intrigue with Spain."

CONGRESS ALIENATES THE FRONTIERSMEN

The American frontiersmen took the initiative in this correspondence. Two of their propositions, those of d'Argès and White, made to Aranda and Gardoqui respectively, we have already discussed, and we have seen how, although they were only partially accepted by Spain, they contained ideas that made a seductive appeal to the embarrassed Floridablanca. Before taking up the third proposition, that of James Wilkinson, and observing how it was received at court, we must inquire into the circumstances that disposed these secular backwoodsmen to conspire with the government of Torquemada.

One of the most powerful forces in American political life in the 1780's, whether in the West, the East or the South, was particularism. Traditions of British local government and the practice of colonial times had given it factual currency. Montesquieu's theory of the geographical influence in politics had given it the dignity of an idea, and the Revolution had consecrated it. The people of the Atlantic coast had nothing to learn from the Mississippi Valley in this respect. What the frontiersmen did was merely to take a widespread idea and reinterpret it in conformity with their peculiar necessities.

By the very mode of its settlement the West of our period was dedicated to particularism. Its communities were established by the individual initiative of land speculator and pioneer in flat defiance of the colonial governments of North Carolina and Virginia — as in the case of the Holston settlements of western North Carolina and Richard Henderson's colony of Transylvania in Kentucky — or with at most the passive acquiescence of the revolutionary state governments, as in the case of Cumberland.[2] By their own efforts these settlements maintained themselves, receiving from the foster-parent state little more than the skeleton of government, which they themselves had to invest with living substance. The frontiersmen felt that the Atlantic States were much more interested in Western lands than in Western people, and that even with the best will in the world legislatures sitting at Williamsburg, Virginia, and Hillsborough, North Carolina, were incapacitated by remoteness and the intervening mountains from giving good government to the Mississippi Valley settlements.

Current ideas with regard to natural frontiers and the economic basis of political systems pointed to the erection of these Western communities into separate states with equal membership in the Federal Union, if indeed they remained a part of it at all.[3]

The example of the American Revolution, so vividly recent, exerted a powerful influence over the frontiersmen, who now thought of themselves as playing the part of oppressed colonists, with the Atlantic governments in the rôle of tyrant formerly filled by George III.[4] Declaiming in the manner of Patrick Henry and Samuel Adams against taxation and misgovernment, the frontiersmen followed the process through its various stages of conventions, petitions, and remonstrances to the culminating step, a declaration of independence. At first, however, they sought only what the Atlantic colonists had at first tried to secure from England: recognition as autonomous members of a federative empire. This was the situation from 1783 to 1786, when the indignation of the frontier was directed against the individual states alone and the frontiersmen professed devotion to Congress.

In 1786 the situation assumed a new and dangerous aspect. The frontiersmen's illusion of a beneficent Congress was shattered and many of them began to question the advisability of a continued union with the Atlantic States on any terms whatever. This change of sentiment was due in part to the resolution of Congress authorizing the conclusion of a treaty with Spain that would close the Mississippi to American shipping for a generation. The "secret" resolution of Congress was adopted in August, 1786, and by the following December it was common property in Kentucky. The indignation of the people there was white-hot, and they protested that they had been sacrificed for the benefit of Eastern fishermen and farmers.[5]

Other grievances increased their ire against Congress. The state of Franklin had applied for admission to the Union and had been rebuffed. Might other frontier communities expect more friendly treatment? The Indian policy of Congress was still more offensive to them. Unable to protect the Kentuckians against the Northern tribes, Congress seemed actually to favor the Southern Indians over their white neighbors in western North Carolina. Its commissioners negotiated a treaty with the Cherokee Indians in December, 1785, that aroused keen resentment in North Carolina and Virginia, not merely among the frontiersmen but on the Atlantic coast as well, for it restored to the Indians, under a perpetual guarantee, lands granted and settled under the authority of the state of North Carolina. One of the leaders of the state of Franklin, Alexander Outlaw, declared that the commissioners of Congress who negotiated this treaty were forcing the frontier people to give up their "just Right," and Patrick Henry roundly affirmed that Congress's whole treatment of the Southwest revealed the determination of the jealous Northern majority in that body to prevent the development of the South and Southwest.[6]

"THE MEN OF THE WESTERN WATERS"

The result was that by the end of 1786 there were many people in the West who were threatening not, merely separation from the parent states on the Atlantic, but secession from the United States. It was no longer autonomy but outright independence that the more radical frontiersmen were planning, and this new phase of particularism was all the more dangerous because its goal was a new Union, a Mississippi Valley republic. The very phrase with which they described themselves, "the men of the Western waters," suggested unity by indicating the bond of union: all of these settlements were situated on the waters of the Ohio on or near the Cumberland plateau. Indian affairs and the navigation of the Mississippi were matters of common interest in these settlements, and when they were not managed to the satisfaction of the people there, inflammatory addresses were circulated and committees of correspondence formed in Kentucky, Cumberland, Franklin, and even western Pennsylvania.[7] So far the frontiersmen had closely and consciously imitated the patriots of '76, but there was still one step that they had not taken: they had not yet sought foreign aid against the oppressor. There was curiously enough much talk of British intervention,[8] but it came to nothing. The current of the rivers that passed their doors pointed to Spain as the nation that should play the part of France in this second American Revolution. Floridablanca, however, was no Vergennes, and Wilkinson no Washington.

It was commerce, as we have said, that formed the substantial basis of the Spanish intrigue, commerce by the Mississippi and Alabama Rivers, commerce already established and commerce only dreamed of. Some question has been raised as to the genuineness of the frontiersmen's interest in the navigation of the Mississippi. It was said at the time, and has been repeated since, that the opposition to Jay's proposals of 1786 came not from bona-fide inhabitants of the West, but from land speculators and anti-Federalists; that the volume of commerce on the river was too small to justify the outcry raised against Jay's proposals.[9]

It is true that land speculators were extremely active in exciting this opposition,[10] but it is difficult to draw the line between speculators and frontiersmen, since most of the leading frontiersmen were engaged in land speculation. It is also true that the volume of American commerce on the Mississippi was very small. In the three years 1782–84 the port records of New Orleans show that arrivals at that port from the American settlements were only ten flatboats, and that their total cargo consisted of 2640 barrels of flour. In the three years 1785–87, owing to the closing of the river by royal proclamation, there was not a single American arrival at New Orleans. In 1788 the only arrivals were James Wilkinson's five flatboats, whose cargo consisted largely of tobacco. In 1789 there were no arrivals. In 1790, after the reopening of the river by Spain, eighteen flatboats arrived with miscellaneous cargoes, principally tobacco, beef and flour.[11]

The volume of this commerce is certainly not imposing and it was one-sided, for goods were almost never sent up the river to the American settlements. The first impression gathered from these statistics must, however, be corrected by two considerations. In the first place, they are incomplete, since a great deal of smuggling went on and since a large part of the exports from the American settlements stopped at Natchez and so was not recorded in the New Orleans office. In the second place, not even the most complete and reliable statistics would give us an accurate index of the importance of the Mississippi River to the Western settlements of the United States. The leaders of the frontiersmen were for the most part men who lived in the future, who were engaged in real estate developments, and whose success in their enterprises depended upon the possibility of assuring prospective purchasers of land a ready outlet for their products. The Mississippi offered the only possible means of exporting bulky products of the soil, for freight rates over the mountains were prohibitive. Even in the case of manufactured goods, freight charges from Philadelphia to Knoxville amounted to about forty per cent of the cost in Philadelphia.[12] Ever since the line of settlement passed beyond the tidewater region, the American frontiersman has been profoundly interested in all questions relating to transportation, and it would have been surprising indeed if frontiersmen who could become so excited over the building of a turnpike or the digging of a canal had taken no interest in the opening of the Mississippi, that most gigantic and comprehensive of all their transportation problems.

THE ROMANTIC TRADESMAN

James Wilkinson, merchant, took it on himself to lead his fellow-frontiersmen out of the wilderness. A brevet brigadier general during the Revolution, he often led the Kentucky militia against the Indians after its close. Employed in the commissary department during the Revolution, he soon became one of Kentucky's most active merchants. Connected, though not implicated, with Benedict Arnold, he used the same cyphers, "aprons" and other devices in his correspondence with the Spaniards that Arnold had employed in his correspondence with the British. Wilkinson was a romantic tradesman. "My passion is military fame," he once confessed,[13] and it was his ambition to make himself the "Washington of the West"; but he also had another passion, and one not so frankly confessed: to make himself the Willing of the West, the merchant prince of the Ohio Valley. So heavy were his shipments to New Orleans after his first visit there that Governor Miró felt obliged to write him a letter of protest, even at the risk of offending his only agent in Kentucky.[14]

When Wilkinson first came to Kentucky in 1784, it was merely as the agent of a mercantile company in Philadelphia; but with the Irishman's usual flair for politics, he succeeded in taking a prominent part in the numerous Kentucky conventions of the next few years.[15] When the events of the troubled year 1786 alienated the frontiersmen from Congress, he quickly sensed the trend of frontier sentiment and got in touch with the Spanish officials of Louisiana. His opportunity came with the action of his rival for military fame, George Rogers Clark, in confiscating at Vincennes the property of some French traders who were subjects of Spain. Wilkinson and his friend, Colonel Richard Anderson, speaking as the mouthpiece of the law-abiding citizens of Kentucky, wrote the Spanish commandant at St. Louis reprobating the violence of Clark and his accomplices. These two letters, Wilkinson's written in French, were delivered by their messenger, who was doubtless the bearer of more interesting verbal assurances from these Kentuckians. Their overtures were well received, and it was no doubt to this episode that Wilkinson owed his success, where so many others had failed, in getting safely past the Spanish posts on his way to New Orleans.[16]

WILKINSON'S MEMORIAL AND THE SPANISH COURT

Here he remained for three months in constant intercourse of the most friendly nature with Governor Miró, Intendant Navarro and the governor's secretary and interpreter, Armesto. On September 5, 1787, just as

Floridablanca was issuing the orders relating to d'Argès's mission, Wilkinson presented to Miró and Navarro a memorial [17] which was doubtless the joint product of their three minds. In this memorial he pointed out that the population of the American West was increasing with great rapidity, and that discontent was keeping pace with growing numbers; discontent with Spain for closing the Mississippi and with Congress for acquiescing in its closure. The consequences to Spain might be disastrous, for the Westerners were determined to open the river to their commerce and the weak defences of Louisiana could not withstand an invasion. There were, however, two means, and only two, by which a catastrophe might be averted and the situation turned to Spain's advantage. The government should either build up a Spanish party in Kentucky by a judicious manipulation of commercial regulations on the Mississippi, and then foment a revolution that would result in secession from the Union and the formation of a close connection with Spain; or it should adopt an immigration policy with such liberal concessions in the way of land grants, religious toleration and political privileges as would depopulate Kentucky and fill the waste spaces of Louisiana. In either case James Wilkinson was to occupy a privileged position as the sole agent of Spain. He preferred the first of these measures and asked that he be given a monopolistic control of exportations from Kentucky down the Mississippi, justifying this extraordinary demand on the ground that such power was necessary to enable him to build up a Spanish party in Kentucky. Two weeks after submitting this memorial he was on his way home. We shall see in the next chapter how he fared on his return to Kentucky.

Miró and Navarro welcomed the proposals eagerly and in a joint despatch forwarded the memorial to the court with a fervid recommendation.[18] Their enthusiasm is easily understood. Wilkinson had by all accounts a pleasing presence and a plausible manner, and the Spanish officials were keenly alive to the American menace, against which Navarro had for seven years been urging his government to prepare. The device that he had recommended — the economic strangulation of the American West by the closing of the Mississippi — had proved a failure. The means of defence in Louisiana were scanty, and its governors had no information service to warn them of an impending invasion. Their first warning would be the appearance of the invaders. To these considerations we must add the common desire to merit promotion and win fame by rendering a signal service to the crown.

Their joint despatch was dated September 25, 1787, and Miró expected to have the court's answer by April, 1788. He actually received it in March, 1789. The delay was due not to Spanish slothfulness, but to the weightiness of the matter and to the fact that when Wilkinson's memorial reached Madrid (January, 1788),[19] the fate of d'Argès's mission and the related negotiation of Gardoqui was still unknown to Floridablanca. It was not until April 19, 1788, that Gardoqui wrote his final report on this subject, informing the secretary of state that neither d'Argès's mission nor threats nor persuasion could secure a treaty from the moribund Congress of the Confederation and that the negotiation must be suspended until the adoption of the new federal constitution and the establishment of the new government, both of which were still problematical.

Even after the arrival of Gardoqui's despatch, there was still reason for delay. Untimely death had recently deprived Floridablanca of two advisers on whose counsel he was accustomed to rely in questions relating to the Mississippi Valley, José and Bernardo de Gálvez. There remained only one other person who possessed both the requisite knowledge of the affairs of Louisiana and the confidence of the court. That person was Martin Navarro. Relieved of the intendancy at his own request, he left Louisiana in May, 1788, for Spain. On his arrival the papers relating to Wilkinson's memorial were submitted to him for his advice and he was consulted on other matters relating to Louisiana.

By this time (October, 1788) a mass of information had accumulated in Floridablanca's office that related in one way or another to Wilkinson's proposals, and it gained added value from the fact that it proceeded from many independent sources, from Havana, New York and St. Augustine as well as from New Orleans. Three important facts were brought out in high relief by this information : first, that Floridablanca's American policy of 1787 must be modified, since Congress was impotent either to make a treaty or to restrain its frontiersmen from attacking Spain in America ; second, that there was a general disposition in the southern and western parts of the United States to drive the Spaniards out of Louisiana and the Floridas ; and third, that many Americans, Germans, Irishmen and Frenchmen were desirous of settling in those provinces as Spanish subjects.[20] In the light of this information, Navarro submitted his recommedations on Wilkinson's memorial. Calling attention to the failure of the system that he himself had recommended in 1781 and that had been adopted in 1784 — namely, the

strangulation of the American West by the closing of
the Mississippi to American commerce — he pointed
out the urgent necessity of a new system and recommended the adoption with modifications of both of
Wilkinson's proposals.[21]

On November 20 the Junta de Estado, or Council of
Ministers, met and decided as follows: Wilkinson was
substitued for d'Argès as Spain's agent in Kentucky,
but neither of his alternative plans was adopted outright. His proposal that Spain foment a revolution in
the American West was flatly rejected. The Junta
declared that until the frontiersmen established their
independence Spain could form no connection with
them. Nor did the Junta temper this refusal in any way.
The correspondence with Wilkinson was to be continued, but neither Miró nor any other Spanish official
was authorized to spend a single *peso* in encouraging a
frontier revolution or to make any promises to the
revolutionists or any engagements with them. The
Floridablanca of 1788 was on this point in perfect
agreement with the Floridablanca of 1778. However
much Spain might wish to profit by revolution, the
Spanish monarchy could not afford to be implicated
in fomenting it, least of all in a country so close to its
own dominions. Nor was Wilkinson's proposal with
regard to immigration and commerce on the Mississippi
adopted in the form in which he had made it. Instead
of granting him the monopoly right to issue permits for
the use of the river — a measure which he declared essential both in order to build up a Spanish party in Kentucky and also to stimulate emigration to Louisiana
— the Junta decided to permit all the American frontiersmen without exception to use the Mississippi as
far south as New Orleans subject to a fifteen per cent

duty, which might be reduced to six per cent in individual cases at Miró's discretion. Instead of making Wilkinson its sole immigration agent in Kentucky, the ministry established general rules for the admission of immigrants and welcomed all comers. Land grants, equal commercial privileges with other Spanish subjects, and religious toleration were promised all immigrants who took the oath of loyalty and became bonafide settlers. The decision of the Junta took the form of a royal order to Miró dated December 1, 1788, and received by him in March of the following year.[22]

To regard this order as solely or even primarily a document in the history of the "Spanish intrigue" would be utterly to misunderstand the policy of the Spanish government. The order had three objects. The first was to mollify the American West; the second, to encourage a revolution in that region by indirect means that would not implicate the Spanish government; the third, to secure immigrants for Louisiana and West Florida. The first object was apparently considered by the Junta of greater immediate consequence than the second, for in deciding upon the concessions to be granted the Americans on the Mississippi it adopted not the system which Wilkinson had declared necessary to precipitate a revolution, but a system which would appease the wrath of the American frontiersmen. Most important of all was the third object, immigration, for while the Mississippi was opened under restrictions to the Americans, their privileges were far inferior to those of Americans who would emigrate to Spanish territory and become Spanish subjects.

The immigration policy that Floridablanca, with the approval of the Junta, adopted in this crisis represents a heroic effort on the part of Spain to adapt its ancient colonial policy to the needs of its frontier provinces, Louisiana and West Florida. The *cédula* of 1782 had liberalized the commercial system of these colonies, and the royal order of December 1, 1788, similarly liberalized their immigration system. Formerly none but Spaniards and Catholics had been permitted to settle in the colonies of Spain.[23] Now two of them were thrown open to aliens and heretics, who were not only permitted but encouraged to settle there, to become Spanish subjects, to accept free lands, to enjoy all the privileges of subjects of His Catholic Majesty. The importance of the grant of religious toleration can hardly be overestimated. The king of Spain was still the Catholic king, Catholic above all others. Toleration was utterly at variance with the whole of Spanish policy, and its grant in the case of Louisiana and West Florida shows the importance that the Spanish government attached to the development of those provinces. It was an experiment forced upon Spain by the requirements of its frontier conflict with the United States, a device adopted to aid Spain in that most vital phase of the frontier conflict, the competition for immigrants.[24]

SETTLING THE GOTHS AT THE GATES OF ROME

A foolhardy experiment, one is inclined to say, this attempt to make silk purses out of sows' ears, Spanish subjects out of American frontiersmen; to turn the Clarks, Seviers and Robertsons of the American West into faithful vassals of the Catholic king. When Thomas Jefferson heard of this policy of "settling the Goths at the gates of Rome," he wrote in high glee: "I wish a hundred thousand of our inhabitants would accept the invitation. It will be the means of delivering to us peaceably what may otherwise cost us a war." [25] In the light of Spain's subsequent experience in West Florida and Mexico's in Texas, the policy seems to have been suicidal; and indeed the inimitable Wilkinson in his "Memoirs" claimed the gratitude of his countrymen on the ground that this immigration policy, adopted by Spain on his recommendation, had facilitated the acquisition of Louisiana by the United States.[26]

And yet there was reason in this madness, reason that appears if we remember the form in which this question of policy was presented to the Spanish government. The form was this: Would the American frontiersmen be less dangerous to Spain in Louisiana or in Kentucky? The geographical unity of the Mississippi Valley required the problem to be stated in these terms. It was not an abstract question of the merits of toleration or the docility of the Americans, but a very concrete problem of protecting the Spanish dominions against the thousands of turbulent Americans in the Ohio Valley. Spain had first tried through diplomacy (1782–83) to check the growth of the American settlements in the Ohio Valley. This had failed. She had then tried to effect the same purpose by closing the Mississippi to American commerce (1784–87). This too had failed. She had simultaneously given diplomacy another trial in Gardoqui's mission, and his tedious negotiation (1785–88) had likewise failed. The day of the Mississippi Valley had arrived. Its development by the hand of the white man was progressing rapidly. This development was taking place not in the Spanish dominions, whose population increased slowly, but in the territory of the United States, where a much more liberal system than the Spanish prevailed.

Those who settled in the Ohio Valley — that is, in

the territory of the United States — were not only lost to Spain, but might also easily become the enemies of Spain. The Spanish government must both increase the population of its own frontier provinces and diminish the population of the American border settlements. The quickest way to effect this double purpose was to attract settlers from the American frontier into Louisiana.

In any case, even had Louisiana not been in need of immigrants, its safety required the reduction of the neighboring American settlements. Unstable equilibrium characterized their social and political life. Resentment against Spain might cause an invasion of Louisiana. Disaffection towards the United States might result in secession from the Union. Moreover, many of these frontiersmen regarded their present settlements as temporary and wished to move further down the Mississippi nearer its mouth. Why not make it possible for them to do so under Spanish rule? Individually they did not seem formidable to Spain. It was their situation that made them dangerous. The lack of an established government made them unruly and the lack of a market made them discontented. Their chief military advantage over Spain lay in their remoteness, which made it possible for them to conduct in the profoundest secrecy their preparations for an invasion. All this would be changed if they were settled in Louisiana or in the district of Natchez. There they would from the outset be accustomed to a firm governing hand, and would have a ready outlet for their products; and there, if they could not be trusted, they could at least be watched.

There are two other considerations that must be kept in mind if we wish to understand Floridablanca's adoption of this immigration policy. In the first place, all his informants assured him that the people of the Western settlements were for various reasons indifferent or hostile to the United States, that they were for the most part either of foreign extraction — French, German, Irish — or were refugees from the Atlantic States — Loyalists, debtors, criminals. Such people could the more readily be made docile Spanish subjects, as they were not bound by ties of sentiment to any other country, and the strong government of Spain would restrain their wayward tendencies. In the second place, a somewhat similar experiment had already been made in Natchez district and the results had been very favorable. The district, conquered by Bernardo de Gálvez in the recent war against England, was inhabited almost entirely by people of English and American origin, most of whom were Protestants. For seven years now since the close of the war they had lived quietly under Spanish rule, manifesting scant sympathy for the Georgia commissioners at the time of the Bourbon County episode, and little disposition to rebel. The contentment of this growing district gave Floridablanca some reason for thinking that Spain might govern large numbers of Americans with success.[27]

We shall return later to the operation of this immigration policy. For the moment we need only note that its success depended on the government's ability to provide a market for the immigrants' products, on its giving them a decided preference over the inhabitants of the American settlements in the use of the Mississippi, and on its ability to secure them immunity from the Indian attacks that vexed the American settlements. Without these incentives to emigrate, the American frontiersman might as well remain with his freer fellows on the Cumberland, the Kentucky and the Holston. As for the other objects of the royal order of December 1, 1788, the frontiersmen would certainly be highly pleased with even the partial opening of the Mississippi to their commerce, but Spain must be careful to give no new offence; and we shall see in the next chapter whether they were inclined to rebel for Spain's benefit without the aid of Spain.

CHAPTER VIII

THE UNION PRESERVED

WHILE Floridablanca was considering Wilkinson's memorial and while the resultant order was on its way to New Orleans, events were taking place on the American frontier which seemed to give immediate promise of the revolution that Floridablanca desired but was not willing to pay for. To Wilkinson's protestations of partiality for Spain on behalf of Kentucky were added similar declarations by leading men in Franklin and Cumberland. The Spanish government might be justified in thinking that the Southwest was of one mind, and that its mind was set on secession and on an alliance with Spain. As it turned out, however, there was, so far as Franklin and Cumberland were concerned, only a brief intrigue with Spain, and no conspiracy. There was no plot, and there were no conspirators. Overtures there were, inquiries and offers; but the frontiersmen — and it was they who took the initiative — soon found that their interests and those of Spain were irreconcilable. The intrigue was still-born because Spanish policy could not grant what the frontiersmen desired as the price of allegiance. There was no conspiracy because Spain would not conspire. In Kentucky the situation was different, and the intrigue went further and lasted longer than in the other western settlements.

INTRIGUE AND LAND SPECULATION : FRANKLIN

Gardoqui's interest in an intrigue with the frontiersmen was revived by the arrival of d'Argès in New York early in 1788, and he urged James White to visit the Western settlements in the interest of Spain. White, who had just heard of Sevier's defeat in a factional conflict with Colonel John Tipton and thought that it would incline Sevier to form a connection with Spain, consented and set out for the West about May 1, 1788.[1] He found the situation in Franklin even more favorable than he expected. For several years Sevier had been engaged in an undertaking with other land speculators, among them William Blount and Wade Hampton, to establish a colony at Muscle Shoals. As we have seen, this speculation was at first a private enterprise closely connected with the creation of Houston County (1784) under the authority of the state of Georgia. After the establishment of the state of Franklin it became a part of the expansionist programme of that state, and was linked with Georgia's projected campaign against the Creek Indians. Georgia's abandonment of the plan of campaign at the end of 1787 brought about the collapse of Sevier's Franklin government, which was signalized by his defeat in the affray with Tipton in February, 1788. From February until July of that year, he lived among the disorderly squatters of the extreme frontier, harrying the Indians and marking their lands for settlement, his interest in the Muscle Shoals scheme still unabated. According to his own story, White found little difficulty in persuading Sevier and other Franklinites to enter into an intrigue with Spain. In July, Sevier wrote Gardoqui a friendly letter. In September, after his arrest had been ordered by Governor Johnson and after North Carolina had failed to ratify the federal constitution, he wrote two more letters to the Spanish envoy. In the briefer of these two letters, which probably gives us Sevier's chief reason for appealing to Spain, he informed Gardoqui of his Muscle Shoals project and asked that Spain use its influence with the Indians to facilitate the colony's establishment.

That the execution of this scheme was the Franklinites' chief object in their intrigue with Spain appeared still more clearly when James White, returning to New York, was sent by way of Havana to New Orleans to continue the intrigue with Miró. White's own written statement, the report of the governor of Havana, and the letters of Gayoso, then in Havana on his way to Natchez, all show White's eagerness to secure Spanish support for an extension of the state of Franklin down the Tennessee beyond Muscle Shoals, and to persuade Spain to open the Alabama River as well as the Mississippi to the colonists of this frontier state.

Such a scheme was incompatible with the interests and policy of Spain. The Spanish government was opening the Mississippi partially and reluctantly, fearing contraband trade; the opening of the Alabama would greatly increase the risk of smuggling. The Spanish defensive system depended in large measure on Indian alliances, and Spain could not afford to offend her savage allies by countenancing a further intrusion upon their lands. Spain was seeking to break up the autonomous American settlements in the Mississippi valley, and the project of Sevier and White would, if carried into effect, bring the American frontier two hundred miles further down the Tennessee and dangerously close to Mobile and Natchez.

When White arrived in New Orleans (April, 1789), Miró had just received the royal order of December 1, 1788, in answer to Wilkinson's proposals. In conformity with this order he drew up his reply to White, informing him of the partial opening of the Mississippi to the Western Americans and of Spain's inability to negotiate with the frontier settlements so long as they remained a part of the United States, and urging the frontiersmen to settle as Spanish subjects in Spanish territory. Verbally he tried to persuade White to incite the people of Franklin and Cumberland to declare their independence, but he gave no assurance as to how Spain would aid the revolutionists or what treatment it would accord them when their independence was established. The court's ultimate decision in 1790 was in effect a confirmation of Miró's provisional reply to White. These mountaineers who longed for the plains could get no help from Spain for their expansionist project, and so Sevier abandoned the intrigue.

INTRIGUE AND INDIAN RAVAGES : CUMBERLAND

In Cumberland likewise the intrigue never got beyond the preliminary stage.[2] As soon as each side perceived what the other wanted, the correspondence came to an abrupt end. Unlike the maturer and expanding Holston settlements, Cumberland was still an insecurely established outpost of the Southwestern frontier. Its remoteness and its scanty population scattered in a long thin line of "stations" along the Cumberland River, made it an easy victim to Indian attacks. Its competition in the Southern fur trade brought down upon it the wrath of Panton and McGillivray, and at the same time that the Creek began their war on Georgia in 1786 they assailed Cumberland. For the next three years they harassed it unmercifully. McGillivray boasted at one time that he had broken up the settlement, and Robertson admitted that trade and immigration had been stopped by the Indian ravages and that in a period of six months forty-eight of the settlers were killed by the Indians. North Carolina gave but little assistance. To their piteous complaints Governor Johnston replied with the hard truth that theirs was the common lot of frontier communities. The Kentuckians would not admit Cumberland's plea for incorporation in their proposed state, and Congress showed no disposition to defend a country that it had often and in vain asked North Carolina to cede to it.

The men of Cumberland cast about desperately for a remedy. In April, 1788, they sent a delegation to McGillivray offering to give him a town lot in Nashville and to put themselves under Spanish protection if only the Indians would cease their murderous attacks. A few months later, having heard no doubt rumors of the landing in East Florida of William Augustus Bowles,[3] reputed enemy of Spain and the representative of British trading interests in the Bahamas, and of McGillivray's momentary alienation from Spain and friendship for Bowles, Robertson wrote McGillivray hinting that Cumberland would gladly join him in the conquest of the neighboring Spanish colonies. McGillivray, however, was soon reconciled to the Spaniards and gave Robertson no encouragement. This was the situation that produced the Spanish intrigue in Cumberland. The intrigue was Cumberland's last resort in securing relief from Indian attacks as it had been Sevier's last resource in securing aid for his Muscle Shoals settlement.

Lack of space forbids us to follow the development of the intrigue in detail. It is enough to say that it had its origin in Gardoqui's letter of April 18, 1788, to Elisha Robertson and in the suggestions of one of Spain's French subjects at the Illinois, the trader André Fagot; that Andrew Jackson, recently arrived in Nashville, and James Robertson and Daniel Smith, colonel and brigadier general respectively of the militia, were the chief agents in the intrigue; and that their objects in undertaking it were to induce Spain to restrain the Indians, to frighten North Carolina into ceding its western territory to Congress, and incidentally to secure commercial privileges from Spain on the Mississippi.

UNDERSTANDING AND ANTAGONISM

Though James White apparently had nothing to do with their writing, his arrival in New Orleans coincided with the delivery of letters to Miró from James Robertson and Daniel Smith. These letters, like Wilkinson's to the commanding officer of St. Louis in 1786, were written in carefully guarded terms; but again as in Wilkinson's case a confidential messenger delivered the letters. Fagot, the bearer of Smith's letter, assured Miró that the frontiersmen were burning with eagerness to rebel and form a connection with Spain.

Miró replied similarly with an unincriminating letter illuminated by the most urgent verbal incitement to rebellion. Both messages, as we have seen, were entrusted to White, and they were in fact the same replies that the governor sent to Franklin, White serving as the messenger to both settlements. In the case of Cumberland, Miró added personal letters to Smith and Robertson that contained little beyond polite phrases, assurances of good will, a vague promise to continue to use his good offices with the Indians for the relief of Cumberland, and a pressing invitation to settle in Louisiana.

Miró's reply showed that the Cumberland settlers had as little incentive as those of Franklin to continue the intrigue with Spain. Incessant Indian attacks proved that Miró was either insincere or that he was unable to control the Indians. The navigation of the Mississippi was, although under considerable restrictions, open to the settlers at Cumberland in accordance with the royal order of December 1, 1788, whose substance was communicated to them by White. The Spanish immigration policy, as outlined in Miró's reply, showed in the clearest possible manner the conflict of interest between the frontiersmen and Spain. Men like James Robertson were dedicated by years of perilous hardship to the success of their settlements, in which they had material and spiritual interests at stake. Spain was evidently determined that they should either emigrate or rebel. To emigrate was to sacrifice all that they had achieved and all that they hoped for in Cumberland. To rebel against the United States was to put themselves at Spain's mercy; and what terms could they expect from His Catholic Majesty? The answer to this question was indicated by the terms offered immigrants to Spanish territory: a narrow measure of religious toleration, and no privileges of local autonomy. Moreover, Spain was an absolute monarchy, with none of those constitutional guarantees of life, liberty and property consecrated by English and American tradition. Another reason why Smith and Robertson lost interest in the intrigue may be that Miró subordinated them to Wilkinson, informing the latter of their advances and writing them in September, 1789, letters which Wilkinson himself drew up and delivered at Nashville on his return from New Orleans to Kentucky.[4]

The effect of Spain's policy was apparent even while White was still in New Orleans. He became increasingly reserved as he perceived the trend of Spanish policy, and Gayoso became correspondingly suspicious of his sincerity and fearful of the Americans' ambitious designs. The alienation of these two men is the clearest proof of the irreconcilability of the interests of Spain and the frontiersmen. Both were possessed of a high degree of intelligence and of an accurate knowledge of conditions in their respective countries, and intimate association over a period of several months facilitated an exchange of views and sentiments. Their disagreement arose not from misunderstanding but precisely from mutual comprehension. Upon his return to Cumberland, White abandoned the intrigue and was active in dissuading the frontiersmen from emigrating to Louisiana. Smith and Robertson wrote the governor of North Carolina in such a way as to let him see, without revealing their part in it, that Spanish influence was at work in Cumberland. Protesting against the presence of a Spanish immigration agent there, they urged the cession of North Carolina's western territory to Congress in order to "quiet the minds of the people." In September, 1789, there was held at Nashville a convention which Miró had expected to declare the independence of Cumberland, but which in fact petitioned North Carolina to make the cession to Congress. It was a fortunate coincidence that the new federal government was established just at the time when these frontiersmen discovered how little Spain could do for them.

THE KENTUCKY SEPARATISTS

In Kentucky, which was justly regarded by Miró and the Spanish ministry as the most important of the Western settlements of the United States, the Spanish policy of 1788 had a similar effect. It must be remembered, however, that the court's reply to Wilkinson's memorial of 1787 was not received by Miró until March, 1789, when the most favorable moment in Kentucky was long past. The influence of the delay is hard to estimate, for on the one hand the court's silence hampered Wilkinson, who could give the Kentuckians no authoritative assurance of Spanish aid or even of Spanish sympathy; and yet on the other hand the court's reply of December 1, 1788, would not have aided Wilkinson in the least even had it arrived a year earlier. Although the conflict of interest between Kentucky and Spain was not so keen as it was between the North Carolina frontier settlements and that power, yet it was evident from the court's reply that Spanish policy required Kentucky first to commit itself to secession and then to make the best terms with Spain that it could.[5] The order also contained a provision which Wilkinson had warned in his memorial of 1787 would be fatal to the building up of a Spanish party in Kentucky, namely, the opening of the Mississippi to all the Western Americans.

Despite these unfavorable circumstances, there can be no doubt that there was a separatist party of considerable strength in Kentucky. The particularistic tendencies common to all the frontier communities of that day were reinforced in Kentucky by the presence of a larger number of men of position and education than the other western communities could boast. Accustomed to command and familiar with the current theoretical justifications of particularism, they found extremely irksome a distant and unintelligent rule and provided capable leadership for the separatists. For nearly a decade a group of such men kept up an intermittent intrigue with Spain. What the strength of their following was we cannot say, but it is unthinkable that men of the intelligence of James Wilkinson, Harry Innes and John Brown would have risked their high standing in Kentucky had they not known that their dangerous intrigue had considerable support and consequently a reasonable chance of success. Mere rascality or greed alone will not account for the persistent intrigue of these men with Spain, although Wilkinson and Innes were ready enough to capitalize their connections at New Orleans. Wilkinson, the best paid of them all, did not receive a penny from any Spanish official until his second visit to New Orleans in 1789. As the court had not yet pensioned him, he was then advanced $7000 as a private loan by Miró and gave security for its repayment.[6] It was not until 1792 that the king finally granted him the pension of $2000 a year recommended by Miró. Moreover, the commercial advantages over the other westerners enjoyed by Wilkinson and his associates were not great, and Wilkinson's first and largest commercial venture in his relations with Spain was not at all successful.[7]

Altogether it seems highly probable that there was a powerful separatist party in Kentucky in the decade from 1786 to 1796; but to call it a "Spanish" party would be misleading. Even Wilkinson, who over and over protested his own devotion to Spain, warned Miró that the other separatists would not tolerate the idea of subjection to His Catholic Majesty and that Spain could hope for nothing more than an alliance with independent Kentucky.[8] Remembering how leaders in the other frontier communities, Franklin and Cumberland, had tried to exploit the intrigue for their own ends, we may safely conclude that the Kentucky separatists were seeking to use Spain as a cat's-paw to pull the chestnut of Kentucky independence out of the fire.

The climax of the Spanish conspiracy in its first phase came with the convention of July, 1788, when, according to Wilkinson, Innes and Sebastian openly urged the convention to carry Kentucky out of the Union.[9] We know but little of the proceedings of that convention, or of the considerations that led the convention to reject the proposal. It was obvious, however, that the analogy so often drawn by frontier agitators between their situation and that of the Atlantic colonies in 1775 was far from perfect. Even admitting genuine grievances and a diversity of interest, the numbers, wealth and political experience of the frontiersmen were inadequate for the maintenance of an independent state, and their geographical situation was extremely likely to entail either a conflict with Spain or subjection to it. The time for independence had not yet arrived.

This was the judgment of the convention, it seems, for that body decided to await the result of the new federal experiment; and when the substance of the royal order of December 1, 1788, was communicated to Wilkinson it gave the separatist cause another blow, if we are to believe the arch-conspirator.[10] In the face of this check and of changed conditions, notably the establishment of the new federal government, Wilkinson descended to New Orleans a second time in June, 1789, in order to look after his business affairs and bring the conspiracy up to date.[11] On his return to Kentucky he continued his correspondence with the Spaniards and played a waiting game, hoping for better times. His hope was fulfilled several years later and under very different conditions, which will be discussed in another place.

Meanwhile the governments on the Atlantic coast had heard reports of the progress of the Spanish intrigue and rumors of a British intrigue in the West. Alarmed at the prospect of disunion, they took measures to placate the Westerners. The legislatures of Virginia and North Carolina, both on their own account and in the interest of the frontiersmen, passed resolutions (1788) asserting the inalienable right of their citizens to the navigation of the Mississippi. Virginia gave encouragement to the movement in Kentucky to form a separate state and secure admission into the Union. North Carolina extended government facilities in its West, creating in November, 1788, a district to which it gave the name "Miro" and erecting new counties. In December, 1789, it pardoned Sevier and restored him to his former office of brigadier general of militia. In November of that year it again ceded its western territory to Congress, as Smith and Robertson had so often requested it to do, and this time the act was not repealed. Congress accepted the cession without delay.

WASHINGTON AND THE WEST

The United States government also was forced to modify its policy with regard to the West. The proposed treaty with Spain was not negotiated. Even General Washington, whose respect for discipline was offended by frontier turbulence and who at first thought the time had come to "speak decisively" to the frontiersmen, was so alarmed in 1787 by the ferment in the West that he advised that Jay's offensive proposals be quietly dropped.[12] In July, 1788, the Con-

gress of the Confederation adopted a resolution defer-
ring the Spanish negotiation until the establishment of
the new government of the United States, declaring
that its citizens had a natural and inalienable right to
the navigation of the Mississippi.[13]

When the new government was organized in 1789,
one of its chief problems was to conciliate the out-
raged West. Washington's diary for the years 1789
and 1790 shows that he was keenly alive to the frontier
problems involved in Indian affairs, Spanish relations
and land speculation.[14] There was a manifest design
in his administration to convince the Western frontiersmen that a new era had begun, that Eastern provin-
cialism was no longer in the ascendant in national
councils, and that Western interests would be safe in
the hands of the new federal government. The appointment of Jefferson instead of Jay as secretary of state
was reassuring to the West,[15] for Jefferson had taken
the lead in opposing Jay's recommendation regarding
the Mississippi. Even Hamilton, the representative
of the commercial interest of the North, let it be known
that he regarded the free navigation of the Mississippi
as indispensable to national prosperity.[16]

Conciliation of Western sentiment was also apparent in the federal appointments to office in the West.
William Blount, whose connection with land speculation was known far and wide and had been the subject
of scandalous gossip in North Carolina in 1786, but
who had influence among the frontiersmen and was
recommended for the office by Daniel Smith of Cumberland, received the appointment of governor of the
Southwest Territory and superintendent of Indian
affairs in the South.[17] As brigadier generals under him
were appointed John Sevier and James Robertson,

Boundary Line
between the United States
and
The Southern Indians,
1783-1795

(Based on C.C.Royce, *Indian
Land Cessions in the United States*)

Creek Boundary, 1783
Cherokee   "   1785
Creek   "   1790
Cherokee   "   1791

Blount's associates in land speculation. Their connection with the Spanish intrigue seems not to have been suspected. In Kentucky the Spanish conspirators received some of the choicest appointments in the gift of the federal government. Wilkinson's treasonable activities had been reported to Washington in 1789,[18] and yet in October, 1791, he was commissioned lieutenant colonel in the United States Army, and was promoted to the rank of brigadier general the following March.[19] Sebastian was appointed United States attorney-general and Harry Innes judge for the district of Kentucky.[20] The influence of their fellow conspirator, John Brown, member of Congress from Kentucky, doubtless weighed heavily in these appointments, but it is difficult to avoid the conclusion that the federal administration shrewdly turned a blind eye to the delinquencies of such men as Wilkinson and Blount, whose appointment would prove its catholicity and attach to the Union these men of influence in the wavering West.

In Indian affairs also the frontiersmen were conciliated by Washington's government. Preparations were made for a campaign against the Miami and Wabash Indians who had been harrying Kentucky. The obnoxious Cherokee treaty of Hopewell of 1785 was scrapped and, on July 2, 1791, a new treaty with the tribe was negotiated on behalf of the United States by William Blount.[21] In this treaty the Cherokee made a cession of land that carried the boundary a hundred miles farther down the Tennessee. In 1790 a large cession of land, though not so large as the Georgians wished, was secured from McGillivray and the Creek chiefs in the treaty of New York, which will be discussed again in another connection. In pursuance of this treaty federal garrisons were established on the Georgia frontier.

Another frontier grievance was remedied when Kentucky was admitted to the Union in 1792. Cumberland and the people of the defunct state of Franklin were within the bounds of the Southwest Territory whose government, organized in conformity with the system established in the Northwest Ordinance of 1787, contained a promise of statehood when the population of the territory should warrant it.

We have now seen how disaster very nearly overtook the United States in its frontier conflict with Spain, how it was averted by the force of cultural antagonism and by a conflict of interest between Spain and the American frontiersmen, and how the new federal government under Washington cultivated the friendship of the frontiersmen with studied care. In the next phase of the Spanish-American conflict, which will be discussed in the remaining chapters, there were two factors of great importance that had not existed in the first phase of the struggle: the new government of the United States, and the French Revolution with the attendant mutation of alliances and ideas.

CHAPTER IX

YAZOO

IN the course of the year 1790 the New World contributed two barbaric names to the vocabulary of international diplomacy : Yazoo and Nootka. A year earlier these were familiar to none but Indians and a few venturesome fur traders. A year later the frontier of their fame had receded to the national archives of the states concerned in the controversies that had raged over the Yazoo River and Nootka Sound. But throughout the year 1790 and well into the following year, one or both of these names was on the lips of statesmen in Whitehall and State Street, at San Lorenzo and Versailles, and well-informed observers perceived the bond that united the Yazoo country on the Lower Mississippi with Nootka Sound far up the California coast. While one Scotch fur trader's activities on the Vancouver brought the British government to the verge of war with Spain, capitalists and frontiersmen of the Southern States brought on a similar crisis between the United States and Spain by their effort to break the Scot Panton's monopoly of the Southern Indian trade. The intricate intrigues of these two years imperilled first the integrity of the American Union and then the existence of the Spanish empire in North America.

LAND SPECULATION AND THE TREATY-MAKING POWER

First came the Yazoo episode. The establishment of the new federal government influenced in many impor-

tant respects the development of the American West.
The new government brought to the Westerner's door-
step and into his home the principle of close federal
union, and yet the settlement of the West had been
conceived and executed in a spirit of particularism.
What its inhabitants thought of the new plan of government it is hard to say, for, while we have many evidences of widespread opposition to its adoption, we
also know that its adoption was followed by the immediate collapse of the first intrigue between the frontiersmen and Spain.

There was one clause in the Constitution of 1787
which made the whole instrument unpopular in the
West. This was the clause granting the President and
two thirds of the Senate the treaty-making power.
The reason for the frontiersmen's opposition to this
clause has seldom been understood by historians, for
they have generally assumed that what the "men of
the Western waters" feared was that this power would
be used to carry into effect Jay's plan of 1786 for bar-
tering away the use of the Mississippi for a generation.
It is true that a great deal was made of this point in
the Virginia ratifying convention of 1788, and that
Patrick Henry did raise the spectre of the Spanish
treaty in order to defeat the proposed constitution. It
is also true that, while Madison disposed of Henry's
argument so effectually that it could have no further
weight with any reasonable person, ten of the fourteen
members from the district of Kentucky voted against
the constitution; and that their opposition seems to
have been due to the clause in question. Since these
Kentucky members seem to have been at least normally
intelligent persons, we must look elsewhere for an
explanation of their action; and the explanation is

not far to seek. It was not in reality the treaty with
Spain that they feared, but treaties with the Indian
tribes or "nations" as they were then called. Although
the sovereignty of these tribes was not recognized,
the various state governments, the Congress of the
Confederation and after it the new federal government
concluded treaties with them as if each tribe were a
sovereign state. For example, the treaty of New York
between the United States and the Creek "nation,"
which will be discussed in this chapter, was negotiated
by the President and ratified by and with the advice
and consent of the Senate precisely as were Jay's treaty
with England and the treaty of San Lorenzo with Spain.
Now, while Madison could demonstrate with finality
that the treaty-making clause would not lead to the
surrender of the Mississippi claim, neither he nor any
one else could convince the frontiersmen that the new
government's policy in Indian affairs, its treaties with
the Indian tribes, would be equally unobjectionable
to them. For after all the Congress of the Confederation had not consummated, though it had authorized,
the surrender of the Mississippi; but, on the other hand,
it had pursued an Indian policy that was most offensive
to the frontiersmen of the Southwest. Its treaty of
Hopewell with the Cherokee, of which we have spoken
elsewhere, had alienated expansionists and land speculators throughout the South.

Hence when it was proposed in the new constitution
that the federal government be given still greater power
in Indian relations, there was general alarm among all
those interested in Southwestern expansion. Patrick
Henry, who was speculating extensively in Southwestern
lands, declared that there was a conspiracy on the part
of the jealous Eastern States to check the development

of the Southwest, and that the chief devices by which the conspirators designed to effect their purpose were the closing of the Mississippi and the protection of the Southern Indians.[1] Arthur Campbell of south-western Virginia and Harry Innes of Kentucky took the same position, Innes going so far as to declare that in his opinion the interests of East and West were irreconcilable in Indian affairs and many other matters, that the West could never expect fair treatment from the dominant Eastern majority, and that the only remedy lay in the establishment of Western independence.[2]

It seems probable that this state of mind was one of the chief causes of the outburst of land speculation in the Old Southwest in the years 1789 and 1790, for a stronger federal government would be better able to prevent the development of that region. The expansionists must act before the national government was established firmly enough to interfere with them. Patrick Henry, whose notorious hostility to the new system we have already had occasion to mention, was one of the most active of this group of speculators, and lamented that age prevented his seeking refuge in the Southwest from national tyranny.

THE GEORGIA LAND COMPANIES OF 1789

In 1789 the first group of Yazoo companies, less notorious but no less important than the vintage of 1795, secured provisional grants of land in the Southwest from the state of Georgia.[3] There were three of these companies. The Tennessee Company, under the leadership of Zachariah Cox and with support in the Holston settlements, secured the Muscle Shoals district. The Virginia Company, among whose members were Patrick Henry and a wealthy merchant and fur trader, David Ross, obtained a grant on the Mississippi as close to Chickasaw Bluffs as Georgia's territorrial claims would permit. The third and most active of these groups was the South Carolina Yazoo Company, whose organizers were South Carolinians and whose grant, lying on the Mississippi between the Yazoo River and the lands of the Virginia Company, included the important site of Walnut Hills at the mouth of the Yazoo River. Altogether some fifteen million acres were included in these three grants.

Like Bourbon and Houston Counties of 1784–85, these speculative schemes of 1789 were organized under the authority of the state of Georgia, but there were two important differences. In the first place, the state did not provide in the latter case for the extension of its political system over its western territory. It simply sold three enormous tracts of land, and made no attempt, through the establishment of county governments or otherwise, to supervise the founding of the new colonies or to establish any political connection with them. Moreover, since Georgia did not recognize the claim of Congress to this territory, it is difficult to see what bond was expected to unite the new colonies with the United States. In the second place, the South Carolina Yazoo Company, the most important of this group, made a determined effort — as had Sevier and White in their recent intrigue with Gardoqui and Miró — to enlist the support of the Spanish government. The speculators of 1784–85, it will be remembered, acted either independently of Spain or even in direct opposition to it. This change of attitude indicates the impression that Spain had made on the Americans in the short space of five years. The lesson of the Bourbon County fiasco had not been lost upon them. In

short, the particularist tendencies that had long characterized land speculation in the South were never more
strikingly in evidence than in these schemes of 1789.

Many ambitious speculators, busy in 1788 with their
private schemes, were drawn into the larger enterprise
of the Yazoo companies. George Rogers Clark, George
Morgan, James O'Fallon, James White, John Sevier, the
Baron von Steuben and others had approached the
Spanish government, through Gardoqui and Governor
Zéspedes of St. Augustine, with proposals for the establishment of colonies in Spanish territory or under
Spanish protection.[4] Their proposals were due, at
least in part, to the widespread report of Wilkinson's
favorable reception at New Orleans in 1787.[5] O'Fallon's
earliest correspondence with Zéspedes contains references to Wilkinson's visit to Miró and was apparently
designed to discredit him with the Spanish government
in order that O'Fallon might supplant him as Spain's
agent in the Southwest. It seems likely that the proposals of George Rogers Clark to Gardoqui for the establishment of a colony in Upper Louisiana were, like
those of O'Fallon, made in consequence of Wilkinson's
rumored success at New Orleans. In 1786 Clark had
seized the goods of Spanish merchants at Vincennes in
retaliation for the closing of the Mississippi, and had
threatened to invade Louisiana; but in 1788, just at
the time of Wilkinson's return to Kentucky from New
Orleans, he wrote Gardoqui proposing to establish a
colony that would protect the dominions of His Catholic
Majesty. The attempt of Sevier and White to secure
Spanish support for their Muscle Shoals project has
already been discussed; and it will be observed that
they broached the subject to Spain only in 1788, after
Wilkinson's return from New Orleans. In the same year

Joseph Martin wrote McGillivray in connection with
a colony that he proposed to establish on the Tombigbee
River, presumably under Spanish authority. Wilkin-
son himself was seized with the rage for speculation
that his return had done so much to cause, and addressed
Gardoqui a letter proposing that he, John Brown,
Sebastian and Harry Innes establish a colony under
Spanish authority in the Walnut Hills district.[6]

THE YAZOO PROJECT

Most of these speculators were drawn into the ambitious project of the South Carolina Yazoo Company.
James O'Fallon was appointed general agent of the
company. On his arrival in Kentucky he engaged
James Wilkinson, and later George Rogers Clark, to
support the company's undertaking. John Sevier,
hearing of the plan, had already written asking admission to membership, and his services were accepted.[7]
The organizers of the company were probably associated
with earlier speculative schemes, such as Bourbon and
Houston Counties, in both of which several South
Carolinians were interested, among them Wade
Hampton.

One of the directors of the company was "poor Tom
Washington," as O'Fallon called him two years later
when Tom was hanged in South Carolina for counterfeiting.[8] The other directors were William Clay Snipes,
Isaac Huger and Alexander Moultrie, reputed men of
fortune and influence in South Carolina. The last two
certainly bear names that are respectably familiar in the
history of the state, and Moultrie had but recently held
the office of governor. Their agent, James O'Fallon,
was one of the most verbose and unimaginative liars
that ever penned a letter. His copious but undisci-

plined vocabulary convinced the undiscriminating of his erudition, but few were deceived by his numerous and equally undisciplined lies. Formerly a doctor and formerly also, it was said, a Catholic priest, he threw himself into Charleston municipal politics at the close of the Revolution, aiding the popular party in its effort to drive the dominant conservatives from power. The failure of this attempt induced O'Fallon to try his talents elsewhere, and, as we have seen, it was the report of Wilkinson's journey to New Orleans in 1787 that pointed out to this Irish Catholic his next field of endeavor.

His race and faith made it easier for him to approach Governor Zéspedes of the neighboring town of St. Augustine. Zéspedes was not at all favorably impressed by O'Fallon's colonization proposals, but since rumors were rife that the American frontiersmen were planning to invade the Spanish dominions, he encouraged the Irishman's correspondence as a source of information that might prove valuable. In order to keep O'Fallon longer in suspense, he directed him to forward his colonization scheme to the court through Gardoqui, the proper channel for communications from citizens of the United States. Don Diego was quite as skeptical as Zéspedes, but, with the same object as the governor of St. Augustine, he replied with vague courtesy to O'Fallon's proposals, promising to forward them to the court.[9]

This Spanish connection got O'Fallon nothing from Spain, but his expectations in that quarter and his influence with the South Carolina Yazoo Company seem to have been responsible for the company's determined effort to secure the support of the Spanish government for its colony. Director Moultrie wrote

Alexander McGillivray and the wealthy Benjamin
Farrar of Natchez, while Tom Washington approached
another influential inhabitant of Natchez district,
Peter Bryan Bruin, in order not only to enlist their
individual support for the company, but also through
them to conciliate Spain.[10] The democrat O'Fallon,
however, was its chief ambassador to the Bourbon
autocracy. With the company's secret instructions in
his pocket O'Fallon journeyed to Kentucky. These
instructions [11] directed him to win the friendship of the
Choctaw and Chickasaw Indians, to proceed at once
to occupy the company's grant and to assure the
Spaniards of its ardent desire to cultivate amicable
relations with them and of its determination to establish an independent state which would serve as a
barrier between the United States and the Spanish possessions in North America. The comprehensive commercial designs of the company are manifest in the
letters of O'Fallon and still more in those of Moultrie
and Washington. They included the slave trade, trade
with the Indians and land speculation; and Walnut
Hills was designed as the *entrepôt* for the commerce of
the whole of the Mississippi Valley above that point.
It was but natural, however, that in letters intended
for Spanish eyes the political aspect should be emphasized. Moultrie wrote of the large amount of European
capital engaged in the enterprise and the anti-federalism
of its American members. O'Fallon fairly outdid himself in expressions of devotion to Spain and of abhor-
rence for the United States.[12] Postulating an Irishman's
hereditary love for Spain and misrepresenting shame-
lessly and foolhardily the nature of his relations with
Zéspedes and Gardoqui, he pictured the company as
converted by his influence into zealous Hispanophiles

panting for an alliance with the Bourbon monarch against the United States. At the very same time that he was writing in this tone to Miró, O'Fallon addressed an equally perfervid letter to President Washington, denouncing Spanish tyranny and offering to conquer New Orleans with the company's forces and turn it over to the United States government, if only the administration would give the company's enterprise its approval.[13]

Unscrupulous as he was, O'Fallon could not dissimulate. Indeed, one is inclined to accept Wilkinson's interested but apt description of him as a "vain blockhead." Even when his first obligation was to reassure the Spaniards, he could not resist the temptation to boast of his strength and to warn Miró that, in case Spain refused to sanction the enterprise, the company would resort to the use of armed force and would have the aid of thousands of soldiers from Cumberland, Franklin, Kentucky, the British in Canada, and even — through a suicidal charity, we must suppose — of the United States government itself.

The absurd maladroitness of this "vain blockhead" must not blind us to the importance of the project. It carried on a powerful tradition of American life, the tradition of colonization by capitalistic enterprise. It made a strong appeal to the interest of the investor and, as a venture in state-making, it caught the imagination of the romantic. Many people of influence in the South Atlantic States and on the Western frontier were committed to its prosecution, and it was legitimated by a grant from the state of Georgia. It was a far more formidable undertaking than Richard Henderson's Transylvania Company, so influential in the founding of Kentucky, and it gave greater promise of success. For the new federal government, its success would be a calamity. It would alarm the Indians and perhaps precipitate that general Indian war which Washington was striving so earnestly to avoid. It would bring on a crisis in the relations of the United States with Spain. If Spain sanctioned the establishment of the colony, it would undoubtedly be on condition of alliance or incorporation, thus imperiling the territorial integrity of the United States and prejudicing infinitely the pending diplomatic negotiation. If on the other hand Spain refused to sanction the settlement and opposed it with armed force, war might result, and the United States government, as much as it might deplore the cause, would almost certainly be involved. Hence the execution of the scheme must at all costs be prevented.

CHECKMATING THE SPECULATORS

One of President Washington's first steps was to issue a proclamation warning the public against the lawless projects of the companies.[14] Georgia's territorial claims, though still disputed by Congress, were not called into question by the proclamation, which was based on the federal government's control of Indian relations and on the treaties of Hopewell of 1786 whereby the perpetual possession of the lands involved was guaranteed to the Choctaw and Chickasaw tribes by Congress. Governor Blount of the Southwest Territory was directed to enforce this proclamation, and a mission was sent to the Indians to prevent them from giving any aid to the companies.[15]

Washington's next step was to prevent McGillivray and the Creek Indians from supporting the companies' project.[16] This was especially necessary because of the strength of the tribe, McGillivray's influence over them and the other Southern Indians, and the efforts of the South Carolina Yazoo Company to draw him into their project. The company claimed that it had succeeded in doing so, and letters from Moultrie and others to McGillivray on the subject were found by Panton among the half-breed's papers during his absence from home in 1790, but, other than his own statement that he gave them some encouragement in order to discover their designs,[17] there is no evidence that he actually joined the company. Even had he done so, Panton would certainly have used all his powerful influence to destroy the connection, for all of these schemes were obviously designed to break his monopoly of the Southern fur trade. Washington, however, could not be certain of this, and in any case he could not afford to rely on this British favorite of the Spanish government for the performance of a service so essential to the interests of the United States. The federal government itself must detach McGillivray from any connection he might have formed with the Georgia land companies.

There were other pressing reasons for the conclusion of a treaty with the Creek. The war between these Indians and the Georgians had continued intermittently ever since its outbreak in 1787, despite the repeated efforts of the Congress of the Confederation to secure peace, and Washington feared a general Indian war in the West. One of the very first measures of his administration was the appointment of a commission of three influential and disinterested persons to go to the Georgia frontier, inquire into the grievances of both parties, and arrange an accommodation. Again the negotiation ended in failure. The immediate reason for the breaking off of the conferences was apparently

McGillivray's dislike for the chief negotiator, Colonel David Humphreys, whose overbearing manner seemed intolerable to the sensitive half-breed. McGillivray's first impulse after his withdrawal was an Indian's impulse: to avenge himself for the Connecticut Yankee's insults by scalping the Georgia frontiersmen; but Miró urgently advised him not to continue hostilities, and he thought better of it.[18]

There was a deeper reason for the failure of the negotiations. While the Spanish government repeatedly urged McGillivray to make peace with the Georgians, Miró as often charged him to confine himself to a treaty of friendship and limits, never to agree to any terms that conflicted with the treaty of Pensacola of 1784, and above all to refuse to make any concession to the Americans in respect to trade or sovereignty.[19] This latter point was all the more important because of its bearing on the negotiation pending between the United States and Spain. While McGillivray had been deeply offended with Miró in 1788 because the latter, on orders from the court, had cut off the Indians' munitions supply in order to induce them to make peace with the Georgians, his resentment had led to no more serious consequences than his brief intrigue with Bowles, which we have already mentioned. The breach was soon healed, Miró reopened the Spanish magazines to the Creek, and McGillivray professed himself the unwavering champion of Spanish interests. Just before he and his fellow-chiefs left to meet the American commissioners he received through Panton, Leslie and Company a fresh supply of munitions which, as Panton prophesied, enabled him to "talk strong" in the ensuing conference. Unable to agree with the commissioners on trade, limits or sovereignty, McGillivray needed little provocation to make him break off the negotiation and return to his plantation on the Coosa.

The commissioners naturally laid all the blame on McGillivray and declared war inevitable, and the secretary of war, General Henry Knox, was of the same mind. It was felt in government circles, however, that the commissioners were not themselves blameless, and that, as Senator Maclay put it, Knox was moved by the very natural desire to "labor in his vocation." [20] As a last resort, Washington sent Colonel Marinus Willet as his personal messenger to invite McGillivray to come to New York with his chiefs and make a final effort for a peaceful settlement. Meanwhile Miró had received with something approaching consternation the news of the failure of the recent peace conference and the imminent danger that the United States would now at last aid the Georgians against the Creek. Once begun, there was no telling where such a conflict might end, for it was commonly believed that the Indians' ravages had been instigated by Spain. Miró therefore urged McGillivray to accept at once any offer that might lead to the renewal of negotiations, and only cautioned him not to forget his obligations to Spain. This was the situation when Willet arrived, and, in view of Miró's admonitions, it is not surprising that McGillivray accepted the invitation and set out for New York with more than a score of chiefs and interpreters without waiting to consult Miró or even Panton.[21]

McGillivray riding on horseback and the chiefs seated sedately in waggons, the cavalcade journeyed northward. Fêted at Richmond, the party was met at Murray's wharf in New York by a military escort and by the largest crowd that had assembled since Washington's inauguration fifteen months earlier. The necessities of the federal government and the incipient romantic movement secured for these noble savages a warm welcome. Presented to the secretary of war and the president, they were lavishly entertained by government officials and others, including the Order of St. Tammany, and in turn regaled their hosts with a war dance.[22]

THE TREATY OF NEW YORK

This flattering reception and the distribution of pensions among McGillivray and his companions secured the terms desired by the United States government. The treaty was concluded on August 7, 1790, and a week later McGillivray went so far as to sign an oath of allegiance to the United States.[23] By the treaty, the Creek recognized the sovereignty of the United States so far as their towns lay within its limits. McGillivray gave up his claim to the boundary of 1772, though the territorial concessions that he made were not extensive enough to satisfy the Georgians. All traders without a license from the United States government were to be excluded from the Creek towns. The latter were authorized to expel by force any intruders on the lands guaranteed them by the treaty. Although this clause appeared in the earlier treaties of Hopewell, McGillivray wrote Miró later that in this case it was directed against the Georgia land companies, and that he was repeatedly urged during the conferences preceding the treaty to break up the companies' settlements, should any be made.

Two secret articles were added.[24] One of them was written under the influence of the Nootka crisis that had just arisen between Spain and England. It was provided that in case the Creek trade by way of the Floridas should be interrupted by war or otherwise, $50,000 worth of goods annually might be imported duty free through the United States into the Creek country. It is possible that the whole treaty as well as this article was agreed to by McGillivray because of the Nootka crisis. War between Spain and England seemed inevitable, and the defeat of Spain and the disorganization of Panton's trade, at least for a time, seemed no less certain. The treaty of New York`was McGillivray's provision against the rainy day that seemed at hand.

The other secret article provided that in satisfaction of his claims against the state of Georgia McGillivray should receive a pension of eighteen hundred dollars a year from the United States government. This was three times the amount of the only remuneration that he was receiving from Spain at that time, namely, a salary of six hundred dollars a year as the commissioner of Spain among the Creek Indians. The munificence of this new pension must have had great weight with McGillivray, who lived in the generous manner of a Southern gentleman and, like most Southern gentlemen, was often embarrassed for ready cash.

In the triangular contest between the United States government, Spain and the Georgia land companies for the support of the Creek Indians, the former had apparently won a complete victory.[25] So far as McGillivray's relations with Spain were concerned, the victory was not lasting. Panton's friendship and the alternate threats and persuasion of Miró and Carondelet, who raised his salary first to two thousand and then to thirty-five hundred dollars, delayed its execution several years.[26] The mere fact that the treaty was negotiated, however, was in itself an achievement of lasting importance. Despite Carondelet's attempt in 1792 to demonstrate its invalidity, the treaty was negotiated with at least as much formality as most of Carondelet's treaties with the Southern Indian tribes, and as most treaties between white men and Indians. Consequently it afforded the United States what a strong power usually seeks in a treaty with a weaker neighbor : a legal basis for future penetration. Since the application of the treaty was restricted to the Creek towns lying within the United States and since most of the Creek towns were situated in the territory still in dispute between Spain and the United States, the precise significance of the treaty remained in doubt until the two powers came to an agreement as to the location of the southern boundary of the United States. In two respects the treaty was immediately beneficial to the United States : The imminent resumption of the Georgia-Creek war was averted, and McGillivray's aid was enlisted against the Georgia land companies. In both respects, it is curious to note, Spanish interests and Spanish policy coincided with those of the United States.

CHAPTER X

NOOTKA

In 1789, Spanish forces seized a British vessel in Nootka Sound, which, Spain claimed, lay within its territorial waters. The interests of British fur traders, already active in that region, led their government to make an issue of the case. A peremptory demand for satisfaction was addressed to the Spanish government in May, 1790, and Pitt began to concert with William Augustus Bowles and Francisco de Miranda plans of attack against Spanish possessions in North and South America.[1] The affair at once became public property and created a great sensation in Europe and America. The insignificance of the offence, the doubt, arising from the uncertainty as to the rights of the two countries, whether any offence at all had been committed, the curtness of England's language in addressing a supposedly friendly power, and the rapidity and scale of its preparations for war created the impression that the British were determined to fight on no matter what pretext while Spain's ancient ally, France, was crippled by the Revolution.[2]

THE NOOTKA CRISIS AND THE YAZOO PROJECT

The Nootka crisis, whose influence on the treaty of New York we observed in the preceding chapter, exerted an even profounder influence on the development of the South Carolina Yazoo Company's enterprise. The company's confidential instructions of 1790 to O'Fallon had directed him to assure the Spanish colonial officials that its intention was to establish a

colony which would serve as a barrier between the
United States and the Spanish dominions and to form
a close connection with Spain. What the Nootka crisis
did was to cause O'Fallon, with or without the company's consent, to convert the colonization project into
a plan of conquest, with Louisiana as the prize.

O'Fallon's first letters to Miró from Kentucky were
conciliatory enough, and he cultivated Wilkinson,
whose partiality for Spain was notorious. Wilkinson
responded readily. Indeed, he had written the company
in 1789 and again early in 1790, before O'Fallon's
arrival, setting forth the importance of enlisting the aid
of Spain and intimating that he himself was the very
man for that task and for the general agency of the
company in the West. Unfortunately for the company,
O'Fallon's appointment had already been made. Moultrie answered Wilkinson to this effect, and sought to
placate him with the offer of a share. The offer was
accepted and for a few months all went well.[3] Wilkinson
may have been sincere, for his interest in such an enterprise had been shown by his application through
Gardoqui, which we have already mentioned, for
authority to establish a colony in the very same
territory now claimed by the company. He may have
been further disposed to support its project because the
separatist movement in Kentucky had come to a halt.
Conscious of failure and fearing exposure, he wished at
the same time to render a compensatory service to
Spain and to provide an asylum for himself. Whatever
the reason, he supported the project energetically for
a few months and wrote Miró urging him to recommend
it to the court.

Suddenly in August, 1790, he wrote Moultrie sever-
ing his connection with the company. Both to Moul-

trie and to Miró, to whom he sent a copy of his letter to
Moultrie, he explained his action on the ground that
O'Fallon had changed the whole character of the
undertaking and was perfidiously planning to invade
Louisiana with British aid. One may suspect that the
prospect of a commission in the expedition against the
Miami and Wabash Indians had its influence in detach-
ing from O'Fallon's colonial enterprise a man who once
declared, "My passion is military fame." [4] It cannot
be doubted, however, that O'Fallon's plans had
changed and that the Nootka crisis was the cause.
This crisis offered the frontiersmen a golden opportunity. Those of them who were godly were for the
most part Protestants with no stomach for popery.
The ungodly frankly longed for the silver mines of
Mexico. Godly or not, they all resented the payment
of a duty of twenty-one per cent for the use of a river
which, they told themselves and all the world, God and
Great Britain had given them to use free of charge.
Yet as often as the frontiersmen had been tempted to
invade these invitingly defenceless provinces, as often
had they been restrained by the reflection that, even
though they might take New Orleans, Spain would still
control the Gulf with its navy and the mouths of the
Mississippi would still be closed.

The Nootka crisis seemed to solve the difficulty by
offering the Kentuckians what was needed to make the
conquest of Louisiana complete: the coöperation of a
British fleet in the Gulf. It also seemed likely that a
British land force from Canada would descend the
Mississippi and join in the assault. Washington was so
alarmed at the prospect that he took the advice of the
cabinet on the course that he should follow in case
British troops attempted to pass through the territory

of the United States in order to attack Louisiana. Differing in their opinion on this point, Jefferson and Hamilton were agreed that the navigation of the Mississippi and the control of the territory about its mouth were of the greatest importance to the United States. In Kentucky also the crisis was earnestly discussed.[5] British intrigue in Kentucky had long been rumored in the Atlantic States and, while rumor exaggerated the danger, it was true that a British agent from Canada, a Colonel John Connolly, had appeared in Kentucky in 1788 inciting the backwoodsmen to insurrection. This tradition seemed to point the way to O'Fallon, who, moreover, learned just at this time that Miró was urging the Southern Indians to attack any Americans who might attempt to settle in the companies' grants.[6] An indication of the changed character of the enterprise is that the pro-Spanish Wilkinson was now supplanted as O'Fallon's chief adviser by George Rogers Clark, whose name both before and after 1790 was so often associated with plans for invading Louisiana. The new union was sealed by the marriage of O'Fallon, aged fifty, to Clark's youngest sister, aged fifteen; "an additional proof of his circumspection and good sense," remarked Wilkinson.[7]

This change of front was fatal to the company's project. The Nootka crisis was soon over, for the Spanish government, unable to secure aid from revolutionary France on satisfactory terms, was forced to yield to England. The freebooters of Kentucky were disappointed in their hope of securing the coöperation of England's navy. Spain's control of the Gulf was unbroken, and a mere land conquest of Louisiana was as futile as ever. All that O'Fallon had accomplished

was to give Spain irrefragable proof of his duplicity.
With England aloof and the Spanish and United States
governments hostile, success was all but impossible.
The company's *coup de grâce*, if we are to believe
Wilkinson, came from no less a person than himself.
He tells us that by sending a certain Captain Manning
to South Carolina to inform the company's directors of
O'Fallon's prodigality and incompetence he induced
them to refuse to honor O'Fallon's drafts on them.
His credit ruined by this stroke, O'Fallon's enterprise
had collapsed; [8] and the simultaneous execution of
"poor Tom" Washington for counterfeiting cannot
have raised the company's prestige in either South
Carolina or Kentucky

The projects of the other two Georgia land companies
also came to nothing. Patrick Henry of the Virginia
Company yielded with bad grace to Washington's proclamation against the speculators, but was consoled
when the paper money with which he was to have paid
the state of Georgia for the company's grant rose in
value with Congress's assumption of the state debts. [9]
The Tennessee Company, under the energetic leadership of Zachariah Cox, actually made a settlement at
Muscle Shoals despite the opposition of Governor
Blount, who had lands of his own to sell. The settlement was, however, broken up by a band of Creek Indians sent out by McGillivray. [10]

SHORT'S MEMORIAL ON THE MISSISSIPPI

The Yazoo projects and the Nootka crisis were also
responsible for the resumption of the negotiation between Spain and the United States. Since the Congress
of the Confederation had by its resolution of 1788
bequeathed the problem to the new government,

neither Spain nor the United States had formally attempted to reopen the discussion. Floridablanca expected to find the new federal government more compliant than the old Congress, but, warned by Gardoqui that some time must be allowed for its consolidation, he was not pressing. Gardoqui was permitted to return to Spain on leave (1789), and when, shortly after his arrival at court, he was appointed to the newly created post of director of colonial trade his place in the United States was not filled. Jáudenes and Viar, the young men brought over with Gardoqui in 1784 to assist in the work of the legation, were commissioned as Spain's agents in the United States, but they were not given the rank even of *encargado de negocios* (chargé d'affaires) for the conduct of the ordinary business of the office, and no provision whatever was made for the resumption of the negotiation of a treaty. The Spanish government took the position that since the first conferences had been terminated through the action of the old Congress the first overtures for another parley must come from the new government. To fill the diplomatic hiatus, Floridablanca had adopted a more liberal immigration policy and had taken up the western intrigue, which was designed primarily to guard against the danger of an invasion of Louisiana by the frontiersmen of the American West, though it was also hoped that the partition of the United States might ensue. The various intrigues with the frontiersmen, however, soon demonstrated a fundamental conflict of interest. Spain's object in the intrigue was to enfeeble the American border settlements. The frontiersmen's object was almost invariably to promote the prosperity of communities already established or to found new autonomous colonies on the American model within or near the dominions of Spain.

Simultaneously with reports of the Yazoo and Nootka affairs another proof of the futility of the Western intrigue reached Floridablanca. At the same time that Miró wrote to the court about O'Fallon's proposals, he confessed the failure of Wilkinson's scheme to separate Kentucky from the Union.[11] Since, as these disturbing notices showed, the American West did not respond to direct treatment, and since to Floridablanca diplomacy and the Western intrigue were but alternative methods of restraining the frontiersmen, it was clearly time to resume the interrupted negotiation with the United States government. A hopeful indication of the American government's sweet reasonableness in Western questions was afforded by its vigorous opposition to the Georgia land companies.

It was in these circumstances that Floridablanca received from William Short, the chargé d'affaires of the United States in Paris, a memorial insisting that without delay Spain permit the citizens of the United States to exercise their right to the free navigation of the Mississippi River. Short had a brother living in Kentucky,[12] and was bound by ties of close personal friendship to James Monroe and Thomas Jefferson. Monroe was one of the leaders of the Mississippi party in the old Congress, and one of the most resolute opponents of Jay's treaty project of 1786. Jefferson's solution of the difficult problem so clearly stated by Jay — how to secure the navigation of the Mississippi from Spain without going to war — was to take advantage of one of the frequent European war-scares, in which Spain was usually involved, and to extort a favorable treaty as the price of neutrality.[13]

When the Nootka crisis arose, these connections left no doubt as to the course Short should follow. Drawing up a vigorous memorial on the right of the United States to the free navigation of the Mississippi, he submitted it to Vergennes' successor in the foreign office, Montmorin, who transmitted it to Floridablanca through the French chargé in Madrid.[14] That the French government, still nominally bound to Spain by the Bourbon Family Compact, was willing to be involved in so delicate an affair and one in regard to which the Spanish court was very sensitive, may perhaps be attributed to the influence of Lafayette, the strong man of France at that juncture. Not only was Lafayette sympathetic towards the republic to whose establishment he had devoted years of his youth, but he was personally involved in the negotiation between Spain and the United States. In 1783 he had used all his influence to get Floridablanca to accept the stipulations of the Anglo-American treaty with regard to the southern boundary of the United States and the navigation of the Mississippi, and had received from the Spanish minister an equivocal reply that became the subject of heated discussion at a later time.[15]

Another factor which probably inclined the French government to forward Short's memorial was its resentment at Floridablanca's insistence on a formal reply to his note demanding the aid of France against England in the Nootka crisis. The French government finally replied, but hedged its assent about with conditions unacceptable to Spain, and Montmorin probably welcomed the opportunity offered by Short's memorial to retaliate for the embarrassment that Floridablanca had caused him.

Spain's situation was extremely uncomfortable. The united hostility of the English and the Americans, so long feared by the court, seemed about to be realized just as Spain was estranged from her one ally by the French Revolution. Gardoqui, to whom, as a specialist in relations with the United States, Floridablanca referred Short's memorial, dwelt on the Anglo-American menace and urged an accommodation with the United States. His report is especially interesting because it seems to suggest a surrender to the United States on the questions of limits and navigation in return for a defensive alliance and a mutual guarantee of the possessions of the two powers in America.[16]

TWO ROYAL ORDERS

Upon receiving this report, Floridablanca issued simultaneously two orders covering the relations of Spain with the United States. One of these orders related to the frontier situation and was sent to the governor of Havana for transmission to Miró and Gayoso.[17] The governor was informed of the court's rejection of the South Carolina Yazoo Company's project and was instructed to prevent any settlement by the Americans in the territory between the Tennessee and Mississippi Rivers, all of which Floridablanca, in conformity with the Instruction of 1784, styled Spanish territory. The order approved Miró's decision to establish a fortified post at Los Nogales, or Walnut Hills, in order to anticipate the company's designs on that site. The correspondence with Wilkinson was ordered to be continued, though the question of his pension was still left unsettled. Finally, a copy of Short's memorial was enclosed and Miró was informed that negotiations were in progress for the regular and peaceful settlement of all the points at issue between Spain and the United States.[18]

The other order was sent to Jáudenes and Viar, Spain's agents in the United States. Expressing His Majesty's pained surprise at the tone of Short's memorial and especially at his complaint against the dilatoriness of Spain, Floridablanca very properly pointed out that it was the United States that had broken off the previous negotiation, and that Short's memorial was the first intimation Spain had received of his government's readiness to resume it. However, continued Floridablanca, His Majesty wished his agents, Jáudenes and Viar, to give a proof of his good will towards the United States by informing the president of Spain's willingness to conclude a comprehensive treaty. The United States might send suitable persons with the proper authority to Spain, or, if they preferred, the king would send his plenipotentiary to the United States.

The choice of the envoys to Spain was a matter of some moment to that power, as the above summary of the order suggests. The action of the United States in response to this invitation illuminates its policy towards Spain and is one of the clearest proofs that it was not seeking to negotiate an equitable treaty but to maneuver Spain into a complete surrender. A sincere desire to negotiate would have led the United States to select acceptable envoys for the Spanish mission and to despatch them promptly. Nothing of the kind was done. Before the appointment was made Jefferson had a conversation with Jáudenes in which he asked the Spanish agent if Carmichael, the American chargé at Madrid, would be acceptable as the plenipotentiary for this negotiation. Jáudenes gave it as his opinion, merely personal but quite positive, that in view of the wording of the invitation his appointment would not be satisfactory to the Spanish government, and that moreover His Catholic Majesty would never agree to a treaty unless the emissaries sent by the United States were persons of accomplishments and distinction.[19]

Despite this warning the United States government not only failed to send public characters of distinction to Spain, but actually named the unwelcome Carmichael one of the envoys. The other was William Short, who had presented the memorial on the Mississippi, and who at the same time with this temporary mission to Spain was given the permanent post of minister to the Hague. An estimable person, Short was certainly not distinguished enough to fulfill the Spanish requirements. Jáudenes indeed wrote Floridablanca, on the authority of Senator Butler of South Carolina, that Carmichael and Short were almost unknown even in the Senate, and that their appointment was confirmed merely in order to please Jefferson and the President.[20]

It is doubtful whether the American government could have persuaded more prominent persons to undertake the mission, for it was quite clear to any one well informed on the subject that its success was highly improbable. Then why, it may be asked, did the administration make any provision at all for a negotiation? The answer is that, in the first place, the United States could not openly ignore Spain's advances without incurring the odium of unreasonableness and destroying the fiction of patient negotiation; and that, in the second place, it must convince the Westerners that it was doing everything in its power to secure the free navigation of the Mississippi. It was

in order to keep up appearances as economically as
possible that two diplomats already on the government
pay-roll and already in Europe were appointed to conduct the negotiation.[21]

It is also worthy of notice that while Floridablanca's
invitation was communicated to Jefferson in November,
1791, the envoys were not appointed until February,
1792, and Short did not actually arrive in Spain until
a year later, that is, February, 1793. This delay was
explained on the ground that Short's commission had
gone astray;[22] but it is an interesting coincidence
that this extremely long delay took place precisely during the year 1792, a year in which the European
situation was least promising for the success of the
United States in its negotiation with Spain. Spain and
France were still at peace, and a *rapprochement* was in
progress between Spain and England that culminated
in a treaty of alliance and saved Spain from isolation
when she went to war with France early in 1793.
Jefferson still clung to his belief that time was on the
side of the United States, and there can be little doubt
that his enthusiasm for the French Revolution was
heightened by his conviction that it would hasten the
victory of the United States in its conflict with Spain.
As early as 1786 he had written that his only fear was
lest the Spaniards should be unable to hold their territory on the Mississippi "till our population can be
sufficiently advanced to gain it from them piece by
piece;"[23] and the French Revolution seemed at first
to advance the day when the United States might
extend its possessions down the Mississippi to the Gulf.
Certainly Jefferson's enthusiasm was in part justified,
for to Spain the French Revolution was a disaster of
the first magnitude. For the present, however, this

was not apparent to any but the keenest observers. Throughout the year 1792 and most of the following year the Revolution seemed to have the contrary effect, reconciling Spain with her traditional enemy and bringing England and the United States to the brink of war. It was only when the alliance with England turned out badly and the war with France still worse that the despatches of Short and Carmichael and the instructions of their chief betrayed that eagerness for negotiations that they and others after them have read into the earlier policy of the United States.

CHAPTER XI
HECTOR, BARON DE CARONDELET
A MAN OF ACTION

In the meanwhile, events were taking place in Louisiana and West Florida that exercised a powerful influence over the course of the diplomatic negotiation. On December 30, 1791, Hector, Baron de Carondelet, took over the government and intendancy of those provinces from Esteban Miró, who had completed the normal five-year term and who, on account of his age, was permitted to return to Spain. The appointment of Carondelet was, to put it mildly, deplorable. A wise government would have promoted either Arturo O'Neill, governor of Pensacola, or Manuel Gayoso, governor of Natchez, both of whom were of sufficient age and rank and possessed two indispensable qualifications in which Carondelet was absolutely lacking: a thorough knowledge of the English language and an intimate acquaintance with the state of affairs in the Mississippi Valley. Carondelet knew not a word of English, so far as the records show, and was dependent for his translations upon his secretary, Armesto, who, although he was the local schoolmaster, could boast but a mediocre knowledge of the language.[1] Coming to Louisiana from San Salvador, Carondelet was utterly ignorant of the situation in his new provinces. Without the necessary background, without competent advisers at New Orleans, without the temperament that can take advice, and yet at the same time a man of immediate and strong convictions and a lover of direct action, he was probably the worst man that could have been found in the whole colonial service of Spain for the command of these border provinces at such a crisis. He probably owed his appointment to the influence of his wife's family, the Las Casas, who bore a name familiar in colonial affairs since the sixteenth century.[2] Carondelet's brother-in-law, Luis de las Casas, was governor of Havana and captain-general of Louisiana and the Floridas from 1791 to 1796. It may be that the Baron's knowledge of French — he was a Fleming — was considered an important asset, since most of the inhabitants of Louisiana were of French origin.

This man was dominated by a veritable passion for direct action, a passion that may perhaps be explained by his consciousness of his mental limitations. Realizing his inability to deal with a complex situation, he would seek to resolve the most obvious of his perplexities by the use of physical force. Even his handwriting is not that of one who is by nature masterful, a compelling man of action, but rather of a warden of some tranquil college. What has this man to do with war? we ask, as we turn over page after page of yellow paper covered with the prim traces of his pen. And yet violence, war, conquest he would have.

We could hardly find a better case to illustrate the man's temperament than his conduct when he heard in 1794 that Elijah Clarke of Georgia was planning an invasion of the Floridas. Forgetting — or was it perhaps remembering? — that a dozen important and complex questions required his presence at the seat of government in New Orleans, he urged the captain-general to let him lead an expedition in person by way of St. Mark's up the Appalachicola River to attack this freebooter in the desert wilds on the border of the Floridas and Georgia.[3] We suspect that he was fleeing from civil complexity to the simplicity of the battlefield, and that in this as in many other cases a sense of weakness lay at the root of his belligerency.

The result was what might have been expected from the appointment of such a man to such a post. Misinformation that was sometimes merely ludicrous, sometimes dangerously misleading, was sent by Carondelet to the home government. In decoding Wilkinson's important cipher despatches the most amazing errors were made. Sometimes Carondelet's blunders were corrected by his secretary, Armesto, before the despatch was mailed, as for example when Carondelet wrote the secretary of state in regard to the state of "Belmont," obviously confusing Belmont, Kentucky, with the state of Vermont. On one occasion he was thrown into a panic by the report that fifteen thousand men were going to invade West Florida by marching overland from Georgia, and begged the captain-general for reinforcements to resist the invaders. As Miró pointed out, when this letter was referred to him in Madrid, it would have been next to impossible for such a body of troops to pass through the intervening country of the hostile Creek Indians or to support itself even if not attacked by the Indians. On another occasion Carondelet solemnly assured the ministry that a body of hostile troops could march from St. Louis to Santa Fé in twenty-two days. Upon examination it appeared that he based this assertion upon the experience of a single Spanish official who, traveling under the most favorable circumstances, had made the down-stream part of the journey from Santa Fé to St. Louis in that length of time.[4]

Far more serious than such misinformation were his errors of judgment, which seem to have been generally due to his rudimentary powers of discrimination. Instances of these faults will appear in the following pages. For the present it will suffice to call attention to his failure to perceive the wide gulf that separated the freebooters of the American frontier from the federal government, George Rogers Clark from George Washington. Gayoso and Gardoqui were more perspicacious than he, but Gayoso was merely one of Carondelet's subordinates and Gardoqui was appointed secretary of the treasury just after Carondelet's arrival in Louisiana and was consequently not in a position to make his influence felt in the political administration of that province. Some of the consequences of Carondelet's blindness to this distinction will appear in connection with the development of his Indian policy.

THE BARON'S DILEMMA

When he arrived in Louisiana he found the situation serious and represented it to his government as most alarming. Reliance had been placed in four measures for the defence of this province and West Florida: the maintenance of military posts, the Kentucky intrigue, immigration, and Indian alliances. The posts, as Carondelet warned, repeating what Miró had so often said before him to an unheedful government, were in a ruinous state. Most of the forts consisted merely of earthworks which were washing away and a wooden palisade so rotten as hardly to be proof against a musketball. The one regiment assigned Louisiana was far from complete, and was utterly inadequate in the face of the rapidly growing American settlements and an impending war in Europe and America.[5]

The Kentucky intrigue, which had been designed to weaken the United States by dividing it into two rival republics, was almost dead of pernicious anæmia when

Carondelet arrived in Louisiana. The collapse of the first attempt at secession had left Wilkinson nothing to do but play the spy and immigration agent. The rôles were not only unromantic but unprofitable as well, for Spain had not yet granted him a pension, and the return of the seven thousand dollars advanced him as a loan by Miró might be demanded. Under these circumstances and under the pressure of financial difficulties he accepted a lieutenant colonel's commission in the United States Army in October, 1791, and his correspondence with his dear friends Gayoso and Miró languished.[6] A few weeks after Carondelet took over the government of Louisiana he received the court's order granting Wilkinson a pension of two thousand dollars a year dating from January 1, 1789. He hastened to write "our brigadier" the good tidings, and thereafter the exchange of letters became more frequent.[7] Conditions were not yet favorable, however, for a renewal of the attempt at secession, for admission to statehood and the campaign against the Northern Indians placated the Kentuckians for the moment and absorbed their surplus energy and farm products. It was not until 1794 that it was possible to renew the intrigue in earnest, and in the meanwhile Carondelet must seek safety in some other measure.

THE GOTHS REFUSE TO EMIGRATE

Despite an initial success that alarmed land-owners in the American West, the immigration policy had failed as completely as the frontier intrigue. We have seen how in 1787 the court's resolution on the proposals of d'Argès foreshadowed a profound change in Spain's colonial immigration policy, and how this change was effected in the royal order of December 1, 1788. A post was established at New Madrid in the country that George Morgan planned to colonize, and Natchez was raised from a post to a government with the diplomatic Gayoso at its head. Nogales also was thrown open to settlement (1791). Free grants of land were made, the importation of slaves was not only permitted but encouraged, and Protestants were admitted, tolerated and granted all the rights of Spanish subjects on taking the usual oath of allegiance. These measures were designed to depopulate Kentucky, Cumberland and Holston and fill Louisiana and West Florida with settlers.[8]

This remarkable effort at adaptation failed, and the reasons for its failure are not far to seek. In the first place, the political and religious privileges offered the Americans were less than those they already enjoyed, although far greater than Spain was accustomed to grant. As one traveler, Colonel John Pope, remarked, a Spanish subject could not even post a notice of a stray horse without the consent of the military commander of his district.[9] Another observer warned the Americans that Spain was ruled by an absolute monarch and if they settled in Spanish territory they might be compelled to become Roman Catholics within twenty-four hours on pain of banishment.

By the beginning of Carondelet's administration it was clear that no compensatory advantages over those offered by the communities of the American West could be hoped for under Spanish rule. Spanish subjects enjoyed no considerable advantage over the Americans on the Mississippi, for, as Wilkinson told Miró, they preferred paying the duty imposed on their river traffic — from six to fifteen per cent — to the trouble and expense of moving to Spanish territory.[10]

Still more discouraging to immigration was the government's reduction in 1790 of the amount of tobacco purchased on the royal account for the factory at Seville. One of the chief attractions of Louisiana and West Florida in the 1780's was the fact that the heavy purchases of tobacco on the government's account — two million pounds a year at a price of first ten and then eight dollars a hundred pounds — assured the planters a ready market for their tobacco and hard cash in payment for it.[11] A letter written by Joseph Martin to Patrick Henry shows the interest aroused in the American West by this policy, which inclined Martin to establish a colony on the Tombigbee River not far above Mobile.[12]

In December, 1790, a royal order was issued reducing the amount to be purchased annually to the insignificant figure of forty thousand pounds, or, at the maximum price of ten dollars per hundredweight, four thousand dollars' worth of tobacco a year. There were excellent reasons for this reduction. The factory at Seville was overstocked, and the tobacco of Louisiana was said to be of inferior quality. Politically, however, the measure was very unwise, for it was a striking instance of the insecurity of property under the Spanish government. The planters of Natchez presented a petition complaining loudly of the reduction, declaring that it was only the prospect of a ready market that had induced them to settle there, and to contract debts in order to buy slaves and clear lands for cultivation, and that unless two million pounds of tobacco a year were purchased or free trade with foreign countries permitted certain ruin would overtake them.[13] Ezekiel Forman, who came from New Jersey with his family and fifty slaves to settle at

Natchez, found the planters despondent and the situation discouraging when he arrived there in 1790.[14] Wilkinson assigned the change in the tobacco policy as one of the principal reasons for the cessation of immigration from Kentucky; and Gayoso assured the government that with the resumption of its tobacco purchases or the grant of free trade the development of a strong barrier-colony within ten years was a certainty, but that without some such encouragement its growth would be extremely slow.[15] Nevertheless, the government did not resume its liberal purchases, and, as we shall see, the measure of "free trade" that it accorded these frontier provinces in 1793 was narrowly limited.

At the same time that the attraction of a ready market was lost by the people of Louisiana it was gained by the Kentuckians. The United States Army operating against the Northern Indians and the thousands of immigrants that entered the state every year consumed the surplus food-stuffs produced by the Kentucky farmers.[16] Hard times at Natchez attracted few settlers from prosperous Kentucky.

Another of the putative advantages of Spanish subjects soon proved illusory, for the Indians took scalps in Natchez district as well as in Cumberland and Kentucky. Despite all that the Spanish officials could do or say, their Creek allies would not distinguish between Americans who had taken the oath of allegiance to Spain and those who had not. Journeying from the Alabama River through the Choctaw towns they murdered an inoffensive Natchez settler and his family, threw the whole country into a panic, brought immigration to a pause and frightened away some who had already made their homes in Spanish territory. When one of these recent immigrants, Robert Stark, a man of some means and influence who had settled at Natchez in 1790, asked permission in 1793 to return to the United States, he encountered another of the peculiarities of the Spanish system. He was informed that the land granted him in 1790 could not be sold but must revert to the crown, since it had been granted for settlement and not for speculation.[17]

Finally, in considering the reasons for the failure of the immigration policy, it must be remembered that the Spanish system forbade three forms of activity common among the American frontiersmen : local self-government in its various manifestations, such as elections, conventions and associations; public Protestant worship, to which many frontiersmen, especially the Presbyterians and Baptists of the Holston region were devotedly attached; and land speculation, in which almost every frontiersman of any consequence was engaged and which was consistently opposed by the Spanish government.[18] Land grants were made to none but bona-fide settlers, were not always transferable, and varied in size according to the number of adult males, free or slave, in the grantec's family. Some of the American frontiersmen said that Sunday had not yet crossed the mountains, and no doubt many of them could have got on quite comfortably without a Sunday sermon; but one can hardly conceive of an American frontier community, even under the Spanish government, without its political conventions and its land speculators.

Under these conditions it is not surprising that the Spanish experiment failed. The extent of the failure was brought out strikingly by Spain's experience at New Madrid and Nogales (Walnut Hills). In both cases the projects had originated with Americans, the former

with George Morgan and the latter with the South
Carolina Yazoo Company, and both had given fair
promise of success until Spain intervened. As soon as
Spanish authority was extended over the settlements
by the establishment of garrisons, immigration came to
a standstill and the colonies languished with a handful
of apathetic inhabitants.

Even had the policy been successful it was opposed
by so many influential Spaniards — Carondelet himself;
his superior, the captain-general, Luis de las Casas; the
viceroy of Mexico, the Marqués de Revillagigedo; and
the secretary of war — that it would probably have
been modified in any case. As it turned out, the policy
was not merely modified but abandoned during the
conservative reaction in Spain following the excesses
of the French Reign of Terror, and its abandonment
coincided with the surrender of the diplomatic controversy with the United States. In November, 1795,
two weeks after the conclusion of the treaty of San
Lorenzo, the Council of State had under consideration
a colonization plan proposed by a certain Louis de
Villemont of Louisiana, and based on the liberalism
that had inspired Floridablanca's immigration policy.
Times had changed since 1788. Godoy observed
severely that "a Catholic king cannot be indulgent in
the observance of the law of God," and the Council
disapproved of the plan because of "the absolute
impossibility of securing a large number of suitable
colonists from other nations on the proper terms," and
because of its "many highly objectionable features,
notably the freedom of religion and sects." In other
words, Spain at last confessed her inability to colonize
the Mississippi Valley.[19]

CARONDELET'S SEPOYS

Since, for the time being at any rate, Carondelet could place little or no reliance in the Kentucky intrigue, immigration or the fortified posts of Louisiana, there remained by elimination only one of the traditional means of defence against Spain's turbulent American neighbors, namely, the Indian alliances. During this first year of his administration (1792) several events occurred which, given the general situation, convinced him that the United States government was planning the immediate invasion of Louisiana and West Florida and that the Southern tribes of Indians would be an effective weapon with which to repel the invaders.

During the early months of this year, the usual rumors of hostile demonstrations on the American frontier reached Carondelet, together with the news that the United States government was gathering a large force on the Ohio River. Obsessed by fear and unable to distinguish between irresponsible frontiersmen and the American government, he disregarded Gayoso's assurances that the force was destined for service against the Northern Indians, declared that the rape of Louisiana was at hand and frantically besought his brother-in-law, the captain-general, to rush troops and munitions to his defence.[20]

At this juncture (March, 1792) the Baron had an interview that was most unfortunate for him. William Augustus Bowles, the rival of Panton and McGillivray, had just been captured in the Creek nation. Brought to New Orleans, he was questioned by Carondelet about the state of affairs on the frontier. His attractive personality and his plausible manner made the governor

an easy victim to his brazen lies to the effect that the
Creek Indians were overwhelmingly opposed to the
recent treaty of their chiefs with the United States
(New York, 1790), that they were ready to join in a war
against the United States, and that thousands of troops
were being raised by the state and federal governments
in Georgia and the Carolinas to invade the Spanish
provinces. Bowles was simply the tool of rival mercantile interests in the Bahamas who hoped to supplant
Panton and McGillivray; and even had he been most
veracious he had got most of his information by hearsay.
Carondelet, however, was deeply impressed, for his
temperament inclined him to accept Bowles's trans-
parent fabrications as the truth. The situation was
little improved by the adventurer's departure, for
Carondelet then fell under the influence of Panton,
whose voice was always for war.[21]

Another event that moved Carondelet profoundly
was St. Clair's defeat by the Northern Indians, news of
which was received in New Orleans just after he took
over the government from Miró.[22] It was probably this
event which betrayed him into the capital error of
assuming that the Indians were better fighters than
the Americans, that they would form an effective
defence against invasion by the Mississippi and that
they could even intimidate the American frontiersmen
into accepting a Spanish protectorate or drive them
back over the mountains. A worse blunder could
hardly have been made, and there was abundant
evidence to set him right had Carondelet only been
capable of weighing it. Persistent attacks by the war-
like Creek had not destroyed even Cumberland, the
smallest and most exposed of the frontier settlements.
The Indians' fickleness was proverbial, as the Spaniards

had found to their advantage at the siege of Pensacola and to their sorrow in the treaty of New York. The Indians were prone to take the winning side or the side of their latest benefactor. Their mental processes were totally different from those of the white man. Even had they been faithful and docile, they could not have been used as veteran troops as Carondelet planned to use them, hurling them into the fray and withdrawing them at will. They remembered bloodshed longer than a gift, and war once begun could not be terminated at his behest, as he assumed it could.

Even had conditions been as favorable as Carondelet painted them, the Indian alliances would have been of little military value; and conditions were much less favorable. He overestimated the number of Southern Indian warriors and assumed that unity of action was possible among these tribes. In reality their bickerings were incessant, not only between tribes, as for instance between the Creek and the Chickasaw, but within tribes also, as between the upper and lower Creek and between the various factions of the Choctaw.

The Baron was far less judicious than his predecessor in the handling of Indian affairs. On one occasion when an invasion from the Ohio seemed imminent, Miró declared that the Indians were expensive and worthless allies. He very wisely confined his efforts to securing a monopoly of the Indian trade and to forestalling any attempt on the part of the Americans to stir the Indians up against Spain. At the most, he thought them useful for breaking up settlements of land speculators, such as the colony projected by the South Carolina Yazoo Company at Walnut Hills. His policy was defensive and pacific, in accordance with the royal orders on the subject. Carondelet's attempt to convert the Indian tribes into sepoys and the Indian treaties into a military alliance of offence and defence constituted an abrupt departure from Miró's policy, was a direct violation of the express orders of the court, and produced the most deplorable consequences.

THE INDIAN CONFEDERATION

Mistaken as his Indian policy was, it cannot be denied that he executed it with vigor and with the ability that he usually manifested in dealing with simple problems. The situation in the Indian country was most unfavorable to Spain at the beginning of his administration. The treaty concluded at New York in 1790 between the United States and the Creek chiefs led by McGillivray conflicted at several points with the treaty of Pensacola (1784). In the other Southern tribes, American trade and influence were making rapid advances through the efforts of Governor Blount of the Southwest Territory, who was also superintendent of Indian affairs for the Southern department, and of James Seagrove, United States agent among the Creek Indians. Carondelet's first step was to restore order in the distracted Creek Confederacy. This he did by sending out an expedition from New Orleans in February, 1792, to capture the interloper Bowles, who, discarded by Pitt after the Nootka crisis, had returned to the Creek country in December, 1791.[23] Posing as the defender of Muscogean liberties against American aggression and against the exploitation of the Indians by Panton and McGillivray and their Spanish masters, he was in reality the agent of British mercantile interests in the Island of Providence headed by the governor, Lord Dunmore, Virginia's last colonial governor, and by the wealthy merchant, John Miller.

Succeeding where McGillivray, Panton and their henchman Milfort had failed, the governor's expedition captured Bowles by an unscrupulous stratagem devised by Carondelet himself. The adventurer was first sent to New Orleans, where he had the interview with the governor of which we have already spoken, and thence by way of Havana and Spain to a long captivity in the Philippines.

Carondelet then reduced McGillivray to obedience by intimidation, by the influence of Panton, and by the grant of a larger pension than the one paid him by the United States. A Spanish officer of French origin, Pedro Olivier, was sent as the governor's agent to reside in the Creek nation and keep watch on McGillivray. The latter's reduction was merely a part of Carondelet's design of preventing the execution of the treaty of New York, whose consequences would, he thought, be fatal to Spanish influence in that tribe and to the integrity of the Spanish defensive system. McGillivray was induced to sign a new convention (1792) abrogating the obnoxious treaty, and Olivier was instructed to incite the Creek to drive the Georgians out of the territory ceded to the United States. This last measure was too much for even family affection to condone, and the captain-general forced his bellicose brother-in-law to countermand the order.[24] Carondelet complied for the moment, but appealed over Las Casas' head to the secretary of war and continued to stir up trouble between the Indians and the American frontiersmen.

Other measures to strengthen Spanish influence in the Indian country were the appointment of an agent, Juan de la Villebeuvre, to reside among the Choctaw and Chickasaw Indians, and the establishment of a connection, through Panton and one of his traders,

John McDonald, with the Chickamauga towns of the Cherokee, a tribe hitherto beyond the Spanish pale.[25]

Having prepared the ground, Carondelet proceeded to summon the Southern Indians to an assembly at Nogales under Gayoso's presidency for the purpose of forming an alliance against the United States. Had his instructions to Gayoso been carried out at this congress, a war between Spain and the United States would almost certainly have resulted, for it was his plan to form a permanent confederation of the four Indian tribes, to conclude an alliance with this confederation on behalf of Spain, and although the alliance was to be styled defensive, to have the confederation send a delegation of chiefs to the United States government and demand the reëstablishment of the frontier line of 1772, with war as the alternative.[26] Panton had written Carondelet in 1792 that he had things in readiness so that he could let loose "as bloody a war as ever the Southern states have experienced."[27] Carondelet believed him and was ready for war. Gayoso, however, knowing that the Indians were deceitful and intractable and that Carondelet's plan was foolhardy, virtually ignored the instructions. Proceeding with the ostentation and ceremoniousness proper to such occasions, he negotiated a treaty which, while it was merely defensive and failed to provide for the sending of a delegation of chiefs with an ultimatum to the United States, created a confederation of the four Southern tribes under Spanish protection, established a mutual territorial guarantee, and stipulated that henceforth the annual present given each tribe should be delivered to it in a lump in its own territory. This last clause was designed among other things to furnish Spain with a pretext for sending its troops into the Indian country and thus pave the way for the establishment of additional posts. The erection of such a post in the Choctaw country was authorized in the treaty, and consequently in 1794 a Spanish fort was built and garrisoned on the Tombigbee River near the site of the old French Fort Tombecbé. It was called Fort Confederation in honor of the newly formed union of Indian tribes.[28]

It has been said that Carondelet's Indian policy produced deplorable consequences. In the first place, it interfered with the development of the intrigue with the American frontiersmen. As Gayoso pointed out, Carondelet was pursuing mutually contradictory policies. Indian attacks on the American frontier had been moderated in the last three years of Miró's administration (1789–91), but were renewed with redoubled fury when Carondelet took over the government in 1792. The frontiersmen rightly attributed this change to Carondelet's advent; and the intrigue with the frontiersmen suffered in consequence, the intrigue in its second phase being confined to Kentucky, which was more remote than Cumberland and Holston from Spain's Indian allies.[29] Even with the Indians themselves Spain's interests suffered from Carondelet's belligerency, for many of them resented the effort of any white man, regardless of his nationality, to involve them in war with other white men.

In the second place, Carondelet's Indian policy had a most unfortunate effect on Spain's negotiation with the United States. The Spanish agents in Philadelphia, Jáudenes and Viar, were at first on very friendly terms with the administration, but in the course of 1792 Carondelet's pernicious misrepresentations led them to charge the United States with pursuing an Indian policy deliberately hostile towards Spain. One of the principal proofs adduced in support of this assertion was that Governor Blount had distributed among the Indians medals bearing on one side an effigy of Washington and the inscription "Friendship forever," and on the other side, "Peace and trade without end." Such a frivolous charge gave an air of absurdity to their representation, but they pressed their case with the utmost gravity and with the most objectionable vehemence. As Carondelet's policy was unfolded, they saw that it would bring a protest from the United States government; and, on the principle that the offensive is the best defence, they redoubled their vehemence and warned Jefferson that, unless the United States altered its Indian policy, the continuance of peace was highly problematical. Equivalent to a threat of war, which Jefferson wrote Monroe at this juncture was almost certain,[30] their note led the administration to transfer the discussion to Spain and to refuse to receive any further communication on the subject from the Spanish agents.[31] In Spain, as we shall see, this controversy over Indian affairs enabled Short and Carmichael to score the only diplomatic triumph won by the United States in the whole course of this twelve years' negotiation with Spain, and the American envoys owed their success to Carondelet.

CHAPTER XII

THE FRENCH REVOLUTION AND THE SPANISH EMPIRE

VIRTUE AND VITALITY

As Carondelet's frontier policy began to take shape and just as Spain and England were being drawn into the war against France, William Short arrived at Madrid in tardy response to Floridablanca's invitation of 1791. On February 6, 1793, he and William Carmichael, the resident chargé, who held joint powers, informed the secretary of state, Manuel de Godoy, the Duke of Alcudia, that they were ready to begin the negotiation.[1]

It was just at this juncture that the Red Terror in France reached its grand climacteric in the beheading of Louis XVI, royal cousin of His Majesty of Spain and the Indies. No event more disastrous to Spain has ever occurred in its history, for it was thereby involved inextricably in the European wars of the next twenty years, with fatal results to the dynasty, the nation and the empire. Even though we are concerned with only a small corner of the colonial and diplomatic fields, and that for a brief period of time, we shall have abundant occasion to note how cruelly Spain suffered from the convulsions that shook its neighbor to the north. In Spain, as in England, liberalism was brought into disrepute by the excesses of the French republicans, and, as we have seen, an interesting experiment in immigration policy, based on religious toleration, was abandoned in the conservative reaction of the 1790's at the Spanish court. In the following pages it will appear how, in other respects as well, such as colonial commerce and finance, Indian trade and international relations, the results of the French Revolution handicapped Spain in its bloodless conflict with the United States.

The king of Spain at that time was Charles IV, whose reign was one of the most disastrous in the history of Spain, or for that matter of any European country. The disaster was all the more poignant because of the fair promise of the preceding reign, which ended with the death of Charles III in 1788. For those who are satisfied with such explanations, it may be said that Charles IV was simple-minded and his queen a nymphomaniac, and that the youthful chief minister, Godoy, was one of the queen's lovers.² If one tests this interpretation by a comparison of the conduct of relations with the United States in this reign and the one that preceded it, the hollowness of it becomes at once apparent. Charles III was possessed of at least normal intelligence and of a most extraordinary chastity, for during the last twenty years of his life he had neither wife nor mistress. His chief minister was no upstart youth, but the tried and true Floridablanca. And yet a crisis was never more incompetently handled than the one that the austere king and his patriotic minister had to face at the outbreak of the American Revolution. If the youthful Godoy had at last to surrender to the Americans, it was because the middle-aged Floridablanca had let slip a golden opportunity and had not been able to rectify his blunder in the nine remaining years of his ministry after the end of the American Revolution.

It is difficult indeed to establish any causal relation between the private morality of the ministers and the issue of the struggle between Spain and the United States. While Godoy lay in the arms of his royal mistress, Alexander Hamilton was similarly engaged with the wife of one of his underlings in the treasury department. It is also an interesting fact that Godoy was a far more industrious person than George Washington.[3] If we consider the case from the point of view of public morality, the situation is not altered. On the contrary, the Spanish government seems to have been punished for its virtues. Loyalty to monarchy induced it to undertake the disastrous war of 1793 with France, and loyalty to the Catholic faith handicapped it hopelessly in the frontier competition with the United States.

What Spain lacked was not virtues but vitality, the power of adaptation. Perhaps she had neither the manpower nor the money-power nor the brain-power to maintain her heritage from another world, but certainly she was unable to adapt herself to the needs of a changing age. For a generation past, enlightened Spaniards had made notable efforts at readjustment; but when the rhythm of change was accelerated by the French Revolution the nation would not, and by its very nature could not, keep pace. Soon hopelessly maladjusted to the new world, the Spaniards resigned the effort, canonized their faults, consoled themselves with reveries of a glorious past, and dreamed away an empire. The most heroic of ministers could have done little more than shake an impotent fist in the face of the storm that broke upon the just and the unjust in 1793.

THE ENGLISH ALLIANCE

Spain's first and most urgent need was an ally. Since the Nootka episode the Family Compact had been as good as dissolved, and for a time Spain stood in dangerous isolation. As the progress of the revolution in France made the renewal of the Compact unlikely, and as the contagion of republican ideas became more menacing, Floridablanca suggested an alliance with no less a power than the ancient enemy, England. His fall and the rise to power of the Gallican Aranda interposed a delay; but Aranda was supplanted by Manuel de Godoy, Duke of Alcudia, in November, 1792, and the English alliance was pressed to an early conclusion.[4] The alliance was of course directed primarily against France, but the treaty also provided that if either power should be drawn into war with another power through its measures against France, the other contracting party must make common cause against the new enemy. Thus if British restrictions on neutral trade with France should result in war between Great Britain and the United States, Spain would be obliged under this treaty to come to the aid of the British.[5]

No matter how much one may sympathize with the Spanish court in the terrible dilemma of 1793, and no matter what cogent reasons it may have had for concluding the English alliance, the fact remains that Britain was the age-old enemy of the Spanish empire, that French aid alone had long sustained the tottering power of Spain in the Indies, and that the French and the Spaniards now set merrily to work sinking each other's ships for the greater glory of Great Britain. The result might have been foreseen. It was foreseen by some, among them the doughty old Count Aranda, who warned his king of the wrath to come, and was rewarded for his pains by dismissal, disgrace, and imprisonment at Granada in the palace of Charles V.

ECONOMIC PENETRATION

On the Spanish frontier in North America the disastrous results of the French Revolution were soon apparent. In the first place, the increasing gravity of the European situation prevented the court from carrying into effect its plan of 1789 for supplying the trade of Louisiana and the Floridas with Spanish goods. Since the colonists had long been accustomed to French and English goods, the court had proposed in 1789 to facilitate the change by duplicating in Spanish factories the articles of common colonial consumption. Martin Navarro, former intendant of Louisiana, was actually sent to France and England, where he secured samples and information with regard to methods of production and marketing; but by the time that he returned to Spain (1790) the menacing European situation had diverted his government's attention to other matters.[6] And yet some provision must be made for supplying these North American colonies. The commerce of Louisiana was regulated by the *cédula* issued in 1782 and limited to ten years' duration, and was in the hands of merchants of France, with which country Spain went to war in May, 1793. To meet this situation, the Spanish government issued in July, 1793, a *reglamento de comercio*, which was to apply to East and West Florida as well as to Louisiana.[7] The *reglamento* contained the apparently liberal provision that these provinces might trade with all friendly nations with which Spain had a commercial treaty; but since Spain was at war with France and had no commercial treaty with the United States, the practical effect of the *reglamento* was to restrict the trade of the colonists to Great Britain. Furthermore, the new regulations required all foreign ships going to and from Louisiana and the Floridas to touch at the port of Corcubión in Galicia, a requirement which its sponsor supported by the touching observation that it would be of great benefit to that little port. This onerous provision was subsequently repealed, in view of the strenuous protest of the New Orleans *cabildo* or town council; but the court had given convincing proof that it was either ignorant of the interests of its North American colonies or was willing to sacrifice them for the benefit of a single insignificant Spanish port.

Worst of all, the French Revolution made it impossible to prevent Spanish subjects in Louisiana and the Floridas from trading with the United States. On the Mississippi Carondelet stretched to the utmost the discretionary power granted him by the Royal Order of December 1, 1788, and reduced from fifteen to six per cent the duty on importations from Kentucky which included fourteen thousand barrels of flour in a single year (1792). In defence of his course, he declared that the exaction of the higher duty would provoke the Kentuckians to invade Louisiana and that in that event they would probably be aided by a creole insurrection, so great was the ferment caused by the French Revolution. As for the seaborne commerce of Louisiana, Carondelet warned that it was falling into the hands of the United States, and frankly admitted that American ships were trading at New Orleans, flying the United States flag on the Atlantic and in the Gulf of Mexico, and hoisting the Spanish flag only when they entered the Mississippi River. In extenuation he not only pleaded the danger of rebellion in Louisiana, but actually espoused the cause of the colonists, arguing economic necessity. Since, he said, the war with France had closed the normal channels of Louisiana's trade, but one market for many of the colonial productions was left and that was in the United States. If this were closed, the colonists would be ruined.[8]

While the court never approved Carondelet's course,

neither did it take effective steps to cut off contraband trade with the United States, and the opening of the Mississippi to the United States shipping under the treaty of San Lorenzo increased enormously the facilities for smuggling. In conclusion, we are justified in saying that the French Revolution had a most disastrous effect on Spanish commercial policy in Louisiana and the Floridas, for it not only prevented the execution of the plan to supply their wants with Spanish goods but actually opened the way to economic penetration by the very nation, the United States, that Spain was most anxious to exclude from contact with its frontier colonies.

THE INDIAN TRADE

In that highly specialized branch of commerce, the Indian trade, the French Revolution again exercised an influence unfavorable to Spanish interests. Spanish policy, as we have seen, was designed to control the territory in dispute with the United States by keeping the occupant Indian tribes, the Creek, Choctaw and Chickasaw, dependent upon Spain, and this was to be accomplished through the medium of trade. By the year 1793, when Spain went to war with France, this policy gave fair promise of success. Spanish influence was paramount among the Southern Indians, whose trade was falling more and more into the hands of Panton, Leslie and Company. The company with stores at St. Mark's, Pensacola and Mobile, and with a business whose capital value in 1794 was estimated by Panton and Carondelet at $400,000, seemed most favorably situated to engross the fur trade as it retreated westward in the face of the advancing American and Spanish frontiers. In addition to long-standing connections among the Indian tribes and to a monopoly protected by the Spanish government, the company enjoyed several other advantages. First among these was its direct communication with England, where its correspondents, Strachan and McKenzie, sold its furs and bought its next year's supply of goods for the Indian trade; and these goods were bought in what was then the cheapest market in the world. Furthermore, economies were made possible by the magnitude of the enterprise; and finally the finances of the company were stabilized by its manifold activities, for it traded not only with the Indians but also, sometimes openly and sometimes surreptitiously, with the colonists; it owned its ships, supplied the Indians with salt from its own salt mine on the Island of Providence, imported slaves, exported timber, and speculated in lands.[9]

Supported by the imprudent but vigorous Carondelet, the company made rapid strides in the period 1792–95. It prevented the execution of the Creek treaty of 1790 with the United States, which would have endangered the company's hold on the Creek trade. It built up a powerful party among the Chickasaw, who had hitherto been largely under the influence of the Cumberland settlers, and even began to penetrate the Cherokee, most of whose towns lay beyond the extremest limit of Spain's territorial claims.[10] In 1794 Fort Confederation and in 1795 Fort San Fernando were built by Carondelet to strengthen the company's hand among the Choctaw and Chickasaw; and Panton's store at San Fernando (Memphis) opened up to him the Mississippi River fur trade and would have made it possible for him to follow the trade as it retreated westward across the Mississippi.

This fair prospect was ruined by the wars of the

French Revolution and the simultaneous rise of a strong federal government in the United States. Spain's war in alliance with England against France (1793–95) resulted in many losses to Panton, Leslie and Company, for they were now unable to secure in England the indispensable supply of guns for the Indian trade. When they invoked Carondelet's good offices, he was forced to send to the United States for the guns and even then was unable to obtain them, since their exportation was prohibited by the United States government. The company suffered further losses through French depredations, as its ships sailed under the British flag; and to the delight of Panton's sworn rivals, the Georgians, a French privateer brought one of his richly laden ships a prize to the port of Savannah.[11]

At the same time, the increasingly vigorous Indian policy of the United States, executed through Blount at Knoxville and Seagrove in Georgia, gave Panton great concern; and when in 1794 he learned that the United States government itself was planning to take over the Indian trade he was utterly dismayed and sought the aid of the Spanish government. As he stated in his memorial, the American project was a tribute to his company's efficiency, since it was equivalent to the admission that private enterprise could not compete with him; but at the same time Panton admitted his inability to hold the field against the United States government.[12]

These and other difficulties led the company to beg the court for a loan and other concessions, urging as the only alternative the purchase and operation of its business by His Catholic Majesty's government. Unfortunately for Panton, the European war, which was in a large measure responsible for his memorial, was also largely responsible for Spain's inability to adopt either of the alternatives that he proposed. Both involved heavy expenditures, and these were lean years for the Spanish treasury. Economy was the order of the day, and we shall soon see how important a part an empty treasury played in bringing about the Spanish surrender to the United States in 1795. Left to shift for itself, the company succeeded in controlling for another generation the trade of the Indian towns nearest the coast; but as early as 1796 one of its members, John Forbes, wrote Carondelet that he was on his way to Knoxville to close out the company's Cherokee trade because of the "proximity and cheapness of the American supplys."

SPAIN RETREATS

To return to the mission in Spain of Carmichael and Short: Until the end of 1793, they accomplished absolutely nothing, and Short was more than once inclined to give up the effort in disgust. The English alliance and a few easy victories over the French made Gardoqui for a few months quite indifferent to the attitude of the United States, and a better man than Gardoqui, appointed plenipotentiary to negotiate the treaty, could hardly have been found to baffle the American commissioners. He had an excellent excuse for putting them off, since they had nothing to offer in return for their extravagant demands. He had an interest in putting them off, since his own family were merchants at Bilbao, and since Spanish commerce, he thought, was being ruined by colonial contraband trade, which would be facilitated by the opening of the Mississippi River to the United States. Finally, he had a genius for putting the Americans off, and not only the

Americans but everyone, for he was a master of evasion and, as the British ambassador wrote, "repeating what falls from Gardoqui" was "next to saying nothing." [13]

Not for long, however, did this happy state of affairs endure. The British alliance, so recently cemented, soon cracked under the strain of the opposing thrusts of Spanish and British interests, first at Toulon, then at Santo Domingo and elsewhere. No longer could the Spanish government stand so unyieldingly on its rights in the American controversy as it understood them, and it is interesting to observe that the first concession to the Americans (many were soon to follow) was made in frontier affairs, in the field of Indian relations. As we have seen, Jáudenes and Viar, instigated by Carondelet, had taken an absurd position in regard to Indian affairs on the Spanish-American frontier, and had maintained their absurdities in such offensive language that Jefferson had transferred the discussion of the subject to Madrid. Making skillful use of the data at their disposal, Carmichael and Short forced Gardoqui and Godoy from one position to another until finally, on January 19, 1794, Godoy surrendered the argument, admitting that the Indian allies of Spain had been the aggressors against the unoffending American frontiersmen and promising to use his authority to prevent the recurrence of such episodes. [14]

Another concession soon followed that of January 19. On March 7, 1794, Godoy laid before the Council of State a copy of the treaty concluded by Gayoso at Nogales in October, 1793, whereby a Southern Indian confederation had been created in alliance with Spain. On Godoy's advice, the King and Council approved the treaty only on the express understanding that it did not contain any provision that might endanger the continuance of friendly relations with the United States. Jáudenes and Viar were informed of their decision and instructed to communicate it to the United States government. And so the treaty that Carondelet had designed as a prelude to war with the United States was used by his government to prove its earnest desire for peace and friendship with that power.[15]

In the course of the first seven months of 1794, Godoy received from various quarters of Europe and America reports which broke down still further his will to resist the Americans and determined him to press to an immediate conclusion the pending negotiation. From St. Augustine and Havana he learned of the imminent invasions of East Florida and Louisiana planned by Elijah Clarke and George Rogers Clark at Genêt's instigation. From Philadelphia he learned of the opposition of the United States government to Genêt's plans and of its inclination to maintain friendly relations with Spain.[16] From London, the Spanish ambassador, Bernardo del Campo, sent him the disquieting news that an envoy from the United States was expected there to negotiate a treaty.[17] Almost every week brought a fresh reason for dissatisfaction with the English alliance. The campaign of 1794 in the eastern Pyrenees was marked by the most alarming succession of victories by the French invaders over the Spanish troops, and already Gardoqui was warning the Council of State that the finances of the crown could not stand the strain of war much longer.[18]

Spain's change of policy in Indian affairs was soon followed by its necessary complement, a modification of its diplomacy. The same spirit that curbed Carondelet's belligerency led Godoy in May, 1794, to request the United States to send a new plenipotentiary to

Spain, a more eminent person than Short and Carmichael and one armed with ampler powers. On May 9, 1794, seven days after the Council of State had discussed many fresh reports of forces gathering in the United States to invade Louisiana and the Floridas, an order was sent to Jáudenes instructing him to lay this request before the President of the United States at the earliest opportunity.[19] Jáudenes did so in August, and it was in answer to this invitation, though after a considerable delay, that Thomas Pinckney was appointed to Spain. Jefferson, who was offered the appointment, declined it.[20]

Under the circumstances, it can hardly be doubted that Godoy's invitation was dictated by a sincere desire for an accommodation, especially when we remember his simultaneous modification of Spain's Indian policy for the express purpose of maintaining friendly relations with the United States. On what terms he intended to conduct the negotiation it is impossible to state with certainty, but we may be sure that a complete surrender was not intended. In view of Gardoqui's influence with Godoy, his advice to Floridablanca on Short's memorial of 1791, and the inclination, recorded in the correspondence of Godoy's office, of Jay and Jefferson [21] to agree to a mutual territorial guarantee in return for the thirty-first parallel and the free navigation of the Mississippi, we may suppose with no great probability of error that Godoy hoped to secure some such settlement before Spain's situation became still more disquieting.

Fate was against him. The French advance continued, funds were exhausted, and even the Spanish aristocracy seemed tainted with republicanism. Early in July, 1794, Godoy received from Jáudenes the startling news that John Jay had been sent by the United States government to conclude a treaty with England.[22] Godoy was terrified. The spectre of an Anglo-American alliance that had so long haunted the Spanish foreign office seemed about to assume corporeal substance; and Spain's tenuous connection with England offered her no security. Albion's perfidy was taken for granted by the Spanish court.

The other portions of Jáudenes's despatches did not afford Godoy the comfort intended. Describing the unstable equilibrium of the American frontier, which might incline the Kentuckians either to secession and alliance with Spain or to an attack on the Spanish dominions, Jáudenes failed to console his youthful chief, for Godoy knew that the former alternative would be as disastrous to Spain as the latter.

The only escape, it seemed, was to forestall England by a quick negotiation with the American government. Consequently Godoy laid the case before the Council of State on July 7, 1794. After hearing a lengthy statement of the diplomatic and frontier situation, the Council determined unanimously to make fresh overtures to the United States.[23] The next two weeks were occupied in drawing up the necessary instructions, Godoy writing out the first draft in his own hand,[24] a rare thing for the first secretary of state to do, even in the time of the faithful Floridablanca. Before the instructions were sent, however, Godoy received from Carondelet letters of such a character as to require the reconsideration of Spain's policy towards the United States and its frontiersmen. The origin and contents of Carondelet's letters and the government's resolution thereon will form the subject of the next chapter.

CHAPTER XIII

THE INTRIGUE INFALLIBLE

"A PREDISPOSITION TO BE DISSATISFIED"

On the American frontier, as well as in diplomacy and commerce, the French Revolution did much to shape the course of Spanish-American relations in the period 1793–95; and for a long time it was uncertain whether Spain or the United States, or either, would be the gainer. There were two ways in which the American settlements between the Ohio and the Tennessee were affected by the European cataclysm. In the first place, fresh currency was given to two ideas already familiar to the frontiersmen, namely, particularism and natural rights; in the second place, boundless possibilities of violence were opened up by the alliance between Great Britain, controlling the Lakes, and Spain, controlling Mississippi, against France, which was the ally of the United States and from which the frontiersmen had for the past decade expected aid in opening the Mississippi.

It seemed very doubtful, in the summer of 1793, whether either Spain or the United States would be able to derive any benefit from the situation thus created. On the one hand, the danger of an invasion of Louisiana by the Kentuckians, long the nightmare of the Spaniards at New Orleans, was increased tenfold. "Natural right" was the frontiersman's chief argument in support of his claim to the free navigation of the Mississippi, and the weighty authority given the idea of natural right by the French Republic increased the frontiersman's sense of injustice, his indignation against the Spanish tyrants who made him pay a six per cent duty at New Orleans. It was not likely that the French government, which had never forgotten Louisiana, would neglect this opportunity to capitalize the Kentuckians' resentment: nor, as it proved, was the opportunity neglected. At the same time, the fever of the French Revolution stirred up sedition among the numerous French creoles of Louisiana and insubordination among the slaves; and the Spanish government, with so many other demands on its feeble energy, was able to do little or nothing for its exposed frontier provinces.

It might be supposed that an international situation so embarrassing to Spain would have been correspondingly advantageous to the United States; but this was not the case. The American government had relied on a European war to enable it to bring Spain to terms; but this war was too gigantic a thing to be manipulated by so puny a power as the infant republic. The character of the European struggle divided the sympathies of the Americans, making it impossible for them to take a decided part, and in 1793 no power was willing to pay a high price for their neutrality. The alliance of their immediate neighbors in North America, Great Britain and Spain, was formidable, in appearance at least, throughout 1793 and 1794. At the same time, frontier particularism received from the French Revolution a new form of expression in the Democratic Societies, several of which were organized in Kentucky from August to December, 1793.[1] The partitioning of Poland was in progress, and the interests of both England and Spain would be served by a partition of the United States. Altogether, the situation was fraught with great danger to the Union in view of the possibility of a secessionist movement in the West, and of the recovery of Louisiana by France [2] and of the Floridas by England.

The greatest danger of all lay in the particularistic tendencies of the frontiersman. Natural in their situation, these tendencies were intensified at this juncture by their dissatisfaction with certain measures of the federal government, such as the assumption and excise acts, and the neutrality proclamation of 1793, and by their resentment at its aristocratic tone and its failure to secure the free navigation of the Mississippi. "Neglectful" and "contemptuous" were adjectives with which the Kentuckians described the attitude of Congress towards them. So obdurate were they in their discontent, and so exasperated was President Washington with their obdurateness that he wrote in August, 1794: "There must exist a predisposition among them to be dissatisfied." [3]

When Edmund Genêt proclaimed a holy war against Spanish tyranny he found a ready response among the frontiersmen from Georgia to Kentucky. George Rogers Clark, O'Fallon, Lachaise, Depeau and Michaud in Kentucky; Elijah Clarke, the Hammond brothers, Tate and Mangourit in Georgia and South Carolina, were his agents in the summer and fall of 1793 in raising legions for the conquest of Louisiana and the Floridas. [4] George Rogers Clark was moved by the bitter discontent of a neglected hero, the Hammonds by a desire to supplant Panton, Leslie and Company in the Southern fur trade, others by love of excitement, by the prospect of plunder, by resentment at Spain's long denial of their "natural rights." Above all, the frontiersmen were opportunists, ready to try any expedient, and Genêt offered them a means of opening the Mississippi. At the same time, there is every evidence of a deep and widespread sympathy among the frontiersmen for the French Revolution. Where sympathy for France had been weakened in the United States since the close of the American Revolution, it was generally due to the influence of merchants trading with England, of Congregationalist preachers scandalized by French deism and immorality, or of Jay and Adams, with their charges of French duplicity in the negotiations of 1782.[5] On the frontier, there was no Jay or Adams, preachers of any denomination were few, and the mercantile interests of the Mississippi Valley settlements demanded the free navigation of the Mississippi, which Genêt offered them. Where there was one William Blount in the West in the 1790's to denounce the "Jacobin incendiary Genêt," there were a dozen Andrew Jacksons to hail the liberator "Boneparte."

The joint land and sea expeditions against Louisiana projected by Genêt in 1793 caused great alarm to the governments of both Spain and the United States. With all his French sympathies, Jefferson looked with favor on the project only as a means of securing the Floridas for the United States.[6] By this stroke the controversy with Spain over the boundary, the navigation of the Mississippi, fugitive slaves and Indian relations would be settled once for all, and the United States would have made a good start towards taking Spain's North American possessions from her "piece by piece," as Jefferson had prophesied in 1786. Washington and Hamilton, however, looked on Genêt's plans in another light, and Jefferson's hopes came to nothing. In December, 1793, he resigned his office, and the Westerners felt that they had lost a friend at court.

The year that followed Jefferson's retirement from the state department was an acutely critical one in the relations of the United States government with its frontiersmen. The chief danger was the possibility of a general insurrection in the West. The remedy lay in the diminution of the frontiersman's grievances, and the magnitude and complexity of the problem required systematic treatment. Accordingly diplomacy was enlisted. One of the principal aims of John Jay's mission to England (April, 1794) was to secure the surrender of the Northwest posts. Monroe, who was sent to France at the same time, was instructed to exert every effort to persuade the victorious republic to extort from Spain the terms desired by the United States. In order to facilitate the Spanish negotiation, William Short was given sole charge of it with the rank of minister to Spain, and Carmichael, no longer a *persona grata* at court, was recalled.[7] In the United States itself a show of force was made to intimidate the seditious when Hamilton and Washington marched against the distillers of western Pennsylvania. To Kentucky, where the situation was more dangerous, the administration wisely sent not troops but a diplomat, James Innes, attorney-general of the state of Virginia and brother of the Spanish conspirator, Judge Harry Innes, to convince the governor and people of that state that the federal government was doing all in its power to secure the free navigation of the Mississippi.[8]

"COCHON DE LAIT" RENEWS THE INTRIGUE

Still more perturbed by the Kentucky ferment was the timorous Carondelet. He was terrified by the vision of Genêt's simultaneous invasions of Louisiana from the Gulf and from Kentucky, aided by the rebellious French inhabitants, who later, in their version of the "Carmagnolle," dubbed Carondelet "Cochon de lait"

and promised him first place on the guillotine.[9] These
dangers induced him to revive the moribund Kentucky
intrigue. While the promise of lasting benefit to Spain
was even less than when Miró conspired with Wilkinson,
this second conspiracy was fraught with great danger to
the United States. The widespread unrest, the dominant political ideas of the day and the instability common to frontier societies made secession far from impossible. While two of the communities that were involved
in the first intrigue, Franklin and Cumberland, took
no part in this second conspiracy, the conspirators in
Kentucky were more numerous and seemed to press
the affair with more seriousness than in 1788, and
Carondelet hoped, as had Miró, that the other frontier
communities would follow the lead of the Kentuckians.

It was James Wilkinson, as we should expect, who
was immediately responsible for the revival of the conspiracy. His correspondence with Miró and Carondelet
from 1791 to 1793 had been languid; but in January
and February, 1794, while Clark was raising his French
legion in Kentucky, Wilkinson wrote Carondelet that
the time had come when Spain must take a decisive
stand in its relations with the Kentuckians. The
people of that state, he said, had at last lost patience
with their incompetent federal government and were
determined to open the Mississippi at once, whether
by secession from the Union or by the conquest of
Louisiana. It depended upon Spain which course they
should follow. Once a revolution was begun in Kentucky, it would be easy, he said, to turn it to Spain's
advantage.[10] There was nothing novel in this information, for it was substantially what Wilkinson had been
writing for several years. What made it impressive was
that he now assured Carondelet that what had long

been threatened was at last to be executed, that the critical moment was at hand, and that the decision between secession and conquest would be made within the next few months. Carondelet had already been deeply impressed by a similar warning from Michel Lacassagne, a French merchant in Kentucky, who had come down to New Orleans in the winter of 1793–94 to collect six thousand dollars on Wilkinson's pension account, and whom Carondelet described in his letters to Godoy as one of the richest and most influential men in Kentucky.[11]

In a series of letters to the secretary of state, Godoy, from April to July, 1794, Carondelet warned him of the dangerous ferment in the settlements of the American West, which, he said, could put 60,000 armed men in the field. He declared that there were only two means by which Spain could preserve Louisiana and the Floridas. The first was the strengthening of its military defences, the repair and construction of forts, the sending of reinforcements, and the stirring up of the Indians against the American frontier. He urged Godoy to secure the coöperation of the British in Canada, for, as he wrote a few months later, Lord Dorchester's notorious speech to the Indians at Detroit showed that the Spanish and English governors were pursuing the same Indian policy. Realizing, however, that the war in Europe might not permit Spain to undertake so expensive a policy, he proposed as an alternative the separation of Kentucky from the Union. All the other Western settlements of the United States, he declared, would follow Kentucky's lead, and thus the colossal republic would be split into two rival powers, which Spain could play off against each other for her benefit, and especially for the protection of Louisiana and

Mexico. Kentucky's separation could easily be brought about, though at no inconsiderable cost to Spain, for Wilkinson's pension must be increased, other leading Kentuckians must be granted pensions, and munitions must be sent to support the revolution. Once the revolution was begun, said Carondelet repeating Wilkinson's assurance, it could easily be given a direction favorable to Spain by the negotiation of a treaty between that power and the Kentuckians opening the Mississippi as far south as New Orleans.[12]

The governor's reasons for urging the Kentucky project on Godoy were, as the foregoing summary indicates, that Louisiana's critical situation, in the face of the Clark-Genêt projects, made some defensive measure an immediate necessity, that a purely military defence would probably be too expensive, and that the only alternative was the revolutionizing of Kentucky. Other considerations, however, seem to have influenced the Baron strongly to urge the Kentucky project upon his government with such vigor. One of these considerations was that to his amazement and chagrin he had just received from Gardoqui, minister of finance, an order removing him from the post of intendant, which, since Martin Navarro's return to Spain in 1788, had been united with the governorship of the province. The loss of pay and prestige led him to protest bitterly to Godoy, who curiously enough knew nothing of the change until he received Carondelet's complaint.[13] This reverse doubtless convinced Carondelet that he must render some signal service that would offset his failure in the intendancy and secure his promotion at the end of his five-year term in Louisiana. An opportunity for such a service was offered by the Kentucky intrigue.

Another consideration that led him to urge the project was his desire to secure free trade privileges for the port of New Orleans, that is, to have it thrown open to the commerce of all friendly nations subject to a six per cent import and export duty. Navarro had urged this measure as early as 1780 and repeatedly thereafter, and Miró had renewed the recommendation.[14] All of them saw the economic and political possibilities of the Mississippi Valley and wished to make Spain the beneficiary. Local circumstances had already led Carondelet to relax the commercial restrictions in Louisiana as far as his discretionary powers extended. By a very liberal interpretation of the royal order of December 1, 1788, he reduced the duty on all importations from Kentucky from fifteen to six per cent. He granted frequent "special permissions" to ships to call at the ports of the United States, and strongly supported the New Orleans *cabildo's* memorial against the commercial regulations of 1793. It was indeed his economic liberalism that brought about his removal from the intendancy of Louisiana, but even then he stuck to his guns and assured Godoy that the economic welfare as well as the loyalty of Louisiana required that New Orleans be made a free port.[15]

The renewed intrigue with Kentucky opportunely enabled the governor to advance another and a compelling argument in favor of this measure. Kentucky, he pointed out, should by all means receive its imports as well as despatch its exports by way of New Orleans. All economic intercourse between the American West and the Atlantic States must cease. New Orleans merchants must undersell those of Philadelphia in Kentucky. In order that this might be done, the cost of European goods in New Orleans must be reduced, and this reduction in turn would be secured if New Orleans were made a free port and its market thrown open to the competition of the merchants and manufacturers of all countries. This was the only means, asserted Carondelet, of converting a fugitive intrigue with the Kentuckians into a firm friendship and lasting alliance.

Before writing these despatches to Godoy, he had received encouragement from other quarters in Kentucky. Judge Harry Innes wrote Gayoso in January, 1794, expressing a willingness to negotiate with Spain, but warning Gayoso that the vague promises hitherto received from Louisiana must be converted into precise assurances before the Kentuckians would take a step.[16] In the correspondence that ensued there was a sharp disagreement between Innes on the one hand and Gayoso and Carondelet on the other as to procedure, but they made some progress towards an agreement.[17] Other correspondents of Spain were Michel Lacassagne, whom we have already mentioned; another French merchant of Louisville, Benjamin Tardiveau, and one of Wilkinson's associates in the earlier intrigue, Benjamin Sebastian, who offered as his chief gage of loyalty to Spain his Spanish surname.

So great was Carondelet's confidence in a favorable decision by Godoy that, without awaiting further orders, he sent Wilkinson large sums of money and urged him to come down in person or to send authorized deputies to conclude the treaty of alliance and commerce with Spain on behalf of Kentucky. The messengers employed by Wilkinson in this correspondence were Henry Owens, a quondam schoolmaster; Henry Collins, whom Wilkinson once described as an "unpolished diamond" and later as a "great villain;"

Thomas Power, the most indefatigable traveler of them all; and the notorious Philip Nolan, "my young friend . . . honorable, discreet, courageous and active." [18]

Despite Carondelet's eagerness to give and Wilkinson's to receive, not all went well. Of the $16,000 sent "our Brigadier" by the Baron in 1794, only $5100 actually reached its destination. Lacassagne pocketed $1400 of the $4000 sent by him. In June, 1794, Carondelet sent another $12,000, half of it by Owens and the other half by Collins, ostensibly in payment of a balance long overdue on a legitimate commercial transaction, but actually to reimburse Wilkinson for his alleged expenses in buying off George Rogers Clark and to provide funds for the prosecution of the intrigue. Owens, who returned to Kentucky by way of the Mississippi and Ohio Rivers, was murdered by the Spanish crew sent with him, and the money was never recovered. Some of the murderers were captured and brought before Judge Harry Innes, who hastened to hand them over to Wilkinson, and he in turn sent them on to the Spanish commandant of St. Louis lest their trial in Kentucky should lead to unpleasant revelations.[19] Collins, going by sea with the other $6000 to Charleston, South Carolina, returned safely as far as Pittsburgh, and finally paid Wilkinson $2500 of the $6000.[20] "Our Brigadier" in his turn disappointed the Baron, for he failed either to descend to New Orleans or to send authorized deputies, and Gayoso detected disturbing contradictions between Wilkinson's statements and those of Innes. Wilkinson explained, however, that the Indian campaign had required his attention, and that more time and money were necessary to prepare the ground in Kentucky, and renewed his assurances of ultimate success. Carondelet accepted his explanations, overlooked the contradictions, and, under the influence of proposals from the "Secret Committee of Correspondence of the West," repeated his fervent representations to the Court for instructions and funds.

THE SECRET COMMITTEE OF CORRESPONDENCE OF THE WEST

Jáudenes and Viar were responsible for the address of the committee just referred to. When in August, 1793, the Spanish agents in Philadelphia learned of Genêt's projects against Louisiana, they sent Carondelet a warning by sea, and despatched as their messenger to New Madrid and St. Louis a young man by the name of Thomas or Medad Mitchell. Since Mitchell was known to Gayoso and Carondelet, Jáudenes and Viar gave him important despatches to the Spanish commandants of Upper Louisiana. Having delivered his despatches punctually, Mitchell continued down the Mississippi to New Orleans, and asked for an appointment in the Spanish service; but Carondelet, after conversing with him, came to the conclusion that he was a restless, unreliable young man, and used the pretext of important despatches for Jáudenes and Viar to send him back to Philadelphia. From Philadelphia Mitchell was once more despatched on a Spanish mission, this time to the American settlements on the Ohio, where he had a conference with David Bradford of Whiskey Rebellion fame, and still more important conversations with the Spanish conspirators in Kentucky. On his arrival in Philadelphia, he wrote out from memory, since he had feared to bring it in writing, the representation of the "Secret Committee of Correspondence of the West." This committee, as we learn from Carondelet's correspondence, was composed of Wilkinson, Innes, Sebastian and James Murray. They put their case bluntly. The coming year (1795) would see either a pro-Spanish revolution in Kentucky or the invasion of Louisiana by the Kentuckians, for the latter were determined to have the Mississippi opened to their traffic. If Spain wished to avert an invasion, she must aid the revolution, sending arms and munitions for ten thousand men, extending liberal credits to the Kentuckians, and opening the Mississippi to them duty free. Definite assurances of Spain's agreement to these terms must be returned to Kentucky by April 1, 1795; otherwise, Louisiana would be invaded without delay. In return for Spain's aid, they offered to guarantee to that power all the territory south and west of the Tennessee River and north and west of the Illinois.

Jáudenes was deeply impressed. Sending a copy of this representation by sea to Carondelet, he despatched another to Godoy, together with a long letter urging this intrigue as an alternative to the negotiation with the United States government.[21] Unlike the timorous Gardoqui of 1788, he wished to direct the intrigue himself, instead of turning it over to the governor of New Orleans.

GODOY MAKES HIS CHOICE

It was just after the Council of State of July 7, 1794 had approved Godoy's proposals and had directed him to make fresh overtures to the United States and just before the consequent orders were issued that Godoy received Carondelet's letters of April 7 and May 1, 1794, promising the certain success of the renewed intrigue. Corroborated by Jáudenes and Viar, Carondelet's optimistic interpretation of the delicate situation in the American West posed directly before Godoy the question of Spain's policy towards the United States and its frontier. Should he carry out his plan of conciliating the American government? This he had every reason to know could be done only at the cost of extensive concessions. Or should he seize the heaven-sent alternative, revolutionize the American West, split the United States into two hostile camps, and so retain control of the east bank of the Mississippi, of the southern Indians and their trade, and of the commerce on the Mississippi?

Such a momentous question was not for one man to decide, and so Godoy laid it before the Council of State on July 25, 1794. After a lengthy discussion, but with no sign of hesitation or dissent, the council advised and the king ordered that the diplomatic *démarche* resolved upon a fortnight earlier should be executed without modification.[22] The Kentucky intrigue was not to be abandoned altogether, but it was subordinated to the negotiation with Washington's government, that is, it was to be continued in order to prevent an invasion of Louisiana while the negotiation was pending and as a last resort in case the negotiation failed. On the following day, July 26, Godoy despatched to Jáudenes the order resolved upon in the Council of July 7 directing him to lay before Washington the new treaty proposals.[23]

Once the decision was made, Godoy adhered to it resolutely, despite the increasingly optimistic tone of the despatches of both Carondelet and Jáudenes. Carondelet's confidential despatch of June 3, 1794, informed Godoy of Harry Innes's overtures and spoke of the success of the intrigue as "infallible." Godoy remained unmoved. His decision, contained in a marginal note on this letter dated September 12, 1794, directed that the results of the proposals of the preceding July to Washington be awaited. Again in a letter of October 8, 1794, Carondelet wrote urgently on the same subject, and again Godoy turned a deaf ear to his entreaty. Even when the secretary of state had read the latter of Jáudenes and Viar enclosing the proposals of the "Secret Committee of Correspondence of the West," he would do no more than authorize Jáudenes to open negotiations with the Kentuckians for the very limited purpose, carefully stated by Godoy, of preventing the spread of ideas unfavorable to Spain and of weakening England's influence with the Kentuckians. Jáudenes was instructed that his course must be in conformity with the order of July 26, 1794. Orders to this effect were sent to Carondelet as well as the envoy in February, 1795.[24]

There are several indications of the considerations that guided the Council of State and Godoy in their decision on this matter. In the first place, the project of making New Orleans a free port, which Carondelet linked inseparably with the Kentucky intrigue, was too progressive a measure for the Spanish court, especially at a time when the very word "free" was in disfavor with all the courts of Europe. Even the scanty privileges accorded Louisiana by the *cédula* of 1782 had excited great opposition in Spain, and although in 1793 they were made somewhat more extensive, it was specified that the use of the word "free" should be avoided, because of its republican connotation. In any case, the Council of State could not bring itself to grant free trade out of hand to New Orleans, and merely referred the question to Gardoqui for a report which, as far as the records show, was never made. It was therefore impossible to adopt Carondelet's proposals for revolutionizing Kentucky, since he insisted that the success of the measure was impossible without the simultaneous grant of free trade to New Orleans.

Other weighty considerations against fomenting a revolution in Kentucky were suspicion of Wilkinson, the fear of a war with the United States, with England and with England's Indian allies, and the great expense that the intrigue and revolution would entail, even if Spain were not drawn directly into the revolutionary war.[25] Spain's finances were in disorder and were inadequate to the military activities already undertaken. Additional burdens could not be borne. At the very same meeting of the Council (July 25, 1794) at which Carondelet's proposals were rejected, Gardoqui, as minister of finance, presented a report showing the staggering expenses of the current campaign and the great difficulties that would attend the raising of funds for another.

Defeated in the competition with the American frontier for immigrants, Spain was forced to reject her successes in other phases of the frontier struggle. The Indian alliances and the Kentucky intrigue were painstakingly brought to fruition by Carondelet, only to be discarded by his more discreet superiors in the moment of success. Where success itself was failure, Spain might as well yield; and so, as we shall see, Godoy finally surrendered the last of Carondelet's gains, the territorial, and with it the points that had given rise to this now hopeless conflict.

CHAPTER XIV
SAN LORENZO: A FRONTIER TREATY
A SOUTH CAROLINA GENTLEMAN

ON October 27, 1795, at the palace-monastery of San Lorenzo a treaty was signed whereby Spain surrendered its dispute with the American republic. It was a crucial document that was signed on that day by Manuel de Godoy, the handsome guardsman of Badajoz, and Thomas Pinckney, South Carolina gentleman; for the treaty of San Lorenzo marks the beginning of the disintegration of the Spanish empire as well as the first stage in the territorial expansion of the United States. The following pages will show how the concatenation of events in a Swiss town, on royal Spanish backstairs, and in the backwoods of North America forced this portentous surrender.

It was in November, 1794, that Thomas Pinckney, minister to Great Britain, was directed by his government to undertake a special commission to the Spanish court. His appointment was made in response not to Godoy's proposals of July 26, 1794, but to his invitation of the preceding May. Curiously enough, the royal order of July 26, the result of such earnest and prolonged deliberation in the anxious Council of State, had not the slightest effect on the course of the Spanish-American negotiation. Its contents were never formally conveyed, by Jáudenes or otherwise, to the United States government, and it played no part in the final negotiation between Pinckney and Godoy. It may at first sight seem incomprehensible that Jáudenes, a diplomatic agent of the humblest rank, should have failed to obey the positive command of his king to communicate to Washington's government the contents of the order. It has been suggested by way of explanation that Jáudenes was engaged in an intrigue with the Kentuckians and was unwilling to have it interrupted, as it might have been had he obeyed the order.[1] The most probable explanation, however, seems to be that just one week before he received the despatch of July 26, he had written informing Godoy of Pinckney's appointment to Spain. Since this appointment tied the hands of the United States government, it would have been worse than useless for Jáudenes to reveal his royal master's eagerness for a treaty.

The period from July 26, 1794, the date of the order to Jáudenes just mentioned, to June 29, 1795, the date of Pinckney's arrival at the Spanish court, was marked by the almost complete suspension of the negotiation between the two governments. The same period, it may be remarked by way of anticipation, was one of intense activity on the Mississippi Valley frontier, where Spanish officials and American frontiersmen ploughed an independent furrow, with little knowledge of the plans of their respective governments and with little regard for their wishes.

The length of this diplomatic hiatus of eleven months was due to Pinckney's delay in reaching Spain; and his delay is in turn explained by various causes. In the first place, one of the considerations that led to his appointment seems to have been Washington's desire to placate the Kentuckians. There was little hope in administration circles that a new minister would succeed where Short had failed; but the whole American West was in a ferment, many Kentuckians angrily demanding that the Mississippi be seized while Spain was engaged in war at home. Something must be done to quiet the clamor on the Ohio; and it is significant that at the same time that Colonel James Innes was sent to Kentucky to convince its governor of Washington's determination to open the Mississippi, the President resolved to accept Godoy's invitation of May, 1794, and send a new and more distinguished envoy to Spain. As one writer has expressed it, the king of Spain asked for a gentleman, and Washington sent him Thomas Pinckney; but it is interesting to recall that first Thomas Jefferson was offered and declined the apparently futile appointment.

MALADROIT DIPLOMACY

In view of the origin of his mission, there seemed to be no reason why Pinckney should proceed post-haste to Spain; and the maladroit policy of the United States government actually delayed his departure from London. So long indeed was it delayed that he lost all the immense benefit that he might have derived from Jay's mission to England (1794). The American government's policy has been called maladroit because it relied on the worst and neglected the best means of extorting the desired terms from Spain. Reliance was placed in the good offices of France, which, it was hoped, would utilize its victories over Spain to secure the terms desired by the United States. This fatuous optimism found its best expression in the letters of James Monroe, American minister at Paris, who wrote in 1795 that France was giving us material aid in the Spanish negotiation.[2] As a matter of fact, the French government was engaged at that very time in a determined effort to secure from Spain the retrocession of Louisiana, and in order to carry its point was exciting Spain's fear of the ambitious Americans and was promising to keep the Mississippi River closed in order to check their westward expansion.[3]

The opportunity neglected by Washington's government was afforded by Jay's mission. The hindsight test is often unfair, and yet it seems strange that Randolph, Jay and Pinckney, the three best-informed persons in the diplomatic service of the United States at that juncture, should all have failed so utterly to perceive the real relation of Jay's mission to the negotiation between their government and Spain. They either knew or should have known by the winter of 1794–95 that the Anglo-Spanish alliance was in danger of dissolution, that the secrecy surrounding Jay's mission and his treaty with Grenville had created great alarm in Spain, and that this Spanish fear of an Anglo-American alliance would be the most effective means of extorting a treaty favorable to the United States. Since, as these three diplomats knew, Jay's treaty did not in fact provide for an alliance between England and the United States, it would seem as plain as day that Pinckney should have hastened to Spain before the veil of secrecy was lifted from Jay's treaty and while Godoy was still haunted by the spectre of Anglo-American union.

Instead, the American diplomats followed the opposite course. On the advice of Jay and with the approval of Randolph, Pinckney deliberately awaited in London news of the ratification of Jay's treaty by the United States Senate; and it was only when he learned that there would be a long delay in the consideration of the treaty that he proceeded to Spain.[4] This maladroit diplomacy secured its immediate object, for Jay's treaty was ratified while Pinckney was in Spain and news of the ratification and the text of the treaty reached Spain a full month before the conclusion of the treaty with

Godoy. As might have been foreseen, and as Pinckney now frankly admitted, this news was prejudicial to his negotiation.[5] It might indeed have wrecked it but for an abrupt change in the European situation which the American diplomats could not have foreseen.

GODOY DESERTS ENGLAND

This abrupt change was brought about by the treaty of Bâle (July, 1795) whereby Spain deserted England and made peace with the victorious French Republic. The negotiation was kept even more profoundly secret than Jay's with Grenville, for Godoy feared to face British resentment until the treaty with France was a *fait accompli*. When we consider the desperate straits to which Spain had been reduced in the winter of 1794–95, it must be admitted that Godoy came off very well at Bâle, for the only price that he had to pay to secure peace with France and the evacuation of the Spanish provinces conquered by French arms was the cession of Spanish Santo Domingo to the republic. Louisiana he stubbornly refused to surrender, possibly out of deference to opinion in Spain, possibly for use in a future bargain.[6]

It was while negotiations at Bâle were in progress that Thomas Pinckney arrived at court (June 29, 1795) ; and of course he was unable to make the slightest progress until that affair was terminated. Once the French treaty was concluded, Godoy gave the North American situation his immediate attention. On August 4, 1795, King Charles IV ratified the French treaty. Ten days later (August 14) the Spanish Council of State completed the diplomatic retreat begun in the time of Floridablanca and decided to surrender the dispute with the United States. In the first stage of the controversy (1780–87), Spain had refused to concede on any terms the navigation and boundary demanded by the United States. In 1787, under the combined pressure of a frontier menace and European complications, Floridablanca had offered boundary concessions in return for an alliance with the United States. In 1791, he was apparently ready to include the navigation of the Mississippi in the bargain; and in the despatch to Jáudenes of July 26, 1794, Godoy had virtually declared Spain's willingness to concede both points in return for a defensive alliance and territorial guarantee. Now in August, 1795, the Council of State decided to surrender both points without exacting the equivalent alliance. What were the considerations that led it to make this momentous decision?

Ever since the publication of Godoy's *Memoirs*, most American historians have been content to repeat his statement that the surrender was due to the secrecy surrounding Jay's treaty and the consequent fear that the treaty included an alliance between Great Britain and the United States.[7] We now know, however, that this product of the blurred memory of an old man in exile is not supported by the facts; for, far from being ignorant of the terms of Jay's treaty, Godoy had a copy of it in his possession a full month before he signed the treaty with Pinckney, and far from facilitating, Jay's treaty actually rendered more difficult Pinckney's negotiation. Even before the publication of its terms Jay's treaty had ceased to be a decisive factor in shaping Spanish policy. It was not even mentioned in the lengthy minutes of the Council of State of August 14, 1795, when the surrender to the United States was agreed upon.

It was not Jay's treaty with England but Godoy's treaty with France that made possible Pinckney's triumph at San Lorenzo. By concluding a separate peace with France at Bâle, Godoy violated Spain's treaty of 1793 with England and he knew that as soon as he had made peace with the former he would have to face the angry resentment of the latter. Even in 1794, while the unnatural union was still in existence, the perfidy of Albion had been taken for granted at the Spanish court. After the treaty of Bâle, the danger seemed tenfold greater. Godoy's best informant, the trusted ambassador Bernardo del Campo, showered him with letters from London in August, September and October, 1795, warning him to prepare immediately against British aggression.[8] The blow might fall in Santo Domingo, or in Mexico, or somewhere else; but in any case it appeared certain that Great Britain was about to assail some colony of Spain in the neighborhood of the Gulf of Mexico. In that case the attitude of the United States would be of the utmost importance. An alliance with the Americans would be of great value; their neutrality at least was indispensable, and Thomas Pinckney could not be suffered to leave Spain unsatisfied. Hence it was that only ten days elapsed between the Spanish ratification of the treaty of Bâle and the decision of the Council of State to yield to the United States in the matter of the boundary and the navigation of the Mississippi. Six months after San Lorenzo, Godoy himself gave this explanation of its terms. In a conversation (May, 1796) with Earl Bute, the British ambassador, Godoy complained that Britain's hostile preparations against Mexico in 1795 had forced him to make extensive concessions to the United States.[9]

BACKSTAIRS INTRIGUE

It was not only Spain's insecurity in Europe and America, but also Godoy's insecurity in Spain that led to the capitulation at San Lorenzo. Most precarious was the royal favorite's situation in the summer and early fall of 1795. Heavy taxation had created intense discontent, and military reverses had done much to discredit the youthful minister's conduct of affairs. So cordially was he hated at this time that he rarely showed his face in public; and on one occasion, when the court was moving from one royal estate to another, the danger of popular violence was so great that he deserted his own carriage and took refuge with the king and queen.[10]

One result of this widespread discontent was the Malaspina plot, a typical backstairs episode of the old régime. In it were implicated Antonio Valdés, one of the most influential, though the laziest, of Godoy's colleagues in the ministry; the confessors of the king and queen; and the naval officer and explorer, Malaspina, an Italian by birth. The object of the conspirators was simply to persuade the king to get rid of Godoy, who they said was endangering the monarchy by his incompetence; but to the favorite their intrigue seemed nothing less than treason. To meet the crisis, he first set to work to remove the chief grievances, which were military reverses and heavy taxation. Clearly the only way to remove both grievances at once was to make peace. Peace was accordingly made with France, and, to avert war with the United States, the treaty of San Lorenzo was signed. Having thus strengthened his position, Godoy proceeded to crush the conspiracy, imprisoning the confessors, exiling Malaspina, and forcing the resignation of Valdés. Finally, to justify himself against the charge of incompetence, he read before the Council of State a review of his services to the crown, and one of the two achievements on which he laid most emphasis was the treaty of San Lorenzo.[11]

From Spanish backstairs to the backwoods of North America may seem a far cry, and yet backwoods as well as backstairs played an important part at San Lorenzo. Had not Spain's frontier policy proved a failure by 1795, and had not Godoy been acutely conscious of the failure, it hardly seems probable that he would have made so complete a surrender of the Mississippi Valley controversy. Had the Indians proved themselves trusty allies, had immigrants poured into the Floridas and Louisiana, had the West rebelled just as Spain desired, and had the Spanish treasury been equal to the ever-mounting demands of its frontier provinces, Godoy might well have tried to placate the American government with the commercial treaty that it so eagerly desired.

CARONDELET COURTS THE KENTUCKIANS

While diplomacy drifted in the doldrums from the summer of 1794 to the summer of 1795, Carondelet fought the Americans tooth and nail on the frontier. His object was twofold: To defend Louisiana, and to aid Spanish diplomacy by tightening Spain's grip on the Mississippi Valley. In Miró's time, this object had been pursued through Floridablanca's immigration policy, with the Kentucky intrigue playing a distinctly subordinate part, since the court considered it a remote possibility. Upon Carondelet's arrival in Louisiana (1792), he had modified the immigration policy beyond recognition, and since the Western intrigue gave but faint promise of success, he had devoted all his energies to the elaboration of an aggressive Indian policy. Baffled in this effort by his unsympathetic superiors and the intractable Indians, and threatened with invasion from Georgia and Kentucky, he had welcomed with open arms the treasonable overtures of General James Wilkinson and Judge Harry Innes in the early months of 1794. At the same time, the Baron began to execute a plan that he had long had in contemplation: the military occupation of the east bank of the Mississippi River up to its junction with the Ohio.

The Kentucky intrigue was nothing new, as we have already had abundant occasion to see; but it was now given a decidedly novel character by Carondelet. Hitherto, according to various orders of the court, the revolutionizing of Kentucky had been neither the immediate nor the sole object of the intrigue. Floridablanca's purpose in cultivating it had been to use the Kentucky conspirators as propagandists and information agents for Spain; the revolutionizing of the American West was regarded as a remote possibility; and Spain was to have no open dealings with the conspirators until after they had set up a separate government. Now Carondelet's avowed object was to foment an immediate insurrection in Kentucky, to bring Wilkinson and other leading conspirators into Spanish territory and conclude an alliance with them, and, by supplying them liberally with munitions and money, to aid them in establishing their independence. Thus divided into two rival powers, he said, the United States would no longer be a serious menace to Spain in North America. We have already discussed, in connection with Spanish diplomacy and the royal order of July 26, 1794, his despatches of that year to Godoy on the subject of the conspiracy; but to Wilkinson also, without waiting to receive the court's reply, he began to communicate his designs.

We have no space here to trace the sinuosities of the intrigue, but it may be pointed out that despite the lukewarmness of the American frontiersmen as well as his own government, the Baron continued the intrigue to the bitter end. Already, early in 1795, he had received a disconcerting proof of the indifference to Spain of even the most discontented frontiersmen. After the collapse of the Whiskey Rebellion, David Bradford, one of its leaders, took refuge in Spanish territory; and when he was examined by Governor Gayoso at Natchez he did not even pretend that he and his followers had had any desire to form a connection with Spain.[12] In Cumberland, as Carondelet knew, the Clark-Genêt plan of invading Louisiana had met with a ready response, and he also knew that even in Kentucky, which he regarded as the stronghold of the Spanish interest, many besides Clark were the sworn enemies of Spain.[13]

Nevertheless, the Baron went doggedly ahead with his plans. On July 16, 1795, he wrote Wilkinson a letter that was designed to bring the intrigue to a head at once. "My letter of the first instant," he wrote, "was already signed when I received orders from his Majesty very satisfactory to the Western states: since his Majesty being very desirous of giving them a commerce reciprocaly advantageous to both parties has authorized me to treat privately with the Agents chosen & sent by the State of Kentucky to New Madrid on that purpose. Consequently I send to Colonel Gayoso the necessary instructions, & sufficient powers to agree privately with the aforesaid Agents upon every point and object of this momentous plan. . . ." The letter concluded with the following: "G. W. [General Wilkinson] can aspire to the same dignity in the western states that P. W. [President Washington] has in the eastern." [14] Carondelet knew his man.

This letter was sent to Gayoso with an order directing him to proceed at once to New Madrid, forward it to Wilkinson, and negotiate with the Kentucky envoys who should come down in response to the invitation. His powers were narrowly limited, as he was instructed to conclude only a commercial convention, and even that was to be kept secret at first from all but the "notables" of Kentucky; but we learn from Carondelet's other correspondence that in his shallow optimism he expected this proof of Spain's generosity to effect the separation of Kentucky from the Union. Thereupon it was the Baron's plan to conclude an offensive and defensive alliance with Kentucky and to aid their revolution with ammunition, twenty field guns and ten thousand rifles.[15]

Gayoso ascended the Mississippi to New Madrid, as he had been directed, and from September to December, 1795, he was engaged in correspondence with Wilkinson, Lacassagne and Innes. Wilkinson displayed little enthusiasm at the opportunity of embracing his dear friend, Gayoso, to whom he had once written that he would willingly sacrifice one arm if he might embrace Gayoso with the other. Now he protested that he had a difficult game to play, as he was suspected by both his commander-in-chief, Wayne, and by Washington, and that the ground had not yet been sufficiently prepared in Kentucky. Nevertheless, though he could not visit Gayoso himself, had not consulted Innes, and did not trust Lacassagne, he finally sent a delegate, Benjamin Sebastian, to confer with the Spaniard, adding that, while Sebastian had no power to make a treaty, the conference would undoubtedly forward Spain's interests in Kentucky. In order to prepare the ground in Kentucky and oil the wheels of intrigue, he urgently requested the immediate remittance of twenty thousand dollars and an increase in the amount of his pension. In December, 1795, Sebastian actually descended the Ohio and conferred with Gayoso; but the powers of both were so limited that it was soon decided to adjourn the discussion to New Orleans and, under Carondelet's guidance, concert a plan of action. Arriving at the capital early in January, they were busily engaged in hatching a scheme when, to their consternation, despatches from Havana brought news of the treaty of San Lorenzo.[16]

The witch's pot of intrigue in the West was being stirred up at the same time by the unhappy Jáudenes and Viar. Hardly had Sebastian left Kentucky to join Gayoso when a certain Antonio Argote arrived there, ostensibly to secure recognition as Spanish consul in Kentucky, but with secret instructions to get in touch with the Spanish conspirators and to enlist the services of Governor Shelby in the good cause. An interview with the governor was obtained, and although it was disappointing, Argote was still hopeful of success when news of Pinckney's treaty arrived and paralyzed his efforts.[17]

FORT SAN FERNANDO: FUR TRADER AND LAND SPECULATOR

The extension of Spain's military frontier was, as we have seen, Carondelet's second device for gaining the upper hand in the controversy with the United States. As early as his first year in Louisiana (1792), he had

persuaded the Cherokee to request the establishment
of Spanish posts at Muscle Shoals and Chickasaw
Bluffs (the Barrancas de Margot, or Ecores à Margot,
the site of the present Memphis, Tennessee), both of
which localities, by the way, were outside of the
Cherokee hunting grounds. Various circumstances had
prevented his granting this complaisant request; but in
1794 a step in that direction was taken when, under
circumstances already described, Fort Confederation
was built on the Tombigbie River, well within the
territory claimed by the United States.

Just as the designs of the South Carolina Yazoo
Company had led Miró to occupy Walnut Hills (Los
Nogales) in 1791, so in 1795 the activities of the Georgia
land companies were immediately responsible for the
erection of Fort San Fernando de las Barrancas at
Chickasaw Bluffs. Towards the end of 1794, land
speculators interested in the Yazoo country began
to bestir themselves, perhaps encouraged by the federal
government's assurance that it was at last going to
force a settlement of the dispute with Spain. Gentle
pressure was brought to bear on the Georgia legislature,
and once more in the history of the American frontier
political power was exploited in the interest of land
speculation. Their pockets bulging with shares and
banknotes, the legislators deeded away principalities
for a pittance. Millions of acres of Georgia's western
territory were conveyed to three companies, two of the
grants lying on the Mississippi between Natchez and
Chickasaw Bluffs, and one on the Tennessee River
around Muscle Shoals.[18]

As soon as Gayoso heard of the designs of the companies he hastily forwarded a detachment up the Mississippi to hold the Bluffs until his arrival with well-armed

reinforcements, for he was much disturbed by a visit that Cumberland settlers had paid to the Bluffs in 1794, and by their influence among the Chickasaw. Carondelet, when advised of Gayoso's action, gave his approval, took command of the situation, and despatched instructions, reinforcements and supplies. Most important of all, he persuaded Panton, Leslie and Company to send one of its partners, John Forbes, with a boatload of goods to open a store at the new fort. Again the American land speculator and frontiersman found the Anglo-Spanish fur trader in their path.[19]

As the Chickasaw Bluffs extend for many miles along the Mississippi, the site of the fort was not chosen until after Gayoso's arrival. That done, a review of the troops was held and the construction of the fort begun on May 30, 1795; and since that was the nameday of the Prince of Asturias, Fernando, the fort was called San Fernando de las Barrancas, St. Ferdinand of the Bluffs.[20] Thus the last outpost of Spanish advance in the Mississippi Valley received the ill-omened name of that prince who later, as the notorious Ferdinand VII, lost the bulk of Spain's empire in America.

By the judicious employment of the means usual in such cases — presents, rum and flattery — Gayoso obtained from a friendly faction of the Chickasaw a treaty ceding to His Catholic Majesty the site of the fort and a small strip of territory around it. Panton's store was then established; and, despite vigorous protests from Governor Blount and General Wayne, fort and store were maintained there until the spring of 1797 when, in compliance with the treaty of San Lorenzo, Carondelet ordered its evacuation. Shortly thereafter, having learned of Blount's conspiracy and determined to postpone the treaty's execution, he

countermanded the order; but the second messenger
arrived too late. The lonely garrison had executed the
first order with alacrity, and no attempt was made to
reoccupy the Bluffs.[21]

GODOY LOOKS AT THE MISSISSIPPI VALLEY

In despatches that still glow with pride and tremble
with eager hope, Carondelet informed Godoy of his
achievements in Kentucky and at Chickasaw Bluffs.[22]
In a despatch of June 10, 1795, he reported the establishment of Fort San Fernando, which, he declared,
forestalled the Americans, strengthened Spain's hold
on the Mississippi, and would promote Panton's trade
and Spain's influence among the Chickasaw and Choctaw, at the same time that it advanced the Western
intrigue by facilitating communications with Kentucky.
This conspiracy was the subject of a despatch of July 1,
and the burden of the Baron's song was a plea for funds,
more funds, and still more funds. The plan to revolutionize Kentucky was feasible, he declared, and such a
revolution was almost essential to the safety of Spanish
North America; but tens of thousands of dollars must
be made available at once for propaganda, bribery
and aid to the insurgents. Whether this were done or
not, he continued, still larger sums must be placed at
his disposal to consolidate his recent gains on the frontier. Forts San Fernando and Confederation as well as
the older forts must be strengthened, their garrisons
reinforced, Panton subsidized and the annual Indian
presents increased to meet the competition of the
United States government. Otherwise, he concluded,
Spain must face the necessity of surrender in the controversy with the United States, and all the dire consequences that would flow from the surrender; but

such a calamity need never occur, since, thanks to Carondelet's Kentucky intrigue, Indian alliances and string of forts, His Majesty held the fate of the Mississippi Valley in the hollow of his hand.

These despatches Godoy received more than a week before he signed the treaty of San Lorenzo and almost a week before Pinckney brought the negotiation to a crisis by demanding his passport. Had Godoy been convinced by the Baron's eager optimism, he would have issued the passport that Pinckney had requested but did not expect or desire to receive. The situation thus created was similar in many respects to that of July, 1794. On both occasions the Council of State, on Godoy's advice, had decided to make concessions to the United States in the frontier controversy, and on both occasions, after the decision had been made but before its execution, despatches had been received from Louisiana urging continued resistance and giving positive assurance of success. The parallel was completed when, on October 27, 1795, as on July 25, 1794, Godoy turned a deaf ear to the Baron's rhetoric and consummated the surrender. This time there was no miscarriage. Pinckney was on hand, the treaty was signed, and both the disputed territory and the control of the Mississippi were irrevocably lost to Spain.

We have already intimated that the treaty of San Lorenzo was essentially a frontier treaty. It is of course true that, as we have seen, the European situation was one of Godoy's reasons for concluding the treaty, and that it contained provisions of no little significance in the history of neutral rights on the high seas in time of war. At the same time, it is equally true that by far the most important terms of the treaty related to the Spanish-American frontier: the disputed territory, the navigation of the Mississippi, the right of deposit at New Orleans; and that one of the chief reasons why the Spanish government agreed to these terms was that it had failed, and knew that it had failed, in its frontier conflict with the United States.

That the most important terms of the treaty related to the frontier is so obvious that the mere statement of the fact would be sufficient, since that fact requires not proof but emphasis. It may, however, be well to remind the reader that the navigation of the Mississippi was an essential element in the frontier controversy, for while the exclusive control of the river was still prized by Spain as a means of suppressing contraband trade, it was prized still more as a means of checking the growth of the American West, separating it from the United States, and stimulating immigration into Louisiana and West Florida.

That the fact as well as the terms of the Spanish surrender was conditioned by Spanish failure in the frontier conflict stands more in need of proof; for historians, relying on Godoy's *Memoirs*, have generally explained his course at San Lorenzo by the existing diplomatic situation. These *Memoirs*, however, were written nearly forty years after the event, and contemporary records tell a different story, a story in which the frontier plays a prominent part.

On August 14, 1795, occurred a meeting of the Council of State to which reference has already been made. Two official accounts of the deliberations of the Council have been preserved, each relating to a separate aspect of the subject under discussion. The first of these documents possesses great interest for us, since it throws a flood of light on the reasons for Spain's surrender to the United States and since it has never been utilized by any previous writer on this subject. According to this record, Godoy carefully explained the nature of the controversy to the Council with the aid of documents and maps, and in his exegesis he established two "capital facts." The first of these was that Spain's failure to protest against the Anglo-American treaty of 1783 was taken by the Americans as the silence of consent. The second "capital fact" was the small importance of the disputed territory and the forts contained within its limits; the unsatisfactory state of relations with the "barbarous, voluble and perfidious nations of Indians" of that region, who were incessantly menacing the possessions of Spain; and the undesirability of continuing a very uncertain and very expensive dispute. Godoy concluded with the observation that, even if this controversy were settled according to the "moderate ideas" of the United States, Spain would still have "possessions, peoples and rights quite sufficient, and important to our navigation and commerce in those and other principal parts of the two Americas." [23]

There are many omissions from this document and there are some distortions in it. For example, the "moderate ideas" of the United States had long been regarded as "absurd pretensions" by the Spanish government, and Godoy's novel characterization was simply a sugar-coating to render palatable the bitter pill of defeat. Our interest, however, lies in the second of his two "capital facts," for it shows that the treaty of San Lorenzo was not signed until the Council had canvassed the situation on the Spanish-American frontier and had decided that the chances of success did not justify the continuance of the struggle. From the second report of the Council's deliberations on August 14, and from other documents, we learn that at this time the government was much alarmed by two other developments in the Mississippi Valley, namely, by the activity of British fur traders in the upper Missouri Valley, and by the efforts of Americans to establish settlements at Muscle Shoals and Chickasaw Bluffs.[24]

It may be observed that neither of these reports of the Council's deliberations mentioned the Kentucky conspiracy. Other sources show that Spain did not trust Wilkinson, and was unwilling to incur the expense of revolutionizing Kentucky or the danger of war with the United States. Hence it was that Godoy was unmoved when, on October 18, 1795, he read Carondelet's perfervid despatches about the progress of the western conspiracy. Like Floridablanca, he had no stomach for dealing with the American frontiersmen. His first object was to [check their progress through Spain's frontier, and since that appeared impossible he preferred a treaty with the established government of the United States to an intrigue with its irresponsible frontiersmen.

STRIPPING FOR ACTION

Our task is now done, for we are not concerned either with the details of the Pinckney–Godoy negotiation, or with the execution of the treaty. Pinckney conducted himself most becomingly and quite creditably; but in no essential respect did he get more than Godoy was ready to concede when their conferences began, and he failed to secure either a commercial treaty or a satisfactory article on the right of deposit. His rôle was very much like that of Monroe and Livingston at Paris in 1803, when Napoleon tossed Louisiana into their laps. As for the long delay in the treaty's execution, we must content ourselves with pointing out that a frontier event, William Blount's conspiracy, provided Spain with its chief pretext for postponing compliance with its terms.[25] When Natchez, the chief post in the disputed territory, was at last evacuated (1798), it was no less a person than General James Wilkinson who took possession of it in the name of the United States government.

From what has been said, it should be apparent that the treaty of San Lorenzo did not so much change the situation in the Mississippi Valley as accord recognition to changes that had taken place there since 1783. Even before the treaty was signed, citizens of the United States were enjoying the navigation of the Mississippi River from its headwaters to its mouth. From Kentucky down to New Orleans, their commerce had been legalized by a royal order; from the mouth of the Mississippi up to New Orleans, it was connived at by the governor of Louisiana, who informed his government that no other course was possible. As for the disputed territory, Spain was still in actual possession of it in 1795; but it was by that time apparent that this territory as well as upper Louisiana would fall an easy prey to the United States in case of war. For Spain indeed the treaty of San Lorenzo was one of momentous significance, for it was in effect an admission of the failure of Floridablanca's attempt to make of the Mississippi Valley another Mexico. The admission of failure on the east bank of the Mississippi involved the tacit admission of failure on the west bank as well. The treaty of San Lorenzo of 1795 found its fitting, its inevitable complement in the treaty of San Ildefonso of 1800, whereby Spain retroceded Louisiana to France.

For the United States as well this treaty was one of

great significance. It was a victory not only for the United States over Spain, but also for expansionists in the United States over particularists, both Eastern and Western. It appeased frontier discontent, gave a mortal blow to separatism, and secured the Union from a serious menace to its integrity. It completed the work begun by Jay's treaty and established the frontiers claimed by the United States at the end of the Revolution; and yet it did more than Jay's treaty, for the rights that it established had hitherto rested on a dubious legal basis. By terminating a dangerous controversy and by securing the American government's terms without the formation of the alliance which Spain had long required as the price of concession, the treaty carried one step further the government's policy of cutting loose from the European state system; a policy which, in retrospect, seems a kind of stripping for action in the western hemisphere. Finally, by confirming the United States in the possession of virtually the whole of the east bank of the Mississippi and by validating the Americans' claim to the free navigation of that river, the treaty laid a substantial foundation for the further extension of the new republic in North America.

NOTES

LIST OF ABBREVIATIONS

AHN: Archivo Histórico Nacional, Madrid, Spain.
——, E: ——, Sección de Estado.
——, ——, ACE: ——, ——, Actas del Supremo Consejo de Estado.
——, ——, AJE: ——, ——, Actas de la Suprema Junta de Estado.
A. H. R.: American Historical Review.
AI: Archivo General de Indias, Seville, Spain. Numerals following this abbreviation (e.g., 86–6–16) refer to the *estante, cajón* and *legajo* in which the document was found.
——, PC: ——, Papeles de Cuba.
AME: Archivo del Ministerio de Estado, Madrid.
AMAE: Archives du Minstère des Affaires Étrangères, Paris.
——, EU: ——, États-Unis.
A. S. P., F. R.: American State Papers, Foreign Relations.
——, I. A.: American State Papers, Indian Affairs.
B. P. R. O., F. O.: British Public Record Office, Foreign Office.
C. R. N. Ca.: Colonial Records of North Carolina.
exp.: *expediente.*
H. A. H. R.: Hispanic American Historical Review.
l.: *legajo.*
LC: Library of Congress, Washington.
M. V. H. R.: Mississippi Valley Historical Review.
S. R. N. Ca.: State Records of North Carolina.

CHAPTER I. RIVAL EMPIRES

1. Cf. H. E. Bolton, *Arredondo's Historical Proof of Spain's Title to Georgia*, Introduction, *passim;* and V. W. Crane, "Projects for Colonization in the South, 1684–1732," in M. V. H. R. xii, 23, discussing other and earlier phases.

2. Danvila y Collado, *El Reino de Carlos III;* M. Colmeiro, *Historia de la Economía Política en España;* J. F. Bourgoing, *Tableau de l'Espagne moderne* (2 ed., Paris, 1797).

3. H. I. Priestley, *José de Gálvez, passim.*

4. H. vander Linden, *L'Expansion coloniale de l'Espagne*, 329–37, and map of Upper California in Priestley, *op. cit.*; C. E. Chapman, *A History of California: the Spanish Period*, 216–417.

5. A. V. Goodpasture, "The Watauga Association," in Am. Hist. Mag., III, 110; A. Henderson, *Conquest of the Old Southwest;* Roosevelt, *Winning of the West*, I, 166.

6. AI, 146–3–11, Rendón to J. de Gálvez, Feb. 28, 1783, No. 72.

7. Information given me by Prof. I. S. Harrell. See his recent book, *Loyalism in Virginia*.

8. *Maryland Journal* (newspaper), Tues., Oct. 11, 1785, extract of letter from Caswell County, Frankland.

9. Etting Col. (mss., Hist. Soc. of Pennsylvania), *Old Congress Mss.*, *Autograph Letters*, Wm. Grayson to ——, Dumfries, Sept. 11, 1783; S. R. N. Ca., XVI, 459–60.

10. *Gazette of the State of Georgia* (newspaper), April 14, 1785.

11. J. A. Robertson, ed., "Spanish Correspondence concerning the American Revolution," in H. A. H. R., I, 311. Cf. S. R. N. Ca., XIV, 234–46.

12. Juan F. Yela Utrilla, *España ante la independencia de los Estados Unidos*, II, 187. Referred to hereafter as Yela.

13. *Ib.*, II, 42–43; and see note 4, ch. v.

14. Yela, *op. cit.*, II, 342–50.

15. *Ib.*, I, 477–80; M. Conrotte, *La intervención de España en la independencia de los Estados Unidos*, 164.

16. S. F. Bemis, *Pinckney's Treaty*, 44–65. Referred to hereafter as Bemis.

17. *Ib.*, note 7, pp. 49–50.

18. AI, 146–3–11, Rendón to J. de Gálvez, April 12, 1783, No. 75.

19. This fact was called to my attention by Prof. S. F. Bemis.

20. Yela, I, 305–70, 484–85; Conrotte, 8.

21. Conrotte, 182–88; Yela, I, 480.

22. AHN, E, ACE, Aug. 14, 1795.

Chapter II. Protagonists and Field of Action

1. H. Adams, *History of the United States in the Administrations of Jefferson and Madison*, I, 340.

2. *Secret Journals of Congress, Foreign Affairs*, IV, 45 *et seq.*; A. T. Mahan, *The Influence of Sea Power upon History*, 337, and *The Major Operations of the Navies in the War of American Independence*, 116, 125, 126; A. S. P., F. R., I, 261–63.

3. AMAE, CP, E–U, vol. 32, Otto to Montmorin, Dec. 15, 1787, No. 107 (transcript in LC); *Secret Journals of Congress, Foreign Affairs*, IV, 44–63; Bemis, 170–72.

4. AI, 86–6–7, El Conde de Gálvez to José de Gálvez, Jan. 26, 1784, and draft of (José de Gálvez) to Zéspedes, Jan. 23, 1784.

5. AI, PC, l. 4, Miró to Grand-Pré, Oct. 30, 1787, No. 283, and enclosed *impreso*.

6. AHN, E, AJE, April 26, 1790.

7. AI, PC, l. 177, Floridablanca to the Governor of Louisiana, Oct. (no day), 1791.

8. AHN, E, ACE, Aug. 14, 1795.

9. For a different view, see Roosevelt, III, 127.

10. See below, chs. v and VIII.

11. AI, 87–3–22, Zéspedes to Antonio Porlier, Sept. 8, 1789, No. 12.

12. Navarro's "Political Reflections," in J. A. Robertson, ed., *Louisiana under Spain*, etc., I, 237 *et seq.*

13. AI, 87–3–19, contains a valuable *expediente* on the commerce of Louisiana and the Floridas at this period.

14. Financial reports for Louisiana have been published by C. H. Cunningham in M. V. H. R., VI, 391.

15. Cf. J. R. Swanton, *Early History of the Creek Indians and their Neighbors*, 437–49; A. S. P., I. A., I, 38, 39.

16. "Observations of John Stuart," in A. H. R., XX, 818–20.

17. These figures are only approximate. Gayarré (cf. note 1, ch. III), 172–75; AI, PC, l. 199, Panton to O'Neill, March 15, 1786.

18. P. J. Hamilton, *Colonial Mobile*, 246; cf. note 16, above.

19. Roosevelt, III, 16; S. C. Williams, *The Lost State of Franklin;* reference in note 10, ch. IV.

20. AHN, E, l. 3899, Campo de Alange to the Prince of the Peace, Dec. 2, 1795, reporting the *dictámen* of the *Junta de Generales* on Louisiana.

21. Washington, *Writings* (ed. W. C. Ford), XI, 41–42, 78, and note to p. 43; Rufus King Papers (mss., N. Y. Hist. Soc.), R. King to E. Gerry, June 4, 1786.

CHAPTER III. THE SPANISH BARRIER

1. C. Gayarré, *History of Louisiana*, III: *The Spanish Domination*, 157–60. Referred to hereafter as Gayarré.

2. See below, ch. v.

3. H. vander Linden, *op. cit.*, 403; Gayarré, 1-34, 101-11. See also note 4, below.

4. The original of this *cédula*, dated Jan. 22, 1782, is in AI, 87-3-21. It is published in part in M. Serrano y Sanz, *España y los Indios Cherokis y Chactas*, 15-18; Priestley, *op. cit.*, 4.

5. AI, PC, l. 11, El Conde de Gálvez to Miró, April 24, 1785, and enclosed memorial; *ib.*, 86-7-24, *expediente* on letter from El Conde de Gálvez to J. de Gálvez, Oct. 27, 1785, No. 56.

6. AHN, E, l. 3885, exp. 17, Campomanés to J. de Gálvez, Sept. 14, 1784; AI, 86-6-16, *Copia del Discurso Preliminar sobre Indios*,by Zéspedes, Nov. 16, 1786.

7. W. H. Siebert, "The Loyalists in West Florida and the Natchez District," in M. V. H. R., II, 465.

8. Georgia Papers, 1732-1908 (mss., LC), fol. 116, copy of a circular letter from Gov. Lyman Hall of Georgia, Aug. 25, 1783.

9. AI, PC, l. 203, Panton to Miró, Aug. 31, 1789, and enclosure, and same to same, July 22, 1789; *ib.*, l. 2352, O'Neill to Gálvez, Oct. 31, 1785, No. 3.

10. *Ib.*, l. 203, McGillivray to Panton, Aug. 10, 1789, copy; A. J. Pickett, *History of Alabama*, 429-31 and 342 *et seq.*; L. Milfort, *Mémoire; ou, Coup-d'œil . . . sur . . . mon Séjour dans la Nation Creek* (Paris, 1802), *passim*, to be used with great care.

11. AI, PC, l. 197, McGillivray to O'Neill, March 26, 1784, and same to Miró, March 28, 1784; *ib.*, C. McLatchy to O'Neill, March 4, 1784.

12. AI, 86-6-7, Zéspedes to Gálvez, Aug. 16, 1784, No. 21 *de preferencia*, and enclosures, including Spanish translation of memorial by Panton, Leslie and Co., July 31, 1784.

13. AI, PC, l. 1375, Sonora to Gálvez, May 8, 1786; AHN, E, l. 3901, *extracto* summarizing correspondence on this subject from March 22, 1784 to May 8, 1786.

14. AI, 86-7-15, memorial of Francisco Fernández de Ravago, Feb. 6, 1787, and many other documents relating to this affair; *ib.*, 86-6-16, Miró to Valdés, Nov. 3, 1787, No. 8, and enclosures.

15. AHN, E, l. 3885, exp. 22, contains many documents relating to these congresses, including copies of the treaties; AI, PC, l. 1394, Miró to Ezpeleta, Aug. 1, 1784; Jane M. Berry, "The Indian Policy of Spain in the Southwest, 1783-1795," in M. V. H. R., III, 462 *et seq.*; Gayarré, 160-62; Serrano y Sanz, *op. cit.*, 82-85.

16. AHN, E, l. 3898, El Conde de Gálvez to J. de Gálvez, May 6, 1785, No. 27.

17. AI, 86–6–17, Miró to Valdés, May 20, 1789, No. 180; *ib.*, PC, l. 202, Panton to Miró, April 7 and July 31, 1789.

18. AI, PC, l. 1394, Miró to Ezpeleta, Aug. 1, 1784.

19. AI, 87–1–19, Navarro to J. de Gálvez, April 16, 1784, No. 216.

20. An instance is related in Miró and Navarro to El Marqués del Campo, March 4, 1788, draft: AI, PC, l. 104.

21. *Ib.*, l. 1375, J. de Gálvez to El Conde de Gálvez, May 30, 1784.

Chapter IV. The Westward Course

1. A. Henderson, "The Creative Forces in Westward Expansion," in A. H. R., xx, 86, and "Richard Henderson," in Tenn. Hist. Mag., ii, 155.

2. For the official statement of Spain's boundary claim, see below, p. 70.

3. S. R. N. Ca., xvii, 13–14, 15–16.

4. A. S. P., I. A., i, 17; Georgia Hist. Soc., *Collections*, v, part 2, No. 2, 205–14, 215, 220–21; Knox Papers (mss., Massachusetts Hist. Soc.), vol. xviii, fols. 46, 54, 108; Georgia Records (mss., LC), *Council Correspondence*, Gov. Elbert to Elijah Clarke, June 9, 1785, and *passim;* S. R. N. Ca., xxii, 649–50; *ib.*, xviii, 696–700; *Calendar Virginia State Papers*, iv, 37.

5. AHN, E, l. 3885, exp. 1, "Breve Relacion de las Fronteras medias . . .," cited in note 6, ch. v.

6. F. J. Turner, "State Making in the Revolutionary Era," in A. H. R., i, 70, 251; *Calendar Virginia State Papers*, iv, 45–46; L. P. Summers, *History of Southwest Virginia*, 264–66, 399; Papers of the Continental Congress (mss., LC) 48, 297, Chas. Cumming to the President of Congress.

7. S. C. Williams, *The Lost State of Franklin*, is the latest and best account of this subject.

8. J. H. DeWitt, ed., "The Journal of John Sevier," in Tenn. Hist. Mag., v, *passim*, especially pp. 162, 170–71, 175, 184, 189, 194, 233, 236.

9. S. R. N. Ca., xxii, 699–700.

10. AI, PC, l. 3, Miró to Gálvez, Dec. 10, 1785, No. 258, enclosing copy of letter from L. Chacheret; S. R. N. Ca., xx, 731.

11. A full discussion of this subject, with references, will be found in my article, "The Muscle Shoals Speculation," in M. V. H. R., Dec., 1926.

12. E. C. Burnett, ed., "Papers relating to Bourbon County, Georgia," in A. H. R., xv, 66 *et seq.*; AI, 86–6–15, Zéspedes to Sonora, Dec. 24, 1786, No. 13 *reservada*, and enclosures, show the efforts of the Bourbon County promoters to interest Sevier.

13. AHN, E, l. 3893, Gardoqui to Floridablanca, Havana, Feb. 23, 1785; Burnett, *op. cit.*, 68–71.

14. AI, PC, l. 2352, Miró to Bouligny, Nov. 10, 1785, No. 99; *ib.*, l. 104, Gardoqui to Miró, Oct. 21, 1785.

15. This appears from statistics given by C. H. Cunningham in M. V. H. R., vi, 391–97.

16. Burnett, *op. cit.*, 334–35.

17. *Ib.*, 336; AI, PC, l. 200, McGillivray to Miró, July 25, 1787; *ib.*, Ben James to Mather and Strother, July 23, 1787; *ib.*, l. 11, Bouligny to Miró, Oct. 4, 1785, No. 68; *ib.*, l. 37, O Neill to Miró, July 18, 1787; S. R. N. Ca., xxii, 719–21.

18. AI, PC, l. 1446, McGillivray to (Miró), Jan. 1, 1784, Spanish translation, enclosed in Carondelet to Las Casas, Aug. 23, 1792, No. 43 *res.*; Burnett, *op. cit.*, 299–303; AI, PC, l. 2352, McGillivray to Miró, July 10, 1785, Spanish translation.

19. A. S. P., I. A., i, 49, and references in note 4, above.

20. AI, PC, l. 199, McGillivray to O'Neill, March 28, 1786, announcing the immediate beginning of the campaign.

21. *Ib.*, l. 203, Panton to Miró and Navarro, Jan. 28, 1788; cf. Zéspedes to Sonora, June 12, 1786, No. 7 *res.*

22. AI, 86–6–15, Miró to Sonora, June 28, 1786, No. 136, *res. de preferencia*, and enclosures; *ib.*, PC, l. 4, Miró to O'Neill, June 20, 1786, *muy res.* By Sept. 18, 1786, O'Neill had given the Creek 3750 pounds of powder and 7400 pounds of ball: *ib.*, l. 37, O'Neill to Miró, Sept. 18, 1786.

23. *Ib.*, l. 176–2, Sonora to the Governor of Louisiana, Nov. 12, 1786; *ib.*, l. 1394, Valdés to the Governor of Louisiana, July 31, 1787, copy; *ib.*, l. 1375, Sonora to Gálvez, May 8, 1786.

24. See below, pp. 116, 139.

CHAPTER V. GARDOQUI'S MISSION

1. AI, 86–7–24, (José de Gálvez) to Floridablanca, Dec. 20, 1783, draft, written in margin and at foot of Floridablanca to J. de

Gálvez, Dec. 9, 1783; *ib.*, El Conde de Gálvez to J. de Gálvez, Dec. 20, 1783.

2. AHN, E, l. 3885, exp. 24, Floridablanca to J. de Gálvez, July 29, 1784, and accompanying documents.

3. AI, 87-1-19, Navarro to J. de Gálvez, March 12, 1784, No. 202; *ib.*, PC, l. 3, Miró to El Conde de Gálvez, March 12, 1784, No. 108; AHN, E, l. 3885, exp. 18. A British vessel from Jamaica also appeared and claimed the right of free navigation under the treaty.

4. AHN, E, l. 3885, exp. 2, Navarro to J. de Gálvez, Sept. 10, 1781, and Dec. 15, 1781, both *res.*; *ib.*, J. de Gálvez to Floridablanca, March 26, 1782.

5. Cf. E. S. Corwin, *French Policy and the American Alliance*, 227–28.

6. AHN, E, l. 3885, exp. 20, El Conde de Gálvez to J. de Gálvez, May 23, 1784; *ib.*, Rendón to J. de Gálvez, Dec. 16, 1783, No. 91; *ib.*, exp. No. 1, "Breve relacion de las fronteras . . .," in Gardoqui's handwriting, endorsed: "Pertenece a la carta No. 7 de 16. de Nove. de 1783. de Dn. Bernardo del Campo."

7. AI, 146-3-11, Rendón to Gálvez, Feb. 12, 1785, No. 124.

8. AHN, E, l. 3457, exp. 23, "Instruccion sobre limites de las floridas y la Luisiana y sobre la navegacion del Misisipi," dated July 29, 1784, copy; *ib.*, l. 3885, exp. 24, El Conde de Gálvez to J. de Gálvez, Aug. 4, 1784.

9. This fact was called to my attention by Prof. S. F. Bemis.

10. On the merits of this dispute, see Corwin, *op. cit.*, 230, note 13; R. G. Adams, *History of the Foreign Policy of the United States*, 49; Jay, *Correspondence* (Johnston, ed., 1890–93), I, 248, and II, 1, 296; and Bemis, 51, 52.

11. AI, 146-3-11, Rendón to Gálvez, July 30, 1784, No. 104.

12. AHN, E. l. 3885, exp. 21, "Instruccion para Dn. Diego de Gardoqui . . .," unsigned and undated; AI, PC, l. 1375, (El Conde de Gálvez) to Floridablanca, Oct. 26, 1784, acknowledging the receipt of the royal order of Oct. 2 in regard to Gardoqui's appointment; Conrotte, *op. cit.*, 270–76, publishes the instructions and gives the date as Oct. 2, 1784.

13. Yela, I, 481, and Bemis, 70, erroneously state that Gardoqui's appointment resulted from the proposals of Adams, Franklin and Jefferson to Floridablanca through Aranda. As a matter of fact, Aranda's letter of transmission was written on Oct. 4, 1784, at Paris, two days after the final orders had been issued to Gardoqui.

14. AI, 146–3–11, Miralles to Gálvez, Dec. 28, 1778.

15. Yela, ii, 66.

16. Conrotte, *op. cit.*, 293–95; Yela, i, 382–83, ii, 325–26, 375–77; other documents are in AHN, E, l. 3884, exp. 4, and *ib.*, l. 893.

17. *Ib.*, l. 3894, Gardoqui to (Miguel de Otamendi), no date; AI, PC, l. 104, Gardoqui to Miró, Feb. 14, 1788.

18. E. Channing, *History of the United States*, iii, 408–27.

19. AHN, E, l. 3885, exp. 25, Rendón to Gálvez, April 20, 1784, and enclosed translation of letter from Robert Morris; *ib.*, l. 3893. Gardoqui to Floridablanca, Aug. 23, 1785, No. 14.

20. M. Farrand, *Records of the Federal Convention*, i, 583–84, 603–05; Rufus King Papers (mss., N. Y. Hist. Soc.), King to Adams, Nov. 2, 1785.

21. J. Elliot, *The Debates in the Several State Conventions on the Adoption of the Federal Constitution*, iii, 365–66.

22. *Secret Journals of Congress, Foreign Affairs*, iv, 45 *et seq.*

23. *Ib.*, 81–84. For Jay's first instructions, see *ib.*, iii, 568–71, 585–86.

24. AHN, E, l. 3894, Gardoqui to Floridablanca, Oct. 24, 1788, No. 298.

25. *Ib.*, l. 3893, same to same, Oct. 1, 1786, not numbered; Oct. 28, 1786, No. 124; and Dec. 31, 1786, No. 153.

CHAPTER VI. THE CHEVALIER OF THE ORDER OF
ST. LOUIS

1. AHN, E, l. 3889, exp. 6, Aranda to Floridablanca, April 2, 1787, No. 594, three enclosures. This *expediente* contains many other documents relating to d'Argès. A very different account of Spain's relations with d'Argès and White will be found in Bemis, ch. vii.

2. AHN, E, l. 4255, Campo to Floridablanca, London, July 13, 1787, with long note on cover by Floridablanca; *ib.*, autograph note by Floridablanca, Oct. 8, 1787.

3. AHN, E, l. 3893, "Resumen de cierta conversacion . . .," New York, Sept. 18, 1786, signed "D. G.," i.e., Diego de Gardoqui.

4. AHN, E, l. 3889, exp. 6, memorial by d'Argès. Clark is not mentioned by name, but the allusion is clear. *Ib.*, Floridablanca, to Valdés, August 3, 1787.

5. AI, PC, l. 176–2, Valdés to the Governor of Louisiana, Aug. 23, 1787, copy; AHN, E, l. 3889, exp. 6, (Floridablanca) to Gardoqui, Sept. 5, 1787, No. 5.

6. *Ib.*, Floridablanca to Valdés, Aug. 24, 1787; *ib.*, exp. 5, five documents relating to Gayoso's appointment; AI, PC, l. 176–2, Valdés to Gayoso, Nov. 3, 1787 *res.*

7. Floridablanca to Gardoqui, cited in note 5, above.

8. AHN, E, l. 3889, exp. 6, (Floridablanca) to d'Argès, Oct. 6, 1787, draft; *ib.*, (Floridablanca) to Gardoqui, Oct. 6, 1787, draft; cf. note 23, ch. XII.

9. AHN, E, l. 3894, (Floridablanca) to Gardoqui, May 24, 1788, No. 5, draft; *ib.*, l. 3893 *bis*, Gardoqui to Floridablanca, Nov. 1, 1787, No. 217.

10. *Ib.*, l. 3893 *bis*, a document containing in parallel columns the treaty plans of 1786 and 1787.

11. *Ib.*, l. 3894, Gardoqui to Floridablanca, April 18, 1788, No. 235.

12. *Ib.*, l. 3889, exp. 6, Gardoqui to Floridablanca, Feb. 16, 1788, No. 231; *ib.*, same to same, April 18, 1788, No. 246; *ib.*, d'Argès to Floridablanca, March 27, 1788. On July 6, 1787, Gardoqui had written Floridablanca that there was a chevalier of St. Louis living with much ostentation in Danville, Kentucky, and said to be a French agent: *ib.*, l. 3893, No. 17 *res.*

13. Gardoqui to Miró, Feb. 21, 1788, copy, enclosed in Gardoqui to Floridablanca, No. 246 (see note 12, above).

14. AI, 86–6–8, Miró to Valdés, March 15, 1788, No. 19 *res.*; AHN, E, l. 3889, exp. 6, d'Argès to Floridablanca, May 22, June 17, Aug. 27, 1788, and Jan. 2, 1789 (four letters); Gayarré, 217–18.

15. *Ib.*, Miró to Valdés, March 16, 1790, No. 48 *res.*

CHAPTER VII. INTRIGUE AND IMMIGRATION

1. The Spanish archives are indispensable for the study of the frontier intrigue with Spain, and no comprehensive account, based on those sources, has ever been written. An excellent beginning has been made by W. R. Shepherd (A. H. R., IX, 490) and I. J. Cox (*ib.*, XIX, 794), but much remains to be done. My own articles, based on research in Spain, are in M. V. H. R., Sept., 1925, and Dec., 1926. See also A. Henderson, in Tenn. Hist. Mag., III, 229, and *The Conquest of the Old Southwest;* T. Bodley, Introduction to *Reprints of Littell's Political Transactions,* etc. (Filson Club Publications:

No. 31); and M. Serrano y Sanz, *El Brigadier Jaime Wilkinson*, etc. Mr. Bodley made no use of Spanish sources. Older works dealing with the subject are Gayarré, 193–301; Roosevelt (cf. index); T. M. Green, *The Spanish Conspiracy;* and H. Marshall, *The History of Kentucky.* So far as Wilkinson is concerned, Prof. Shepherd first called attention to the frontier initiative in the intrigue: *loc. cit.,* 491.

2. A. V. Goodpasture, *op. cit.,* 110–12; A. Henderson, "Richard Henderson and the Occupation of Kentucky," in M. V. H. R., Dec., 1914; C. R. N. Ca., IX, 982.

3. E.g., S. R. N. Ca., XXII, 651–52.

4. Wilkinson made this point in his "Essay" or memorial of 1787. See note 18, below.

5. *Calendar of Virginia State Papers,* IV., 242; Green, *op. cit.,* 76–77, 109–10, 385–86.

6. W. W. Henry, *Patrick Henry,* III, 374–77; S. R. N. Ca., XVIII, 483, 756–59, 775–77; XXII, 1005; XX, 761–62; A. S. P., I. A., I, 17; Papers of the Continental Congress (mss., LC), 78, vol. XXI, fol. 481, Sevier to the President of Congress, Nov. 2, 1787.

7. *Calendar of Virginia State Papers,* IV, 242–43; Draper Mss. (Hist. Soc. Wisconsin), 5 XX 18 and 6 XX 105; Green, *op. cit.,* 109–10.

8. S. R. N. Ca., XXII, 676–78, Green, *op. cit.,* 110–12.

9. *Letters of R. H. Lee* (ed. Ballagh), II, 424; Washington, *Writings,* XI, 78.

10. W. W. Henry, *Patrick Henry,* III, 292–97; Green, *op. cit.,* 109–10; Papers of the Continental Congress (mss., LC), 78, vol. XXI, fol. 477, and 150, vol. III, fol. 17; *Gazette of the State of Georgia* (newspaper), April 3, 1788, letter from John Sullivan to Gov. Pinckney. Hugh Williamson of North Carolina, one of the leaders of the Mississippi party in Congress, seems to have been interested in Western lands.

11. Compiled from "Entries and Sailings at the Port of New Orleans" (transcript, Harvard College Library, obtained by Prof. E. Channing from AI); W. W. Carson, "Transportation and Traffic on the Ohio," M. V. H. R., VII, 33.

12. A. S. P., I. A., I, 252.

13. AI, PC, l. 2374, Wilkinson to (Carondelet), Dec. 15, 1792.

14. *Ib.,* Miró to Wilkinson, Sept. 20, 1790. In his *residencia,* Miró was accused of making 2000 *pesos* a year through his trans-

actions with Wilkinson. The charge was not substantiated: AHN, Consejos, Consejo de Indias.

15. Bodley, x, note 11.

16. AI, PC, l. 199. Wilkinson's letter is dated Dec. 20, 1786; Anderson's, Jan. 1, 1786 (*sic*: 1787). I am preparing an article on this subject for early publication in H. A. H. R.

17. AI, PC, l. 2373, contains the original of this memorial, in Wilkinson's handwriting and signed by him. Another copy of the original, which I have not seen, is reported to exist in the archives of the Louisiana Historical Society: See *Publications* of that Society, IX, 45–54. See also W. R. Shepherd in A. H. R., IX, 748 *et seq*.

18. AHN, E, l. 3888 *bis*, Miró and Navarro to (the *Ministro de Indias*), Sept. 25, 1787, No. 13 *res.*, enclosing an English copy and a Spanish translation of Wilkinson's memorial.

19. *Ib.*, *extracto* beginning "Resvda Nueva Orleans 25 de Sepre de 1787 . . .," dated at end: "a 23 de En[e]ro de [17]88."

20. These numerous documents form an *expediente*, which is in AHN, E, l. 3888 *bis*.

21. *Ib.*, Navarro to Valdés, Nov. 11, 1788.

22. AHN, E, AJE, Nov. 20, 1788; *ib.*, l. 3888 *bis*, (Valdés) to the Governor of Louisiana, Dec. 1, 1788; A. H. R., IX, 749–50.

23. AI, PC, l. 4, Sonora to the Governor of Louisiana, Jan. 12, 1786, copy.

24. For another view, see W. R. Shepherd in A. H. R., IX, 492, possibly misled by Wilkinson, *Memoirs of my Own Times*, II, 111–13.

25. Jefferson, *Writings*, v, 316. The phrase alluding to the Goths occurs in a personal letter from Prof. S. E. Morison.

26. Wilkinson, *Memoirs*, II, 117.

27. The best statements of the considerations that guided the Spanish authorities are contained in the letters of Miró and Navarro, referred to in notes 18 and 21, above.

CHAPTER VIII. THE UNION PRESERVED

1. This subject is discussed in detail, with references, in my article, "The Muscle Shoals Speculation," in M. V. H. R., XIII, 365.

2. This subject is discussed in detail, with references, in my article, "The Spanish Intrigue in the Old Southwest: An Episode," in *ib.*, XII, 155.

3. A bibliographical note on Bowles will be found in C. M. Brevard, *A History of Florida*, I, 23, note 21.

4. AI, PC, l. 2373, Wilkinson to Gayoso, Nashville, Nov. 10 (16?), 1789, and Lexington, Jan. 26, 1790; and drafts of (Miró) to Daniel Smith, Sept. 15, 1789, and to James Robertson, Sept. 16, 1789.

5. Cf. Letter from Harry Innes to Gayoso, cited in note 16, ch. XIII.

6. AI, 86–6–17, Miró to Valdés, Dec. 31, 1789, No. 46 *res.*

7. *Ib.*, 86–6–8, Miró to Valdés, June 15, 1788, No. 20 *res.*; *ib.*, PC, l. 2373, (Miró) to Wilkinson, Aug. 6, 1788, draft.

8. *Ib.*, Wilkinson to Miró, Feb. 12, 1789. Wilkinson added that after Kentucky had seceded from the Union the king of Spain could "dictate his own terms."

9. *Ib.*, Wilkinson to Miró, Feb. 12, 1789; cf. Green, *op. cit.*, 186–97, and Bodley, xlvii–liv.

10. AI, 86–6–17, Wilkinson's second memorial, undated, but written on Sept. 17, 1789, and enclosed in Spanish translation in Miró to Valdés, No. 46 *res.*; A. H. R., IX, 751–64.

11. *Ib.*; Wilkinson, *Memoirs*, II, 237 and Appendix, No. I, deposition of Oliver Pollock, June 8, 1808.

12. Washington, *Writings*, XI, 43, note; *ib.*, 163–64.

13. AHN, E, l. 3894, Gardoqui to Floridablanca, Oct. 24, 1788, No. 298.

14. J. J. Fitzpatrick, ed., *The Diaries of George Washington*, IV, 54, 74–77, 87, 90, 95–96, 127, 132–33, 157, 196.

15. Innes Papers (mss., LC), vol. XIX, fol. 3, John Brown to Harry Innes, Sept. 28, 1789.

16. Hamilton Papers (mss., LC), vol. IX, fols. 1138–55, cabinet opinion, Sept. 15, 1790.

17. Draper Mss., 4 xx 18a, Caswell to Sevier, July 12, 1786; A. S. P., I. A., I, 203–06; Pickering Mss. (Mass. Hist. Soc.), *Western Indians*, 1786–1793, fol. 16, Information of Captain Wellbank; "The Papers of General Daniel Smith," in American Hist. Mag., VI, 218–19. Anthony Wayne made a vigorous effort to secure this appointment: Wayne Mss. (Hist. Soc. Pennsylvania), vol. XIX, *passim.*

18. Green, *op. cit.*, note to pp. 250–53; cf. 239 and note.

19. Heitman, *Historical Register of the United States Army*, I, 1037.

20. Bodley, lxix.

21. A. S. P., I. A., I, 124–25.

CHAPTER IX. YAZOO

1. Draper Mss., XI DD 87a, Henry to Joseph Martin, March 10, 1790; W. W. Henry, *Patrick Henry*, III, 412–15.

2. Draper Mss., IX DD 48, Col. A. Campbell to "Mr. Davis" (June, 1788); *ib.*, IX DD 51, Harry Innes to A. Campbell, Sept. 19, 1788.

3. A. S. P., I. A., I, 112–13; C. H. Haskins, "The Yazoo Land Companies," in Am. Hist. Assn., *Papers*, V, 395 *et seq.*; AI, PC, Wilkinson to Miró, l. 2374, April 29, 1790.

4. AHN, E, l. 3894, Gardoqui to Floridablanca, April 18, 1788, No. 252 (von Steuben); AI, PC, l. 104, Gardoqui to Miró, Oct. 4, 1788 (Morgan); AHN, E, l. 3894, Gardoqui to Floridablanca, July 25, 1788, No. 280 (O'Fallon); *ib.*, same to same, same date, No. 282, enclosing Spanish translation of letter from G. R. Clark to Gardoqui, March 15, 1788.

5. AI, PC, l. 2373, Wilkinson to (Miró and Navarro), March 16, 1788; *ib.*, 86–6–8, Miró to Valdés, Nov. 3, 1788, No. 29, *res.*, enclosing a Spanish translation of a news item in the *Pennsylvania Gazette* (Carlisle), Aug. 6, 1788. For O'Fallon, see note 4, above.

6. AHN, E, l. 3894, Gardoqui to Floridablanca, June 25, 1789, No. 316, and enclosures.

7. Draper Mss., *Georgia, Alabama and South Carolina*, V, 72, Alexander Moultrie to John Sevier, March 8, 1790.

8. AI, PC, l. 2374, James O'Fallon to Wilkinson, April 10, 1791, copy.

9. AHN, E, l. 3894, Gardoqui to Floridablanca, July 25, 1788, No. 280, enclosing Spanish translation of O'Fallon to Gardoqui, May 26, 1788; AI, PC, l. 2373, unsigned document in Wilkinson's handwriting, stating that these "crude memorandums" were designed for Miró and Navarro.

10. *Ib.*, l. 202, Moultrie to Farrar, Jan. 24, 1790; l. 203, Moultrie to McGillivray, Feb. 19, 1790, copy; l. 2371, T. Washington to Col. Bruin, March 16, 1790.

11. Draper Mss., *Georgia, Alabama and South Carolina*, V, *South Carolina*, 73, dated March 9, 1790.

12. AI, PC, l. 2371, O'Fallon to Miró, May 13, 1790, and May 24, 1790; *ib.*, l. 1446, same to same, July 16, 1790, Spanish translation, enclosed in Miró to Las Casas, Oct. 7, 1790, No. 9 *res.*

13. *Ib.*, l. 2374, Wilkinson to Miró, March 19, 1791, enclosing copy of letter to Wilkinson from J(ohn) B(rown), Feb. 10, 1791.

14. AI, 86–6–20, Las Casas to Campo de Alange, Aug. 3. 1791, No. 12 *res.*, enclosing copy of Washington's proclamation of March 19, 1791, referring to earlier proclamations of Aug. 14 and 26, 1790.

15. A. S. P., I. A., I, 112–13; "Correspondence of General James Robertson," in American Hist. Mag., I, 192–93.

16. AI, PC, l. 203, McGillivray to Miró (original) and to Panton (copy), May 8, 1790, reported that Col. Willett, agent of President Washington, said that the United States government desired a treaty with the Creek as a means of defeating the Georgia companies.

17. AI, PC, l. 203, McGillivray to Panton, May 8, 1790.

18. A. S. P., I. A., I, 65–68; F. L. Humphreys, *Life of David Humphreys*, II, 4–15; E. S. Maclay, ed., *Journal of William Maclay*, 128–33; AI, PC, l. 202, McGillivray to Miró, Dec. 10, 1789.

19. AI, PC, l. 202, (Miró) to McGillivray, July 22, 1789, draft; l. 4, Miró to O'Neill, March 24, 1787, *muy res.*; AHN, E, AJE, June 14, 1790.

20. A. S. P., I. A., I, 75; Fitzpatrick, ed., *Diaries of George Washington*, IV, 54; Maclay, ed., *Journal of William Maclay*, 174–75.

21. Fitzpatrick, ed., *Diaries of George Washington*, IV, 95–96. Washington, recording a conference with Willett, says they discussed "such lures as respected McGillivray personally . . ."; AI, PC, l. 203, Panton to Miró, July 12, 1790.

22. *New York Journal* (newspaper), July 9, 23, 30, Aug. 3, 10 and 17, 1790.

23. Knox Papers (mss., Mass. Hist. Soc.), vol. XXVI, fol. 145, witnessed by Justice John Blair of the United States Supreme Court.

24. At my request, Prof. S. F. Bemis searched for these articles in the Archives of the Department of State, Washington, and informed me that they are to be found there together with the public treaty. See Pickett, *History of Alabama*, 406, 407.

25. Gov. Zéspedes of St. Augustine sent his secretary, Carlos Howard, to New York in a vain effort to keep McGillivray loyal: AI, PC, l. 1440, Zéspedes to Cabello, June 1, 1790; Fitzpatrick, ed., *Diaries of George Washington*, IV, 132–33.

26. AI, PC, l. 203, (Miró) to McGillivray, Nov. 20, 1790, draft; AHN, E, l. 3898, Carondelet to Aranda, July 7, 1792, No. 4 *res.*

CHAPTER X. NOOTKA

1. W. S. Robertson, *Francisco de Miranda*, in Am. Hist. Assn., *Report*, 1907, I, 266-87; F. J. Turner, ed., "English Policy toward America in 1790-1791," in A. H. R., VII, 706-35.

2. W. R. Manning, *The Nootka Controversy*, in Am. Hist. Assn., *Report*, 1904, 279 *et seq.*, especially ch. x.

3. AI, PC, l. 2374, Wilkinson to Moutier (*sic:* Moultrie), Huger, Snipes and T. Washington, Jan. 4, 1790, copy; l. 2371, Moultrie to Wilkinson, Sept. 5, 1790; l. 2374, Wilkinson to Miró, May 20, 1790, and June 30, 1790.

4. *Ib.*, Wilkinson to Moultrie, Nov. 4 (1790), copy in Wilkinson's handwriting; same to Miró, Feb. 14, 1791.

5. Fitzpatrick, ed., *Diaries of George Washington*, IV, 127; Robertson, ed., *Louisiana under Spain*, etc., I, 263; W. C. Ford, *The United States and Spain in 1790;* AI, PC, l. 1446, Miró to Las Casas, Oct. 7, 1790, enclosing Spanish translation of Wilkinson to Miró, Aug. 27, 1790 (original in l. 2374).

6. *Ib.*, l. 1446, Miró to Las Casas, May 8, 1791, No. 24 *res.*; l. 2371, O'Fallon to (Miró), Jan. 15, 1791.

7. *Ib.*, l. 2374, Wilkinson to Miró, March 17, 1791.

8. *Ib.*, letter cited in preceding note; cf. same to same, May 9, 1791, in *ib.*, in which the *coup de grâce* is attributed to Washington's proclamation.

9. C. H. Haskins, *op. cit.*, 409-12; Etting Collection (mss., Hist. Soc. Pennsylvania), *Old Congress Mss.*, vol. II, Henry to Gen. Charles Scot, July 20, 1790.

10. C. H. Haskins, *op. cit.*, 413; Draper Mss., IX DD 65, Strother to Campbell, Feb. 18, 1791; A. S. P., I. A., I, 112-13; "Correspondence of General James Robertson," in Am. Hist. Mag., I, 192-93; AI, PC, l. 1446, Miró to Las Casas, July 17, 1791, No. 31 *res.*, enclosing translation of McGillivray to Miró, June 8, 1791.

11. AI, 86-6-18, Miró to Valdés, May 22, 1790, No. 50 *res.*, on Wilkinson; *ib.*, l. 177, same to same, same date, No. 49 *res.*, draft, on O'Fallon.

12. *Ib.*, l. 2374, Wilkinson to (Miró), Jan. 26, 1790; Green, *op. cit.*, 326 and note, calls attention to this fact, and says that Wilkinson and Peyton Short formed a partnership that was disastrous financially.

13. Bemis, 170-72.

14. AHN, E, l. 3384, copy in French, dated June 1, 1791.

15. A. S. P., F. R., I, 250–51, 252–57; W. Jay, *Life of John Jay*, II, 187.

16. AHN, E, l. 3889 *bis*, exp. 4, "Estados Unidos/1791/Dictamen que dio D. Diego de Gardoqui . . .," Aug. 22, 1791, signed.

17. *Ib.*, l. 3898, Floridablanca to the governor of Havana, Sept. 28, 1791.

18. AME, Archivo de la Legación de S. M. C., Washington, D. C., Caja No. 5, l. 198, Floridablanca to Jáudenes and Viar, Sept. 6, 1791.

19. AHN, E, l. 3894 *bis*, Jáudenes and Viar to Floridablanca, Dec. 18, 1791, No. 61.

20. *Ib.*, same to same, March 26, 1792, No. 82.

21. A. S. P., F. R., I, 251.

22. AHN, E, l. 3894 *bis*, Jáudenes and Viar to Aranda, Oct. 29, 1792, No. 124.

23. Jefferson, *Writings* (ed. Ford), v, 74–75.

Chapter XI. Hector, Baron de Carondelet

1. AI, 86–6–8, Miró to Valdés, Oct. 8, 1788, No. 121; cf. D. K. Bjork, ed., "Documents relating to the Establishment of Schools in Louisiana, 1771," in M. V. H. R., XI, 562.

2. AHN, E, l. 3899, Carondelet to the Duke de la Alcudia (Godoy), Aug. 20, 1795, personal.

3. AI, PC, l. 2354, Carondelet to Las Casas, Sept. 17, 1794, No. 124 *res.*; Las Casas' reply, Oct. 17, 1794, draft, is in *ib.*, l. 1447.

4. AHN, E, ACE, May 2, 1794; AI, PC, l. 1447, Carondelet to Las Casas, Dec. 30, 1793, No. 99 *res.*; *ib.* 86–7–25, Miró to ——, Aug. 7, 1792, copy.

5. AI, PC, l. 1446, Carondelet to Las Casas, Jan. 13, 1792, No. 1 *res.*

6. Heitman, *Historical Register*, I, 1037; Washington, *Writings*, XII, 158, Washington to Knox, Aug. 13, 1792, commending Wilkinson highly. For Wilkinson's financial difficulties at this time, see Green, *op. cit.*, 326.

7. AI, PC, l. 2374, (Carondelet) to (Wilkinson), Feb. 1, 1792, draft, in the handwriting of Gayoso and Armesto; AHN, E, l. 3898, Carondelet to Floridablanca, Feb. 16, 1792, No. 7 *res.*

8. Though the Spanish sources are abundant, I have not discussed Morgan's project in detail, since it was not executed as he

conceived it, and led to no important results. Those who are interested will find further information in L. Houck, *Missouri under the Spanish Régime*, and in Roosevelt.

9. J. Pope, *A Tour through the Southern and Western Territories*, 28, 33.

10. See references in note 10, ch. VIII.

11. AI, PC, l. 41, (Miró) to (post commanders), Feb. 3, 1790, circular; AI, PC, l. 177, Miró to Lerena, Jan. 17, 1791, No. 32, draft.

12. W. W. Henry, *Patrick Henry*, III, 384–85.

13. AI, 86-7-25, Miró to ——, Aug. 7, 1792, copy; *ib.*, PC, l. 177, (Miró) to Lerena, Sept. 24, 1791, No. 76, draft; *ib.*, l. 204, petition of the inhabitants of Natchez district to his Catholic Majesty, copy, unsigned, and undated; AHN, E, l. 3901, (Floridablanca) to Miró, Dec. 25, 1790; *ib.*, AJE, Dec. 20, 1790; Am. Hist. Assn., *Report*, 1896, I, 979.

14. Samuel S. Forman Correspondence (mss., N. Y. Public Library), 1790–1823, Ezekiel Forman to Samuel Forman, Natchez, April 18, 1790.

15. AI, PC, l. 177, (Gayoso) to Floridablanca, Sept. 10, 1790, draft; *ib.*, l. 2374, Wilkinson to Miró, Dec. 17, 1790, two letters.

16. *Ib.*, Wilkinson to Carondelet, Dec. 15, 1792; l. 2371, M. Lacassagne to Carondelet, Oct. 1, 1794.

17. *Ib.*, l. 2353, Gayoso to Carondelet, Oct. 26, 1792, No. 184; l. 2374, Wilkinson to Miró, Dec. 17, 1790; l. 42, Gayoso to Carondelet, Aug. 6, 1793, No. 338, and Robert Stark to (Carondelet) Jan. 31, 1795.

18. AI, PC, l. 4, Miró to Grand-Pré, Oct. 8, 1787, No. 277; C. M. Brevard, *A History of Florida*, 267–70, Appendix VI: and letter of Robert Stark cited in note 17, above.

19. AHN, E, l. 3890, exp. 34, Luis de Vilemont (*sic*) to Alcudia (Godoy), no date or place; *ib.*, ACE, Nov. 13, 1795.

20. AI, PC, l. 1446, Carondelet to Las Casas, Jan. 13, 1792, No. 1 *res.*, and May 16, 1792, No. 28 *res.*, and enclosures.

21. *Ib.*, l. 2363, Panton to Carondelet, Aug. 4, 1793.

22. *Ib.*, l. 1441, Carondelet to Las Casas, Jan. 18, 1792, No. 11.

23. *Ib.*, l. 1446, same to same, March 13, 1792, No. 6 *res.*, and enclosures; and same to same, Sept. 10, 1792, No. 47 *res.* Grenville denied that the British government had any connection with Bowles: Campo to Aranda, July 20, 1792, AHN, E, l. 3889 *bis*, exp. 10.

24. *Ib.*, l. 3898, Carondelet to Floridablanca, April 4, 1792, No. 19 *res.*, enclosing copy of Carondelet to Olivier, March 30, 1792; Carondelet to Aranda, June 10, 1792, No. 1 *res.*; AI, PC, l. 1446, Carondelet to Las Casas, July 31, 1792, No. 37 *res.*, enclosing a copy of the convention, dated at New Orleans, July 6, 1792; *ib.*, l. 152–1, Las Casas to Carondelet, July 5 and July 7, 1792.

25. See my article, "Spain and the Cherokee Indians, 1783–1795," in North Carolina. Hist. Rev., July, 1927.

26. AI, PC, l. 2353, "Puntos sobre los quales se deve tratar en el Congreso de los indios," Feb. 26, 1793, signed by Carondelet; discussed by Jane M. Berry, *loc. cit.*

27. AI, PC, l. 203, Panton to Carondelet, Nov. 6, 1792.

28. *Ib.*, l. 2353, (Gayoso) to Carondelet, Dec. 6, 1793, No. 12, "Oficio ulto. de la Asamblea."

29. Gayoso freely criticized Carondelet for stirring up the Indians against the Americans: AHN, E, l. 3902, Gayoso to Alcudia, Sept. 19, 1794, No. 1 *res.*, and Alcudia to the governor of New Orleans, Jan. 24, 1795. Cf. Roosevelt, IV, 185.

30. Jefferson, *Writings*, VI, 321–24, 315–16.

31. AHN, E, l. 3894 *bis*, Jáudenes and Viar to Aranda, Oct. 29, 1792, No. 125; l. 3895, same to Alcudia, May 29, 1793, No. 156, and enclosures; and same to same, July 14, 1793, No. 168, enclosing copy of their letter to Jefferson of June 18, 1793; Jefferson, *Writings*, 99, 118, 269–71, 271–73, 314–15, 330–38, 344; A. S. P., F. R., I, 267.

CHAPTER XII.   THE FRENCH REVOLUTION AND THE SPANISH EMPIRE

1. AHN, E, l. 3889 *bis*, exp. 11, Carmichael and Short to Alcudia, Aranjuez, Feb. 6, 1793.

2. There is no biography of Godoy in Spanish. Edmund B. D'Auvergne, *Godoy: the Queen's Favorite*, is well illustrated. Godoy's *Memoirs* are not reliable. There is a good biographical sketch in the *Enciclopedia Universal Ilustrada*. In November, 1792, when he became first secretary of state, his title was Duke de la Alcudia. In September, 1795, Charles IV conferred on him the title of Prince of the Peace, as a reward for having secured peace with France in the treaty of Bâle.

3. B. P. R. O., F. O., *Spain*, 72/38, Bute to Grenville, Aug. 5, 1795, No. 14; AHN, E, ACE, Nov. 22, 1795; Department of

State, *Despatches, Hague and Spain*, I, 150, Short to Sec. of State, Jan. 9, 1794.

4. AHN, E, ACE, Nov. 16, 1792, and Feb. 19, 1793.

5. A. S. P., F. R., I, 278; AHN, E, ACE, July 7, 1794.

6. AI, 87–3–19, contains an *expediente* on this subject.

7. AI, PC, l. 2353, Gardoqui to the Captain-General of Cuba *etc.*, June 9, 1793, copy.

8. *Ib.*, l. 178, (Carondelet) to Gardoqui, May 16, 1793, No. 74 *res.*, draft; *ib.*, l. 104, same to Jáudenes and Viar, Aug. 13, 1793, draft.

9. AI, 86–7–9, Representation to H. C. M., signed by Francisco Xavier Sánchez and others, St. Augustine, Nov. 27, 1794; Pickett, *History of Alabama*, 367; cf. A. S. P., I. A., I, 458.

10. See my article, "Spain and the Cherokee Indians, 1783–1795," in North Carolina Hist. Rev., July, 1927.

11. AI, PC, l. 203, Panton to Carondelet, April 4, 1793, and July 3, 1794; *ib.*, l. 104, Carondelet to Jáudenes and Viar, Sept. 18, 1793, draft.

12. *Ib.*, l. 2354, Panton, Leslie and Co. to Carondelet, not dated.

13. B. P. R. O., F. O., *Spain*, 72/38, Bute to Grenville, Sept. 10, 1795, No. 20, "Most Secret."

14. AHN, E, l. 3889 *bis*, exp. 11, (Alcudia) to Carmichael and Short, Jan. 19, 1794, draft; A. S. P., F. R., I, 445–46.

15. *Ib.*, ACE, March 7, 1794.

16. *Ib.*, l. 3895 *bis*, Jáudenes and Viar to Alcudia, March 13, 1794, No. 213.

17. AHN, E, l. 4249, Campo to Alcudia, March 28, 1794, No. 1.

18. *Ib.*, ACE, Dec. 13 and 20, 1793.

19. *Ib.*, May 2, 1794; AME, *Archivo de la Legación de S. M. C., Washington, D. C.*, l. 201, Alcudia to Jáudenes, May 9, 1794, in cipher, accompanied by a deciphered copy.

20. A. S. P., F. R., I, 469; AHN, E, l. 3895 *bis*, Jáudenes to Alcudia, Nov. 30, 1794, No. 273; W. H. Trescot, *The Diplomatic History of the Administrations of Washington and Adams*, 239–40, 240–45; Washington, *Writings*, XII, 459, note.

21. Yela, II, 342–50; AHN, E, l. 3894 *bis*, Jáudenes and Viar to Floridablanca, Dec. 18, 1791, No. 61; Jefferson, *Writings*, VI, 206.

22. AHN, E, l. 3895 *bis*, Jáudenes and Viar to Alcudia, April 23, 1794, No. 220.

23. AHN, E, ACE, July 7, 1794. The session began with the reading of the letter cited in note 22, above.

24. *Ib.*, l. 3895 *bis*, (Alcudia) to Jáudenes and Viar, "[blank] de Julio de 1794," in Godoy's handwriting.

Chapter XIII. The Intrigue Infallible

1. E. M. Coulter, "The Efforts of the Democratic Societies of the West to Open the Navigation of the Mississippi," in M. V. H. R., xi, 376; W. Jay, *Life of John Jay*, ii, 233.

2. F. J. Turner, "The Policy of France toward the Mississippi Valley," in A. H. R., x, 249, and "Correspondence of the French Ministers to the United States, 1791–97," in Am. Hist. Assn., *Report*, 1903, ii.

3. Washington, *Writings*, xii, 450–53.

4. F. J. Turner, "The Origin of Genêt's projected Attack on Louisiana and the Floridas," in A. H. R., iii, 650; and "The Correspondence of Clark and Genêt," Am. Hist. Assn., *Report*, 1896, i, 930–1107; *ib.*, *Report*, 1897, p. 569; AI, PC, l. 1469, Las Casas to the *encargados* at Philadelphia, May 6, 1794, draft, relative to Abner Hammond.

5. B. Faÿ, *L'Esprit révolutionnaire en France et aux États-Unis à la fin du XVIIIᵉ siècle*.

6. Jefferson, *Writings*, vi, 206; cf. A. S. P., F. R., i, 454–55.

7. AHN, E, l. 3889 *bis*, exp. 11, *minuta*, unsigned and undated, relating to Short's status; B. W. Bond, *The Monroe Mission to France*, 23; S. F. Bemis, *Jay's Treaty*.

8. Washington, *Writings*, 451, note; A. S. P., F. R., i, 454; E. M. Coulter, *loc. cit.*, 388; Calendar of Virginia State Papers, vii, 373–75. Wilkinson sent Carondelet a newspaper containing the correspondence between Col. Innes and Gov. Shelby: AI, PC, l. 3899, Carondelet to Alcudia, July 1, 1795, No. 54 *res.*

9. AHN, E, l. 3899, Carondelet to Las Casas, May 3, 1795, *muy res.*

10. This is the most neglected period of Wilkinson's long intrigue with Spain, and the abundant Spanish sources have hardly been touched. See Gayarré, 358–65; Wilkinson, *Memoirs*, ii, Appendix, Nos. xxxix–xlvi; Green, *op. cit.*, 327–35, 342–69; Bodley, xcv–cxvi; M. Serrano y Sanz, *El Brigadier Jaime Wilkinson*, etc.

11. AI, PC, l. 126, M. Lacassagne to Carondelet, Jan. 20, 1794.

12. AHN, E, l. 3899, Carondelet to Alcudia, No. 31 *res.*, April 7, 1794; AI, PC, l. 2363, same to same, July 9, 1794, No. 38, *res.*, copy; *ib.*, l. 1447, Carondelet to Las Casas, Aug. 18, 1794, No. 123 *res.*

13. AHN, E, l. 3899, Carondelet to Alcudia, March 11, 1794, autograph, personal, endorsed by Godoy: "Ignoro esto . . ." Other documents relating to this subject are in AI, 86–6–10.

14. AI, 87–1–19, Navarro to José de Gálvez, July 20, 1781, No. 62; 87–3–19, Navarro to Valdés, April 26, 1789, No. 3, copy; 86–6–8, Miró and Navarro to Valdés, April 1, 1788, No. 55.

15. AI, 87–3–21, Carondelet to Gardoqui, May 16, 1793, No. 75 *res.*; same to same, Dec. 15, 1793, No. 94; 86–7–15, same to same, Aug. 27, 1792; 87–3–21, note by the *mesa* on letter of Don Honratio Fortier.

16. AI, PC, l. 2371, Harry Innes to Gayoso, Feb. 14, 1794. The two letters of Innes cited in this and the following note seem to me to demolish completely the case that Mr. Bodley has built up for him in *op. cit.*

17. AI, PC, l. 2371, Gayoso to Innes, July 27, 1794, and duplicate dated Aug. 23, 1794; Harry Innes to Gayoso, Dec. 11, 1794; (Gayoso) to Carondelet, March 24, 1795, draft.

18. AHN, E, l. 3899, Carondelet to Alcudia, Aug. 18, 1794, No. 43 *res.*; AI, PC, l. 2374, Wilkinson to (Gayoso), May 25, 1790.

19. AI, PC, l. 2374, Wilkinson to (Carondelet), Jan. 12, 1795, in cipher, and deciphered copy.

20. AI, PC, l. 211, statement of Wilkinson's account, copy in English; see Bemis, illustration facing p. 346; cf. Wilkinson, *Memoirs*, II, 1–120, especially 117–19 and note.

21. AHN, E, l. 3895, Jáudenes and Viar to Alcudia, Oct. 16, 1793, No. 198; AI, PC, l. 2371, M. Mitchell to Gayoso, June 20, 1794; AI, *Estado, Audiencia de Sto. Domingo*, l. 5, Las Casas to Campo de Alange, Jan. 26, 1795, No. 468, enclosing a copy of the committee's representation; AI, PC, l. 211, David Bradford to Gayoso, Natchez, Jan. 22, 1795.

22. AHN, E, ACE, July 25, 1794.

23. AME, *Archivo de la Legación de S. M. C., Washington, D. C.*, l. 201, Alcudia to Jáudenes and Viar, July 26, 1794, principal and duplicate, and two deciphered copies.

24. AHN, E, l. 3899, Carondelet to Alcudia, June 3, 1794, No. 36 *res.*, with *indice* in Carondelet's handwriting stating that the

success of the Kentucky negotiation "le parece infalible," and *minuta* with Godoy's autograph note; same to same, Oct. 8, 1794, No. 47 *res.*, and draft of Godoy's reply, dated Jan. 24, 1795; same to same, Aug. 18, 1794, No. 43 *res.*, with autograph note by Godoy on cover; AHN, E, l. 3895 *bis*, draft of letter from Alcudia (Godoy) to Jáudenes, Feb. 24, 1795.

25. AHN, E, l. 3895 *bis*, fragment of an *informe*, undated, on various letters from Jáudenes and Viar of June 4, 1794.

Chapter XIV. San Lorenzo: A Frontier Treaty

1. Bemis, 244; AHN, E, l. 3895 *bis*, Jáudenes to Alcudia, Dec. 8, 1794, No. 275.

2. B. W. Bond, *The Monroe Mission to France*, 40; Monroe Papers (mss., N. Y. Public Library), (Monroe) to the Secretary of State, March 17, 1795, No. 13.

3. AMAE, CP, *Espagne, Supplément*, vol. 25, fol. 04, Committee of Public Safety to Barthélémy, May 10, 1795; *ib.*, fols. 06–12, Instructions to Barthélémy, same date.

4. Department of State, Bureau of Indexes and Archives, *Despatches, England, T. Pinckney*, Pinckney to the Secretary of State, April 3 and 23, 1795.

5. AI, *Indiferente General*, 146–3–10, Thomas Pinckney to Wm. Short, Sept. 26, 1795. I am preparing for early publication a note on Godoy's knowledge of the terms of Jay's treaty.

6. AHN, E, l. 3370, *carpeta* 13, the original treaty, dated at Bâle, July 22, 1795, together with three secret articles, same date.

7. W. H. Trescot, *op. cit.*, 253–54, quoting from Godoy's *Memoirs;* Roosevelt, iv, 207; H. Adams, *History of the United States*, etc., i, 348–49; E. Channing, *History of the United States*, iv, 146; Bemis, 326–31. Other explanations are advanced by B. W. Bond, *op. cit.*, 40; F. J. Turner, "The Policy of France," in A. H. R., x, 266–67; and F. W. Paxson, *History of the American Frontier*, 85.

8. AHN, E, l. 4247, Campo to Alcudia, July 10, Aug. 7, Aug. 18, Sept. 25, 1795; Godoy, *Mémoires du Prince de la Paix*, i, 349–50.

9. B. P. R. O., F. O., *Spain*, 72/41, Bute to Grenville, May 18, 1796, No. 12.

10. *Ib.*, 72/38, Bute to Grenville, July 19, 1795, "Most secret & private."

11. AHN, E, ACE, Nov. 22 and 27, 1795; B. P. R. O., F. O., Spain, 72/39, Bute to Grenville, Oct. 31, 1795, No. 30, "Most Secret."

12. Bradford to Gayoso, Jan. 22, 1795, cited in note 21, ch. XIII.

13. AI, PC, l. 1447, Carondelet to Las Casas, Aug. 18, 1794, No. 123 *res.*; *ib.*, l. 2354, Address of the Democratic Society of Kentucky, Dec. 13, 1793, Spanish translation.

14. AI, PC, l. 2374, copy in English, with interlinear cipher. The letter given in Bodley, lxxx, was fabricated in 1796: AI, PC, l. 2371, Sebastian to (Carondelet), New Orleans, Feb. 22, 1796.

15. AI, PC, l. 1447, Carondelet to Las Casas, Jan. 30, 1796, No. 154 *res.*

16. *Ib.*, l. 178, (Carondelet) to the Prince of the Peace, Feb. 10, 1796, No. 73 *res.*, draft.

17. AME, *Archivo de la Legación de S. M. C., Washington, D. C.*, l. 69, Antonio Argote Villalobos to Viar, Frankfort (Kentucky), Dec. 15, 1795, March 22, 1796 (two letters): AHN, E, l. 3896, Jáudenes to Alcudia, July 29, 1795, No. 297 and enclosures.

18. C. H. Haskins, *The Yazoo Land Companies, loc. cit.*

19. AI, PC, l. 203, Panton to Carondelet, April 18, 1795; *ib.*, l. 2354, Carondelet to Las Casas, March 4, 1795, No. 131 *res.*; same to same, May 1, 1795, No. 134 *res.*

20. *Ib.*, "Galeota la Vigilante, Diario desde la Salida de Natchez," entry for May 30 (1795).

21. *Ib.*, Carondelet to Gayoso, March 5, 1797.

22. AHN, E, l. 3899, Carondelet to Alcudia, June 10, 1795, No. 53 *res.*, and July 1, 1795, No. 54 *res.*

23. *Ib.*, l. 3384, Montarco to Alcudia, Aug. 17, 1795.

24. *Ib.*, ACE, Aug. 14, 1795; *ib.*, May 27, 1796; AI, PC, l. 2371, Lord Dorchester to Carondelet, Aug. 21, 1794, copy; draft of Carondelet's reply, June 19, 1795.

25. AI, PC, l. 2371, Gayoso to Lt. Pope, May 1, 1797, copy. Panton was suspected of complicity in Blount's conspiracy: *ib.*, l. 1502, Gayoso to Santa Clara, Sept. 24, 1797, No. 22 *res.* See also reference in note 21, above.

INDEX

Adams, Henry, 15.
Adams, John, 188.
Adams, Samuel, 92.
Alabama River, 94, 110, 160.
Alcudia, Duke de la, *see* Godoy, Manuel de.
America, 65, 66.
Anderson, Richard, 97.
Appalachicola River, 154.
Aranda, Conde de, negotiation at Paris, 9–11; advice, 12; succeeds Floridablanca, 18, 174; introduces d'Argès, 78–80, 90; imprisonment, 174.
Argès, Pierre Wouves d', goes to Spain, 78–80; Spanish agent, 81; relation to diplomacy, 82–84; hostility of Gardoqui, 85–88; of Miró, 88; return to Paris, 89; mentioned, 90, 98, 99, 108, 157.
Argote Villalobos, Antonio, 213.
Arkansas, Spanish post, 21; commandant of, 69.
Armesto, *see* López de Armesto, Andrés.
Arnold, Benedict, 96.
Asturias, Prince of, 215.
Augusta (Georgia), 37, 56.

Badajoz, 201.
Bahama Channel, 3.
Bahamas, 164.
Bâle, treaty of, 205, 207.
Barrancas de Margot, *see* Chickasaw Bluffs.
Belmont (Kentucky), 155.
Bilbao (Spain), 180.
Blount, William, governor of Southwest Territory, 20, 120; land speculator, 55, 109; conspiracy, 215, 221; mentioned, 47, 48, 121, 133, 144, 166, 170, 179, 188, 215.
Boone, Daniel, 48.
Bordeaux (France), 22.
Boundary, southern, of United States, 10; Spanish claim, 34, 35, 68, 69, 71, 84, 148, 183, 206; not publicly stated, 54; Count Gálvez on, 64.

Bourbon County (Georgia), attempted establishment, 55–58; mentioned, 60, 81, 106, 127, 129.
Bowles, William Augustus, 112, 135, 140, 163, 164, 166, 167.
Bradford, David, 196, 211.
British intrigue in West, rumored, 119, 143.
Brown, John, 117, 121, 129.
Bruin, Peter Bryan, 131.
Bute, Earl, 207.
Butler, Senator, 150.

Cabildo (New Orleans), 176.
Campbell, Arthur, 126.
Campeche, 2, 7.
Campo, Bernardo del, on growth of Kentucky, 51; on American West, 64; on British hostility, 207; mentioned, 182.
Campomanés, 2.
Canada, 142, 191.
Carmichael, William, 149, 150, 170, 171, 180–183, 189.
Carondelet, Hector. Baron de, appointment and character, 153–156; Indian policy, 163–170; influence on diplomacy, 169, 170, 181, 182; commercial policy, 176, 193, 194; "cochon de lait," 189; relations with Wilkinson, 190–197, 210–213; urges Kentucky secession and free trade for Louisiana, 191–194, 198; court's reply, 198, 200; removed from intendancy, 192, 193; opposes Americans, 209; extends military frontier, 213–216; despatches, 216, 217.
Casas, las, family, 154.
Casas, las, Luis de, 154, 162, 167.
Caswell, Richard, 55.
Cédula of 1782, 35, 36, 66.
Charles III, 2, 172.
Charles IV, 172, 205.
Charles V, 174.
Charleston (South Carolina), 37, 130, 195.
Chattahoochee River, 11.
Cherokee Indians, population, 24;

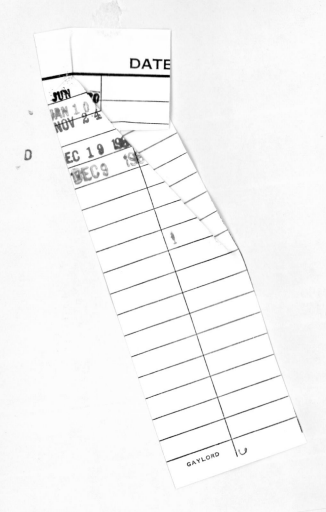